A PASTOR'S LEGACY.

A PASTOR'S LEGACY;

BEING

SERMONS ON PRACTICAL SUBJECTS.

BY THE LATE

REV. ERSKINE MASON, D.D.,

PASTOR OF THE BLEECKER STREET PRESBYTERIAN CHURCH, IN THE CITY OF NEW YORK.

WITH A BRIEF MEMOIR OF THE AUTHOR, BY
REV. WILLIAM ADAMS, D.D.

NEW YORK:
CHARLES SCRIBNER, 145 NASSAU STREET.
1853.

Printed by
C. W. BENEDICT,
201 William Street,

THESE DISCOURSES

ARE AFFECTIONATELY INSCRIBED

TO

THE PRESBYTERIAN CHURCH AND CONGREGATION

IN BLEECKER STREET, NEW YORK.

FOR WHOSE BENEFIT THEY WERE ORIGINALLY PREPARED

By that Pastor

WHOSE FACE THEY WILL SEE NO MORE,

BUT WHOSE WORDS

SPOKEN UNTO THEM WHILE HE WAS YET WITH THEM,

THEY MUST EVER DESIRE TO HOLD

IN GRATEFUL REMEMBRANCE.

INTRODUCTORY NOTICE.

THE day before his decease, DR. MASON expressed the wish that he had selected a few of his discourses, to be bequeathed as a token of affectionate regard for his people. It was then too late for him to undertake the selection. After his death the desire was very generally expressed, and especially by those who had been privileged to sit under his ministry, that a permanent form might be given to those thoughts, which had been to so many the source of profit and delight. By some of his professional brethren, it was proposed that his discourses should be arranged and published in the form of a System of Divinity. Meanwhile, those who were more immediately interested, were desirous of a less pretending volume, containing some of those more practical Sermons, which were still fresh in their remembrance. But who should select them? and on what principle should they be selected, when all were of such uniform merit? The feelings of an auditor are not the best criterion of a pulpit performance. The degree of interest felt in one discourse, more than another, may be owing to some peculiarity in the hearer's own circumstances, rather than any extraordinary excellence in the discourse itself.

The collection of Sermons left by Dr. Mason was large; and there was no clue to the judgment which their author put upon his own productions, or the principle, according to which, he would have made a selection from them for publication.

The responsibility of choosing from a thousand manuscripts, any one of which, for aught that appeared, was neither superior nor inferior to all the rest, was devolved on the Rev. Dr. Van Vechten, of Schenectady, the brother-in-law of Dr. Mason; and the present volume exhibits the result of his decision. The first Sermon in the collection was the last ever preached by its lamented author, as described in the accompanying Memoir. Full of pathos as were the circumstances in which it was delivered, and as is every sentence which it contains, the reader must not expect to discover in a discourse prepared in the debility of the sick chamber, that march and method of style which characterized the productions of the same author, in the fulness of intellectual and physical strength.

CONTENTS.

MEMOIR.

THE life of a Christian minister never can be written. Its *incidents* may be easily mentioned, for they are few. His parentage, birth, education, conversion, ordination, preaching, illness and death, comprise the whole. The *whole?* His real life consists not in striking and startling events. When the streams are flushed with the spring-freshet, overflowing the banks and sweeping away the dams and the bridges, the marvel is heralded in every newspaper; but when the same streams flow quietly along their ordinary channels, making the meadows to smile with verdure, refreshing the roots of the trees and turning the wheels of the mill, they excite no remark, even though their tranquil flow awakens a grateful admiration. Sum up the professional labours of a minister, and give the product in so many sermons, written and delivered!

As well attempt to gather up the rain, measure and weigh it. A certain amount of water you may show, but what of the moisture which has been absorbed by the tender vegetable, and the leaves of the trees? The life of a preacher is spent in addressing the intellect and conscience of his fellowmen. Ten, twenty, thirty years has he preached. How many thoughts, in how many minds has he suggested during such a period! What manifold judgments and purposes, what great hopes and wise fears have had their origin in his own thoughts and words! What sayings of his have been lodged in men's minds, which have worked in secret about the roots of character! Even while despondent himself, because so few visible results of his toil are revealed, his opinions by insensible degrees are growing into the convictions of others, and his own life is infused into the life of a whole generation. It is a peculiarity of his position that he touches the life of his people at those points which are the most memorable and important in their existence. He unites them in marriage; baptizes their children, and buries their dead. He dies, and is soon forgotten by the world. The sable drapery which was hung about his pulpit on his funeral day is taken down; his successor is chosen and installed, and the tide of life rolls on as before. But he is not forgotten by all. His life is not all lost and dissipated. As the manners of a father are acted over in his son, and the smile of a mother will brighten again, after she is dead, on the face of her daughter, so will the sentiments of a minister be transmitted after his ministry is closed, his words be repeated after he has ceased to speak, and all his hopes and wishes live again in other hearts, long after his own beats no more. His biography will not be finished nor disclosed till that day when the secrets of all hearts shall be revealed; and the seals of his ministry will be set, like stars in the firmament for ever and ever. To accommodate to a Christian minister, the language employed by Mr. Coleridge, in reference to Bell, the founder of schools:— "Would I frame to myself the most inspirating representation of future bliss, which my mind is capable of comprehending, it would be embodied to me in the idea of such an one receiving at some distant period, the appropriate reward of his earthly labors, when thousands of glorified spirits, whose reason and conscience had, through *his* efforts, been unfolded, shall sing the song of their own redemption, and pouring forth praise to God and to their Saviour, shall repeat *his* 'new name' in heaven, give thanks for his earthly virtues, as the chosen instrument of divine mercy to themselves, and not seldom, perhaps, turning their eyes toward *him*, as from the sun to its image in the fountain, with secondary gratitude and the permitted utterance of a human love."

There is a wide difference between a Pastor and an Evangelist. To affirm that the latter is never needed and never useful, would be to doubt the truth of the Scriptures and scoff at the Providence of God. The writings of George Herbert prove how early and how deeply imbedded in the English mind, was that conception of the sacred office which is embodied in the idea of one teacher ministering to one people; a relation well described by that significant word Pastor, obviously borrowed from the employment of a shepherd feeding his flock. It was one of the very earliest of English bards, the father of English poetry, who wrote that description of a Parish Priest.

"Yet has his aspect nothing of severe,
But such his face as promised him sincere;
Nothing reserved or sullen was to see,
But sweet regard and pleasing sanctity.
Mild was his accent, and his action free,
With eloquence innate his tongue was arm'd,
Though harsh the precept, yet the preacher charm'd;
For letting down the golden chain from high,
He drew his audience upwards to the sky.
He taught the gospel rather than the law,
And forc'd himself to drive, but lov'd to draw.
The tithes his parish freely paid he took,
But never sued or curs'd with bell and book.
Wide was his parish, nor contracted close

In streets; but here and there a straggling house.
Yet still he was at hand without request,
To serve the sick and succour the distress'd;
The proud he tamed, the penitent he cheer'd,
Nor to rebuke the rich offender fear'd.
His preaching much, but more his practice wrought,
A living sermon of the truths he taught."—CHAUCER.

That confidence which is born of intimate acquaintance, familiar intercourse, and friendly sympathy, contributes more to ministerial influence than the meteoric display of occasional eloquence. "A stranger will they not follow." But it was of quite another thing that I intended to speak when comparing the life of a pastor and evangelist. The latter visits a city for the first time, and preaches with a frequency and power which excite amazement. The secular press heralds it as little short of miraculous that a mortal should be able with no apparent exhaustion, day after day, and night after night, to address changing crowds. The truth is that such an one is leading a life of intellectual recreation. He repeats the same discourses over and over again in the course of his itinerancy, till they are as familiar to his memory, and facile to his utterance as the letters of the alphabet, and he has grown expert in every expression, gesture and intonation. It was the testimony of David Garrick that the sermons of Whitfield, as specimens of oratorical art, never reached their fullest power till the fiftieth repetition. What, for intellectual expenditure is such a career compared with the life of a pastor, preaching to the *same* congregation two or three times a week, month after month, year after year, with increasing interest, profit and power! The late Mr. Sargeant of Philadelphia, after delighting an audience with a lecture on some moral topic, declared to a friend that, for the labour involved, he would prefer to speak at the bar, six times in a week, on cases made to his hand, in the ordinary course of his profession, than prepare one popular lecture on any point on the philosophy of law, once in a month. To the latter the weekly preparations of a minister are the most analogous, yet how few, among the most intelligent, pause to reflect what is implied in the intellectual labours of a pastor like the subject of this memoir, protracted through twenty years, in connexion with the same congregation, with ever-increasing freshness, novelty and delight.

After all, what a poor exponent of a minister's influence is a volume of his sermons! However elaborate their construction, and finished their style, they are but the residuum of a sparkling cup. Those who *read* what once they *heard*, invariably confess to a feeling of disappointment, and can with difficulty be persuaded that the sentences over which their eye passes so languidly, on the printed page, are the very same which, upon their delivery from the pulpit, fresh from the heart and lips of their author, were as a chariot of fire to the devout auditor. The truth is, there is a keeping between the thinking and the speaking of a preacher. His manner may violate all the rules of his art; nevertheless, it is *his own*, and no other can serve so well for the expression of himself. It is *his* emphasis and *his* intonation, *his* pause and *his* look, which alone can give the full and just expression of his own meaning. Think of a sermon of Leighton, its delicacy of sentiment shading off into pure spirituality, delivered by a Boanerges; or a discourse of South, repeated tamely by another, without the author's own burning eye, sharp voice, and stabbing finger.

One advantage, indeed, they may have, who reading the discourses of their pastor, but recently deceased, retain a distinct impression of his form, face and manner, seeming to hear the voice which stirred their hearts when he was living. This, however, is but a shadowy resemblance of a once living reality, gone never to be renewed. "In fact, every attempt to present on paper the splendid effects of impassioned eloquence, is like gathering up dew-drops, which appear jewels and pearls on the grass, but run to water in the hand; the essence and the elements remain, but the grace the sparkle and the form are gone." *

Notwithstanding all these disadvantages, we have collected here some of the sermons of a distinguished preacher, in the form of a Pastor's Legacy; and before their author's form has mouldered away to ashes, the trembling hand of friendship would draw down the covering from the face of the dead, and try to sketch his features, for the recognition of those who knew him.

ERSKINE MASON was born in the city of New York, 16th April, 1805. He was the youngest child of Rev. John M. Mason, D. D., whose fame as a preacher is known on both continents. His mother, Mrs. Anna L. Mason, was the granddaughter of Derick Lefferts, Esq., a prominent and affluent merchant of New York, with whom she resided, her father having died in her infancy. Mrs. Mason was admired from her youth for grace of manners, intelligence of mind, excellent discretion, and cheerful piety.

Singularly fortunate in his ancestry, the subject of this memoir had for his paternal grandfather, Rev. John Mason, D. D., distinguished alike for his scholarship and eloquence. Born in the vicinity of Edinburgh, Scotland, receiving a thorough classical education, competent to write and speak the

* James Montgomery, on Summerfield.

Latin language, in his day the language of the lecture-room and of scholars, he was invited to the pastoral charge of the Scotch Presbyterian church in this city, at that time in Cedar-street. In that pulpit he continued to preach, till his son, Rev. John M. Mason, D. D., became his successor. Descended from an ancestry so illustrious, we may apply to the subject of this memoir the words which Horace first addressed to Mæcenas:

"———— atavis edite regibus ;"

and he followed them with no Iulian steps. Erskine received his name as a tribute of the grateful respect entertained by his father for the late Rev. Dr. John Erskine of Edinburgh, from whom he had received many expresssions of kindness while prosecuting his own theological studies in that city, near the close of the last century. The object of his father's indulgent and hopeful regard, "tender and beloved in the sight of his mother," this youngest of a numerous family of children, displayed in his boyhood more than common intelligence and spirit, which, being accompanied with no special love for study, or effort at sedateness, was the occasion of no small anxiety to his religious parents. In the twelfth year of his age he was removed from home to the family of his brother-in-law, Rev. Dr. Van Vechten, of Schenectady, and joined the school of Rev. Mr. Barnes. Dr. Johnson has very justly said, "Not to mention the school or master of distinguished men, is a kind of historical fraud, by which honest fame is injuriously diminished." The life of Mr. Barnes needed not its tragic end (he was killed by the upsetting of a stage-coach, the day after he had preached on the uncertainty of life) to make his name memorable. The act of entering the school of this judicious teacher, in company with his own brother, James, always correct, high-minded and sedate, was the happy crisis in the life of Erskine, when he awoke to sober reflection and earnest purposes, like the visit of Sir Thomas Buxton to the family of the Gurney's, at Earlham Park.

In consequence of impaired health, Dr. John M. Mason was constrained to exchange the pastoral office in this city for the Presidency of Dickinson College, at Carlisle, in Pennsylvania. Hither Erskine accompanied his father, and was entered a member of the College, in the fourteenth year of his age.

And here I avail myself of the pen of Rev. Dr. Knox, senior pastor of the Reformed Dutch church of this city, the son-in-law of Dr. John M. Mason, who, in a discourse on the death of Rev. William Cahoone, some three years ago, expresses himself as follows:

"A large number of choice young men of this city and its vicinity, attracted by their regard for the venerable President, and the faculty he had gathered around him, followed Dr. Mason to Carlisle, and became members of the College. In the autumn of 1822, a son of the President, *James Hall Mason*, a youth of singular purity and elevation of character, eminent promise and greatly beloved, having just received his degree, and with the ministry in view, after a violent and brief illness, was taken away by death. The event produced a solemn and profound impression throughout the College. The heart-stricken father, who had a short time before parted with a beloved daughter, sat as one astonished. Clouds and darkness were round about the throne. The explanation was not yet. When the bier on which lay the body of his deceased son was taken up by his young companions, to be conveyed to the grave, as by involuntary and uncontrollable impulse, he spake, 'Softly, young men, tread softly, ye carry a temple of the Holy Ghost!'

"This dark and bereaving dispensation, in the wonder-working providence of God, was made the occasion and commencement of a work of grace, the extent and results of which eternity alone will be able to disclose. Of the students who then experienced a change of heart, and subsequently devoted themselves to the ministry of Christ, a majority being of the senior class, I have been able to recall the names of *fifteen;* among them many familiar to us all, such as Mr. Cahoone, Dr. Bethune of Philadelphia, Dr. Erskine Mason of this city, Dr. Morris of Baltimore, Bishop M'Coskry of Michigan, Messrs. Labagh of Long Island, Boice of Claverack, and others, with no less fidelity and usefulness occupying different and important stations in the church. In addition to these, and of the same class with a majority of them, six young men are recollected, who were members of the church previous to the revival, but who probably were more or less influenced during that scene, in devoting themselves to the ministry. These were President Young of Kentucky, Prof. Agnew of Michigan, Mr. Holmes, Missionary among the Chickasaws, Rev. Messrs. Whitehead and Vancleef of our church, and Rev. Mr. Williams, formerly of Salem, N. Y."

"Connected with this revival are various remarkable circumstances. It furnishes a chapter in God's gracious providence, which deserves to be had in admiring and grateful remembrance."

"In its origin it was remarkable. It was as life from the dead. That which, to all human view, seemed to abstract from the anticipated services of the church, and to depress the hearts of the godly, in the early translation of a youth of high and holy promise, became the occasion in the dispensations of Him who worketh all things according to the counsels of his own will, of quickening many souls, and sending into the vineyard of our Lord a band of faithful labourers, who have sustained the heat and burden of the day."

"The work was remarkable in the fact, that although previously many of its subjects were very inconsiderate and heedless of their obligations, and were the objects of great solicitude, those at least to whom we have referred as having been called to the ministry were, every one of them, from the bosom of Christian families, carefully trained in the knowledge of divine things—sons on whose behalf prayer to God had ascended day by day continually."

"Remarkable, in the fact, that, of so large a number brought into the church at the same time, under all the excitement of such a scene, all have maintained their integrity, not one has fallen, or faltered, or backslidden. All have been useful, many of them eminently so."

"Remarkable, in the additional fact, that after the lapse of more than a quarter of a century, this hallowed band has now with a single exception, for the first time, so far as I have been able to ascertain, been invaded by death. With this exception our brother Cahoone is the first of them all to be released from his labours, and taken to his recompense."

Graduating in 1823 Erskine Mason spent a considerable part of the next year with his cousin, the late Rev. Dr. Duncan, of Baltimore, prosecuting his studies under the direction of that distinguished preacher. In the summer session of 1825 he resorted to Princeton, and connected himself with the middle class of the Theological Seminary in that place, where he completed his professional education.

On the 20th October, 1826, he was ordained in the Scotch Presbyterian church in Cedar Street, by the second Presbytery of New-York, and in the next year was installed over the Presbyterian Church of Schenectady.

On the 26th September, 1827, he was married by his father to Miss Mary McCoskry, daughter of Dr. Samuel A. McCoskry, and granddaughter of the celebrated Dr. Charles Nesbit, President of Dickinson College. Mrs. Mason survives her husband with three daughters and one son, all of sufficiently mature age to sympathize with their widowed mother in their common bereavement.

Converted by the grace of God, educated for the Christian ministry, inducted into the sacred office, the true life of Dr. Mason now begins. With the highest models of pulpit eloquence before him, in his own father and grandfather; deeply impressed with the sanctities and responsibilities of his profession, he appears from the very first to have proposed to himself no common-place mediocrity in his pulpit preparations, but eminence of the highest order. Though he was but twenty-one years of age at the time of his ordination, he intended that no one should "despise his youth;" and that no measure of toil should be withheld which was necessary to prevent him as a "workman" from being "ashamed." In a striking passage in one of the Greek tragedies, a character is introduced expressing great surprise, that, amidst all the inventions and attainments of human science and art, there should be found so few to cultivate that *art of persuasion* which is the mistress of human volition, and so the helm of human affairs. The pastor of an educated and intellectual congregation,—the faculty and students of Union College attending on his ministry, Dr. Mason neglected not that undervalued art of conviction, but addressed himself to the understanding of his hearers with a clearness of conception and a depth of thought, which, in the language of the venerable Dr. Nott, "appeared wonderful in so young a man." "His power," such is the continued testimony of this distinguished witness, "was chiefly felt in the pulpit.

He appeared to be conscious that his mission was to preach the gospel; and in the performance of that duty he excelled. He was greatly beloved by his people, highly esteemed by the citizens generally, and his removal from the place was regretted by all, and by none more than by the officers and members of Union College."

The Bleecker Street Presbyterian Church, in New-York, gathered by the persevering labours of Rev. Matthias Bruen, was early called to weep over the remains of their accomplished pastor, who died on the 6th December, 1829, in the thirty-seventh year of his age. To the pastoral office of this church Dr. Mason was unanimously invited; and to this new field was he transferred September 10th, 1830, with the experience of but three years in his profession; and to this people, though often invited elsewhere, did he devote his best services, for more than twenty years, to the close of his life. At the time of his settlement over that people, the Bleecker St. Church was quite above the centre of the city population; that tide of removal and growth which has since made such prodigious advances, scarcely having commenced. An "up-town church," however, afforded accommodations and attractions to those who soon began to change their residence, and such was the ability displayed by the pastor in Bleecker Street, that it was not long before that church was entirely filled; and, for many years after, it occupied a position which gave it pre-eminent advantages over all other churches of the same denomination in the city. Nothing of opportunity was lacking on the one part, and nothing of talent, diligence, and success on the other. The congregations were large and intelligent, and every thing encouraged that purpose which the pastor had formed to devote himself to the one thing of a studious, careful, and excellent preparation for the pulpit. Others might grasp at a different prize, and select a different path, but the composition and delivery of good sermons was the object for which his taste, talent, and judgment of usefulness best qualified him. From that occupation he never suffered himself to be diverted. There are many extemporaneous sermons written out in full. With Dr. Mason, the composition of a discourse was never postponed to some anticipated uncertainty of favourable feeling, or to the last pressure of inevitable necessity. Before he had lost the impulse of one Sabbath he had begun the preparation for another. It was his deliberate judgment, that a minister, special cases only excepted, could serve his people the best, after preaching twice in the day, to pass the evening of the Sabbath at his own home; and seldom did he retire that night without having decided upon the topic which was to be the subject of study and preparation throughout the week. Thus he never lost the headway he had gained; neither weary himself, nor waste time in searching for subjects, or waiting for them "to come to him," as the phrase is which describes the suggestion of topics by accidental association. Adhering to the counsel of our great dramatist,

> "Stick to your journal course: the breach of custom
> Is breach of all,"

he has left a thousand sermons, (of their intellectual and theological excellencies I shall speak hereafter,) written entire in the perfection of penmanship, as the proofs of the wise and faithful manner in which he occupied the pulpit.

In versatility of talent he may have been excelled by others. The richest banker who can draw the largest check does not always carry about with him the greatest amount of small coin. Warmly social in his temperament, Dr. Mason was never garrulous; and that false idea of pastoral duty which many seem to cherish, requiring the consumption of one's chief time in going from house to house, and conversing in the ordinary chit-chat of trifles, he utterly discarded. Because of this was he deficient as a pastor? Who of his people ever knew a substantial sorrow or necessity without his presence and aid? Did Age ever complain of disrespect, or Grief of his want of sympathy, or Suffering that he refused a balm? While the pulpit was the throne of his strength, who could speak, out of it, more wisely than he? If he sometimes appeared to be taciturn, who shall forget that *silence*, in its place, is wisdom as well as speech; that modesty is a beautiful property of greatness, and that he talks to the best purpose, who says the right thing at the right time, and in the right manner? How often has ministerial usefulness been impaired by folly and frivolity of speech. What Dr. Johnson has said of an author's book is equally true of a preacher's public office. "The transition from it to his conversation, is too often like an entrance into a large city after a distant prospect. Remotely we see nothing but spires of temples and turrets of palaces, and imagine it the residence of splendour, grandeur and magnificence; but when we have passed the gates we find it perplexed with narrow passages, disgraced with despicable cottages, embarrassed with obstructions, and clouded with smoke." No one, after being impressed with the dignity of Dr. Mason in the pulpit, lost that impression when meeting him in the familiarities of private life. It was said of some one whose infelicities and imprudencies of manner and conversation were equalled only by his extraordinary endowments as a preacher, "that when in the pulpit one might wish that he was never out of it; but when out of it one could wish that he should never be *in* it." Confidence in the soundness of his judgment, the integrity of his motives, and the sincerity of his piety, is the secret of a preacher's success; let that confidence be shaken by one act of folly, and the rod of his strength is broken. It were well if every preacher of the gospel should bear in mind the last sentiment of the following allegory, by one of the oldest poets in our language.

"Upon a time, Reputation, Love, and Death
Would travel o'er the world: and 'twas concluded
That they should part, and take their several ways.
Death told them they would find him in great battles,
Or cities plagued with plagues: Love gives them counsel
T' enquire for him 'mongst unambitious shepherds
Where dowries were not talked of: and sometimes
'Mongst quiet kindred that had nothing left
By their dead parents. *Stay, quoth Reputation,*
If once I part from any man I meet
I am never found again."*

The discourses of Dr. Mason advertise their own quality. Those which compose this volume are in no respect superior to hundreds more from the same pen. Their first excellence is that they are decidedly *scriptural* and *evangelical.* A French preacher of the reign of Louis XIV, in a sermon to his brother monks, in which he bewails their

* Webster, 1610.

criminal neglect of the fundamental doctrines of the gospel, makes this candid confession: "We are worse than Judas; he sold and delivered his Master: we sell him, but deliver him not." In the preaching of Dr. Mason was no such defect as that referred to in this tremendous satire. He was a *Christian* preacher; and in his eye all truth arranged itself around the cross of Christ, compared with which, the world beside, is, as Leighton well expresses it, one "grand impertinency." I know not how to describe what he was in this regard, so well as in the use of his own words when describing what a minister should be. In a discourse preached by him at Newburgh, October, 1838, before the Synod of New York, of which, in his 33d year, he was then Moderator, which discourse was, by the request of his brethren subsequently printed, entitled "The Subject and Spirit of the Ministry," he employs the following language. I am led to extract largely from this discourse, for the benefit of those who would know the character of its author, for it seems to be a daguerreotype likeness of himself.

"By the gospel of Christ, as an instrument of human conversion, I suppose we are to understand all those principles which cluster around the doctrine of vicarious atonement as their common centre; the lost, ruined, helpless condition of man as a sinner, the provision which the grace of God has made for him, involving the nature, character, the righteousness even unto death of Jesus Christ as the ground of pardon; the regenerating and sanctifying influences of the Holy Spirit, and the promises of good, as well as threatenings of evil, which have been sealed in atoning blood. These, and their correlative truths, usually comprised under the general term of gospel, constitute the exhibition to us of those great facts, in view of which we are brought into the kingdom of God, and prepared for eternal glory. They all give rise to, spring from, or serve to illustrate the sufferings of the Son of God. You cannot find a single doctrinal statement in the New Testament which does not carry you directly to the cross, or for the explanation of which you must not go to that cross. You cannot find a single motive, nor a single explanation, nor a single offer, nor a single warning, nor a single appeal, to which the cross of Christ does not give meaning and power—*that* is the radiating point of light and heat to the whole system. Blot out from the gospel the doctrine of Christ's vicarious atonement, and you rob it of all its vitality; and it remains to be seen what you have left, beyond the frigid influence of infidelity, or what effectiveness your teachings carry along with them to correct the evils of the human heart, to give peace to the human conscience, or to make man like his God.

"It is evident, if what I have advanced is true, that the power of the gospel lies *in the facts themselves*, which it discloses. It is by bringing *them* into contact with the human mind that you secure the results of the gospel; and whatever you may do, however ingeniously you may argue, however earnestly you may labour, however impassioned may be your appeals; you argue, and labour, and appeal in vain, so long as the great facts of the gospel system are not brought to tell with power upon the conscience and the heart. There is such a thing as speculating *about* the gospel, taking up its principles as mere themes of philosophical investigation; approaching it and handling it as a mere theory, which passes sometimes under the name of preaching the gospel, which is, after all, nothing more than exhibiting one's own philosophy; and which, placing that philosophy in the front ground before the human mind, conceals the great facts of the revelation of God; and is, therefore, not only without beneficial result, but prevents those facts from producing their designed effect, standing, as it does, between the mind and their perception.

"I do not mean, by this remark, to cast odium upon what is called the philosophy of Christianity, nor to rebuke as wrong all inquiries into the mode of the truth's operation, and the best methods of presenting the facts of the gospel. Every minister of Jesus Christ must be a Christian philosopher, if he would be '*a workman, that needeth not to be ashamed, rightly dividing the word of truth;*' he must be one, if he would remove the obstacles which a false philosophy has interposed to the influence of the truth; he must be one, if he would work a way for the truth through the varied and almost endlessly diversified windings of the human bosom, and find for it a lodgement in the human mind; and he who cannot be one, is unfit for the office which he exercises.

"And this, what I call the philosophy of Christianity, presents a legitimate field for the exercise of the human mind. There may be diversities here in the *results* at which different minds may arrive; but so long as the facts themselves of the gospel are brought out to view in all their distinctness, the power of the gospel remains, since that power is found not in the philosophy of those facts, but in the facts themselves. When I speak of, and condemn speculations about the gospel, I refer to all attempts to philosophize *away* its facts, or to those laborious arguments which give the mind nothing but philosophy; which make the *rationale*, if I may so speak, the main thing, and truth secondary; which may teach men to reason but not to believe; which may show them how they ought to be convinced, but never convict them; how they ought to repent, but present them nothing in view of which to repent: in fine, which make philosophers, or rather sciolists in philosophy, sometimes; but Christians, never. Let a man philosophize as much as he pleases; but against two things let him be on his guard—philosophizing away the facts of the gospel, and bringing his philosophy with him into the pulpit. He may use it to guide him in his exhibition of truth; he may use it in giving shape to his argument, place to his exhortations, and time to his appeals; but let him never use it *as itself*, an instrument for the accomplishment of saving results. A minister of Christ may in his study be a philosopher always; in his pulpit, never.

"No man can be truly said to *preach* Christ, who is not himself personally interested in his theme. I know that the words of the gospel may be uttered—and the arguments of the gospel may be advanced—and the consciences of men may be plied with the claims and appeals of the gospel. It may be all done with eloquence of diction, and grace of utterance; it may disclose the workings of a powerful genius, and constrain men to do homage to the might of intellect; but there is no *preaching of the gospel*. The science of experience, and the language consecrated to it, may be mastered; but the gospel will not be preached. No man can preach who does not himself perceive the glory of Christ, and know the preciousness of Christ. Spiritual knowledge, spiritual feeling, and the powerful impulse which is derived from principle alone, are essential requisites to a preacher. Without them there may be fire, but it will be false; there may be an unction, but it will be spurious. Under ministrations however clear, however powerful, as exhibitions of intellect, yet unbaptized with the spirit of Christ, not a cord will be touched, not a heart will be moved. Give a man what you please, in point of genius, learning, eloquence, he wants more to make him a preacher—he wants that genius enlightened, that learning directed, and those lips of eloquence touched by the spirit of his master. Let him but be gifted with a spiritual discernment, and the change is amazing. New treasures of every kind will be disclosed; floods of sublime emotion, fields of brilliant imagery, and super-human power of persuasiveness. It is not eloquence, in the proper sense of that term, that constitutes the rod of the ministry; it is the tone of their feeling, the holy unction of their utterance; and this is the result of the impressions of the gospel upon their own souls. This is, in fact, the ground-work of all excellence; the first, the chief element of all pastoral competency; and when we read this remarkable resolution of the Apostles, '*We will give ourselves continually to prayer*,' we seem to have reached the secret of their soul prosperity, their preaching eminence, their wonderful success. They preached the gospel, because they felt the gospel. God was with them, as they were with God.

"Oh! if I am right in my supposition as to the requisites of a herald of the cross; if a man must possess the spirit of Christ in order to preach Christ; is there not room for the inquiry, whether we do indeed preach Christ? and if the spirit of our office is gone, no wonder that its results are absent also.

"The spirit of the ministry is a spirit of self-renunciation, '*We preach not ourselves*.' In the statement of this general principle, and in its truth, we shall all agree, while it is possible that through the deceitfulness of our hearts we may be blind to our constant contradiction of it. It is not only when our aim in our office is the promotion of private interest, that we do preach ourselves. We may pour our severest censures upon the man who would say, '*Put me into one of the priests' offices, that I may eat a piece of bread*,' or give vent to a burst of holy indignation against him who uses his office for the purposes of earthly emolument, while at the same time we may be involved in the same condemnation with himself.

"We may preach ourselves, when we are as far

removed as possible from the influence of mere pecuniary considerations. There are temptations of an intellectual kind, the dangers of which must be seen to be many and powerful by every man who knows any thing of his own heart. They exist in proportion to the greatness or splendor of endowments which God has bestowed upon him who exercises the ministerial office. '*An eloquent man, and mighty in the Scriptures*,' may be above the gratification which thousands and tens of thousands of silver and gold would bestow; and yet he may preach himself, by aiming at the applause of his listening auditory. It is always so with him who is more concerned about the impression he makes upon the minds of his hearers as to the character of his exhibitions of truth, than about the impression he makes upon their minds respecting Christ. Though a man may understand the gospel, he may conceal its glorious object behind the display of his own powers; and he may use that object, as it may serve to fix the attention of men more firmly and exclusively upon himself. He holds up the pole, but the brazen serpent is invisible; and so charms the ears with the sound of the silver trumpets, as to make the people forget the jubilee they are intended to proclaim. Such a man preaches himself, not Christ Jesus the Lord."

Little danger was there that a man holding such

sentiments as these would ever prostitute the pulpit to purposes of mere rhetorical display or intellectual entertainment. The cross of Christ being his theme, there was no imitation of that cardinal fault of a celebrated painter who, in a picture of the Lord's Supper, has made the gold and the silver vessels so large, magnificent and brilliant as to divert the eye of the spectator from the main subject of the piece. He had no ambition to select pearls and diamonds when plainer materials would serve his purpose better. His characteristics were clearness, precision and force. Convinced himself, he sought to convince others. Relying on God, he believed that the truth was capable of being so exhibited as to commend itself to every man's conscience. Studying that truth himself, and feeling its adaptation to his own intellect and heart, his presentations of truth always had the freshness of originality without the least suspicion of that ambition and affectation which often passes by that name. His preaching was argumentative and logical. Commencing with some obvious truth, which all would admit, he advanced step by step, carrying one conviction after another, by a process of demonstration which would admit of no escape till he reached that conclusion, in the application of which he poured out the fullness and fervor of his religious pathos. A distinguished civilian, skilled in diplomacy, and an adept in letters, invited once by a friend, a parishioner of Dr. Mason, to hear him preach, sat in the corner of the pew, at first somewhat listless, then alert, and following the argument with intense interest, till his countenance betrayed the emotion which was working in his heart, exclaimed on leaving the church, "Well, I know not what you who are accustomed to this may think; as for myself, I never heard such preaching before. As Lord Peterborough said to Fenelon at Cambray, 'If I stay here longer, I shall become a Christian in spite of myself.'"

We can always judge of a minister's heart by his public prayers. He who exhibits no feeling in his addresses to God, and wakes to fervour only as he addresses his fellow-men, cannot have much of the vitality of religion. The devotional exercises of Dr. Mason, marked alike by dignity and fervour, correct expression and strong emotion, were proof in themselves that the object of his ministry was to preach not himself but Christ Jesus, and that the grand purpose of his heart was co-incident with that avowed by the great Apostle in these memorable words: "Whom we preach, warning every man and teaching every man in all wisdom; that we may present every man perfect in Christ Jesus, whereunto I also labour, striving according to his working, which worketh in me mightily." A serious-minded, earnest man, who believed the truth, and loved the souls of his people, he could not be persuaded to any trivial topic, nor imitate the cruelty of the Roman emperor, who, in a time of famine, imported costly sands for his amphitheatres, instead of bread for his starving subjects.

A Presbyterian by birth, education and preference, Dr. Mason was too good and great a man to be a bigot. Many of his relatives and intimate friends were members of other communions. His brother-in-law is Bishop McCoskry, of Michigan. Kind and catholic, he was, nevertheless, decided, intelligent and consistent in his preferences for that church to which he was attached. No man was better acquainted with its history, polity and order; as no man, of his age, had greater weight in its counsels. Eventful has that period been, in which he was personally connected as a minister, with the Presbyterian church in the United States. Strong as was his desire to preserve the integrity of that body, which was dear to him by so many ancestral associations, when disruption was made inevitable by no act of his or those with whom he was associated, he did not hesitate for an instant to what body to give his adherence. From that adherence he never wavered, but lived and died in the belief that the right would one day be vindicated, and that they who had suffered wrong would be honoured and blessed at the last. Though young in years, Dr. Mason, at that memorable crisis, was mature in judgment; and when Kent, Wood, Randall, and Meredith espoused and defended the cause of the church to which he was attached, there was no one more competent than he to aid their proceedings, none to whose advice they and his brethren paid so much of respectful deference. Frequently a member, for eight years he was the stated clerk of the General Assembly, by which means his acquaintance was extensive throughout the church, and he was made an object of general confidence and esteem.

In the judicatories of the church his manners were always retiring, and reserved; never obtrusive. He was willing that others should conduct the debate; seldom participating in it, save by some brief suggestion or inquiry, intended to give it direction, the wisdom and pertinency of which was sure afterwards to be vindicated. But when the matter in hand was becoming involved, and perplexity and trouble were likely to ensue, how often, like a pilot in a difficult passage, by the introduction of some resolution, or the suggestion of some amendment, did he contrive the very relief which was needed, covering the entire case, extricating the subject from all embarrassment, and leading the minds of all to an issue of complete harmony. The records of our ecclesiastical bodies will prove that this eulogy on the soundness of his judgment is not exaggerated; and when he died, the general impression throughout the church was, that a standard-bearer had fallen.

The person of Dr. Mason, of full size, and good proportions, was the expression of manly vigour and dignity. Inheriting a sound constitution, he enjoyed, through life, more than ordinary health. He knew but few of those ailments to which his profession are liable, previous to that illness which terminated his life. Invited to the presidency of the Theological Seminary in this city, and to other pulpits in his denomination, we have seen how steadily and perseveringly he addicted himself to the studies and toils of one pulpit. In the year 1846, at the request of his own people, who generously provided their faithful friend and pastor with the means of relaxation, he passed several months in Europe, returning to his ordinary occupations with renewed vigor of body and mind, and fresh resources for instruction. Every thing appeared to promise a long life. One year before his death no one would have suspected that an insidious disease had already begun its secret ravages, by which his labours were soon to be closed. Returning from his annual visit to the country, in August 1850, he gave signs of debility, which at first were regarded but as trifles soon to pass away, but which, continuing from day to day, at length excited the most serious apprehension. When it was first whispered about that Dr. Mason was in a state to warrant solicitude, he in the full prime of life, it was with difficulty that the rumour could be credited. Weeks and months passed by, and his friends, brethren and people were gladdened by his apparent recovery. He was intensely desirous, should God so will, to resume those occupations to which he had been so long and pleasantly devoted. Having sufficiently recovered for the purpose, in the last of December he prepared a sermon from the text, "I said, O my God, take me not away in the midst of my days," the same which is now published as the first in the accompanying collection. Though no one who heard that sermon could fail to apply the utterance of its text to himself, yet, with his characteristic modesty, the preacher made not an allusion to his own case. Unable to endure the fatigue of standing, during its delivery, a chair had been arranged in the pulpit, seated in which, with a voice tremulous with emotion, he preached his last sermon. There was eloquence in the occasion itself; and the simple utterance of the text was enough to start the tear in the eye of those who heard it with mingled gratitude and foreboding. Such was his last "New Year's Sermon," such his last entrance to his pulpit. It was soon apparent that he was gradually sinking under occult and insidious disease and that his work was finished. Deprived of the privilege of glorifying God in active duty, he was now called to the higher and harder testimony of passive endurance. Confined to his chamber he was not without hope and desire of recovery. Strongly did he desire to live; and who has juster views of the value and desirableness of life than a faithful Christian minister! How abrupt the change from the "midst of his days," from plans of study and action yet incomplete, to the silence of the sepulchre! How could he bear to say to his loving, trusting family, hanging about him, that he must leave them without a husband, father and head! For their sakes, rather than his own, he desired, if God should so be pleased, that he might be spared, even as king Hezekiah prayed because of the church and the country which he loved that he might live, even after the prophet had told him he should die. The conduct of Dr. Mason, during his long confinement, was characterised by that calmness and firmness which always belonged to him, but now more than usually softened by the filial resignation of a religious sufferer. More than the splendours of genius, more than the gifts of eloquence are the simple words which reveal the peace and safety of the Christian believer in his last hours. "I have had a long season of trial," said he to a friend, "but I trust it has not been unprofitable. I have had many clear and delightful views of divine truth."

Moved even to tears, he said, on another occasion, "I have had the most glorious and elevating views, such as I never expected to enjoy in this world. It was in the watches of the night, and I feared to sleep, lest I should lose them. But a dark cloud has since intervened—less dark now than it has been. This, however, I can say at all times, Though he slay me, I will put my trust in him. I have no greater comfort than when, under a sense of utter unworthiness, I lie at the foot of the cross."

"A matter of unspeakable thankfulness, is it," said he, "that we are not left to find a place of safety when the hand of disease is upon us. I trust that my eternal interests are safe, and that in the future I have nothing to dread. I have had, in common with all Christians, sore spiritual conflicts; but I believe that the most useful of my labours have been in connection with these scenes of perplexity and trial. Trials, I am sure, were designed to teach us to live by faith."

The evening before his decease he was informed

that, in the judgment of his physicians, he could not survive many hours. He inquired on what facts his medical friends had based their opinion. He differed from them in judgment as to certain particulars. "However," added he, "it matters but little as to time. I am not now to begin and make my preparations. All is safe—all safe."

A friend at his side repeated the familiar words, "The Lord is my light and salvation, whom shall I fear." Taking the sentence from her lips, he completed it—"The Lord is the strength of my heart, of whom shall I be afraid." Again she said, "Thou wilt keep him in perfect peace,"—when he instantly finished the sentence with a decided emphasis—"whose mind is stayed on thee; because he trusteth in thee."

In the evening he engaged in cheerful conversation; with the utmost clearness and calmness of mind made certain dispositions of his estate, signed his will, and sat waiting for his great change to come. Early in the morning he summoned his children about him, and gave them his last counsels. Commending them in solemn prayer to the Father of Mercies, he told them that oftentimes, after preaching in the pulpit, he had retired to his study, and with inexpressible anxiety, had implored in their behalf the blessings of the everlasting covenant.

On the same occasion, addressing his only son, (fourteen years of age) he inquired, "Have you thought what you would wish to do in the world?" The reply of filial simplicity and affection was—"Father, I will do whatever you wish me." "It may not be as I wish," said he, "but if you are prepared for it, my son, my wish is that you may preach the Gospel of our Lord Jesus Christ. It is the greatest work, and the best work. But beware of becoming a minister, unless, by the grace of God, you are prepared for it."

The prayers of many have ascended to God in behalf of this orphan son, that he may inherit his father's gifts and graces, and that he may prolong and transmit the ancestral honours, with which he is enriched, in the ministry of our Lord.

His last day on earth has dawned, and his heart is beating feebler to its rest. "Have you doubts and fears?" whispered a friend. "Doubts! No. Faith is every thing. It is all bright and clear. Have faith." So gently faded his life into the vision of God and the Lamb. About twelve o'clock on Wednesday, 14th of May, seated in his chair, without a struggle, he breathed out his life into the hands of his Redeemer.

On the Friday following, his funeral was attended from the church in which he had officiated so many years. There needed to be no such signs of mourning as those which draped the pulpit, now deprived of its faithful incumbent, to proclaim the sorrow of the occasion. A large concourse of people, with unfeigned grief in their hearts, pronounced his eulogy by testifying that his death was a public bereavement. There, in front of the pulpit, lay the calm remains of the Pastor, who had been brought to the house of God for the last time, to address his brethren, people and friends in speechless tenderness.

The dirge was sung, prayer was offered, some words of consolation were uttered, and devout men bore him to his burial. The early spring blossoms were opening and falling as he was laid in the sacred spot he had, a year before, prepared at Greenwood. The sun had gone down before the act of interment was finished; but we knew that it would rise again; and as we gazed, through our tears, upon the descending form with which were associated so many memories of friendship, love and religion, this was our only consolation, that he would live the life everlasting.

Through the generous regard cherished for his memory by his parishioners, a beautiful monument of white Italian marble, chaste and simple in design, but highly finished in its execution, has been erected on the spot where sleep his remains. On one side is the following inscription:

ERECTED

BY THE BLEECKER STREET PRESBYTERIAN CHURCH,

IN MEMORY OF

THEIR LATE PASTOR,

REV. ERSKINE MASON, D.D.

DIED 14 MAY, 1851,

ÆT. 46.

AN ELOQUENT MAN, AND MIGHTY IN THE SCRIPTURES,

IN DOCTRINE

SHOWING UNCORRUPTNESS, GRAVITY, SINCERITY,

SOUND SPEECH THAT COULD NOT BE CONDEMNED;

A PATTERN OF GOOD WORKS;

LOOKING

FOR THAT BLESSED HOPE, THE GLORIOUS APPEARING OF THE GREAT

GOD, AND OUR SAVIOUR, JESUS CHRIST.

On the reverse side:

DESCENDED

FROM ANCESTORS ILLUSTRIOUS IN THE CHRISTIAN CHURCH,

He was Himself

AN ORNAMENT

TO EVERY DOMESTIC AND SOCIAL RELATION.

In the Spanish gallery of the Louvre at Paris, there hangs a celebrated picture by Murillo, founded on an old legend, which represents that a certain monk was called to die, when engaged in writing his own biography. Grieved at the abrupt termination of his unfinished task, the fiction goes, that he sought and obtained permission to return to the earth to complete his work. Wonderful is the power with which the immortal artist has embodied the conception. There is the monk seated in his cell, intent on his solemn toil. It is not the ghastly face and form of the dead, but the conception of a man who has been dead, and who has returned etherialised and vivified through and through with the life and motives of Eternity.

That legendary fiction will have no reality with any. No one who goeth hence returns to finish the work of life. But there is intensity of motive enough in the sober truth that every man is actually engaged day by day in writing that autobiography, which neither time nor eternity will efface. It may be written in high places or in low, in public remembrance or in the honest heart of domestic affection, but we are writing fast, we are writing sure, we are writing for eternity. Happy is he who, through the grace of God assisting him, like the subject of this memoir, records such lessons of kindness, truth and wisdom, that when he is gone, he will be held in grateful remembrance; happier still to have one's name written in the

Lamb's Book of Life, that when every memorial and monument of his earthly history has perished, he may ascend with the Son of God, to Honour, Glory, and Immortality.

DEATH IN THE MIDST OF LIFE.

"I said, O my Lord, take me not away in the midst of my days." —PSALM cii. 24, *first clause*.

I SHALL not trouble my hearers upon the present occasion, with any enquiries as to the authorship of the Psalm from which my text is selected, nor as to the circumstances in which it was originally uttered. Whether designed to represent the private experience of the writer, or to exhibit the low and depressed condition of the church in time of great trial, is immaterial to the purpose I have in view, which is to bring out, and for a few moments insist upon a thought, which lies upon the very surface of the passage before us.

As we read our text, we perceive it to be a prayer, an earnest, impassioned prayer, a prayer against death; and the fact which gives it its earnestness and impassioned energy, is that he who offers it is in "the midst of his days." There is a peculiarity then about death coming in the prime of life, which does not belong to it at any other time, or in any other circumstances, and which renders it especially repulsive and terrible. True it is that to one at all alive to its connections, it must, at any time, be appreciated with the most painful emotions. To one standing upon the threshhold of life, or farther advanced engaged in active business, engrossed with earthly cares, or when the bustle and anxiety of the world, so far as he is concerned, are over, whether he be in health and prosperity, when life is most joyous, or in sickness and adversity, when many of the strongest ties to earth are sundered, it is still the same repulsive subject of thought, never able to command a welcome from the human mind. Youth dreads it, manhood dreads it, old age dreads it, sickness and health alike dread it; and while irreligion trembles, faith itself is sometimes staggered in view of it.

There are, however, some circumstances in which death is less terrible than it is in others. When the ties that bind us to earth are few, and the considerations which render life valuable are feeble, the desire to live cannot be strong. Disappointed hopes, defeated plans, withered joys, enfeebled frames, taking so much as they do from the brightness, and promise of the world, must, proportionably, weaken our wishes to remain amid its scenes; if to this you add, a weanedness from the world upon principle, an expectation of death; and satisfactory evidence of a preparation to meet its issues, you have a condition in which it loses to the mind much of its terror.

But in the light in which we now look at it, there are none of these considerations to take aught from its horrors. It is death coming to one in the prime of life, in his full strength, and in circumstances in which it is least expected; coming when the dangers of youth are over, when the system has reached its maturity, when the world is invested with the greatest degree of importance, when man thinks he is about to take that position to which he had long looked forward, and to which all his previous training and labours have been but preparatory. It is death coming to one who had not in his dreams even looked upon it to be possible as an immediate event, and who having been at ease and quiet in reference to it, has made no preparation to meet its issues. This is death in its most appalling form. There are here no disgusts with life, no disappointed hopes, no enfeebled frames, no tottering steps, to make this world undesirable, and there is no sympathy in the spiritual things to make the coming world attractive: and O how many, how many even among ourselves to-day, are there to whom death, should he now approach, would he be thus appalling!

I put the question to my hearers in middle life, are your views, feelings, purposes, circumstances, such as you would wish them to be in the hour of your departure to meet your God? I speak to-day upon the supposition that men in middle life are very apt to look upon death as an improbable event, so far as they are concerned, and to make their calculations, and shape their course accordingly. This is the fact upon which I would fasten your minds, showing you some of its reasons, and pointing out some of its effects.

I offer then here, this general remark, that with no class of men is the desire for life so strong as those of whom we are speaking; and knowing as we do the influence of desire over belief, how conclusive seem those arguments which conform to our feelings, we cannot be surprised to find the improbability of dying assumed as a settled matter. True, the mere wish to live is not confined to any particular age or condition of human life. The youth who is just coming forward upon the stage of action, clings with tenacity to his earthly existence, while the aged man, of whom it may be said, that the days have come and the years drawn nigh in which he has no pleasure, looks forward to his approaching dissolution with feelings of great reluctance. In both these cases, more especially in the last, the desire for life seems to be instinctive, rather than the result of any reasoning from external circumstances and relations. Childhood has scarcely reached the point when the strongest reasons for a wish to live have begun to operate. Old age has passed the point where their influence terminates.

But the man in middle life has reached that point, where all these reasons are perceived most clearly, and their influence is felt most deeply. There is something more than a mere instinctive desire of life which makes him cling to his earthly existence. There are reasons taken from his circumstances and relations, which render life to him very important. The ties which bind him to the world are now the strongest. Hithereto, his earthly associations had been few and ephemeral. There are scarcely any responsibilities involved in the connections of youth, and though in these connections, the feelings may be ardent, they are transient. A change of place, and breaking up of associations, does not seem to be a matter of great importance to a youthful mind, because it can so easily adjust itself to the new circumstances into which it may be thrown. In old age the connections of society have been dissolved by the hand of time; most of those with whom our old men mingled their sympathies and counsels are gone, while they who once were dependent upon them no longer need their care and support.

But it is very different with a man in the vigor of life. He has taken his place in society, and is now sustaining his most important earthly responsibilities. His connections now are most intimate, his attachments most strong, his associations most enduring. He is surrounded by those who depend upon him for support, submit to his control, and look to him for counsel. He is the centre of his family, of the social circle, and alive to all those great interests which excite the attention and engage the feelings of the community. His place is in the hall of science, in the chamber of legislation, among those who sustain the interests and carry forward the designs of society. Mind now is most active, and active, not about the pastimes of youth, but about matters essential to the welfare of himself, of his connections, and the community at large. I need hardly say that these are the circumstances in which life not only appears to be, but actually is, most important to man and to society generally. Death never is more melancholy in its aspect than when it takes one away from amid the necessary activities of human life. The youth dies, and the parental heart feels the pang, and may drop a tear over departed worth. The aged sire dies, and the recollection of former counsels and activities and deeds of goodness depresses the spirit, but the whole machinery of the domestic circle and of society goes on as usual, and so far as essential interests are concerned, the loss in these cases is scarcely felt.

But when one dies in the midst of his days, the case is vastly different; now essential interests suffer; from many their entire earthly dependence is removed; the main spring of the domestic machinery is gone, and in the varied relations of life, his place must be supplied before the interest of those relations can be well sustained.

To this we might add, that the spirit of enterprize is now most active. Man is forming plans which will require years to develope, and those plans constitute the objects of his existence, the centre of his heart's warmest feelings. You cannot go out amid the busy scenes of life, and find a man in his prime, whom death suddenly arresting, should not carry away from unfinished plans and unexecuted purposes. Generally men calculate upon the completion of their designs, and upon receiving the fruit of their labour; very few sow when they do not expect to reap, or engage in plans which are to bring them no profit: and hence it is that our men in middle life calculate with almost perfect certainty upon a continuance in this world; they cannot think that their main designs shall never be executed, and their favourite points never reached, and they suffer their wishes to run away with their judgments, and presume in accordance with the dictates of their hearts.

It is not to be denied, my brethren, that there is not a little in the history of man which tends to foster this very state of mind. Judging from the ordinary developments of Divine Providence, we should be forced to the conclusion that the securities against death, and what are commonly termed the chances of life, are greater in manhood than at any other period of existence; and the scenes through which we have passed ere we reached manhood have been such as to lead us to estimate these securities too highly. It is a fact, I apprehend, that fewer men die at the meridian than at any other point in human life. The majority of our species are gone from the stage of action before they reach their prime, and of the remainder, the larger proportion die after they have passed their prime. This fact, I apprehend, can point to both natural and moral causes in its explanation. At middle life the human system has attained its greatest strength; is less liable to many of those accidents, and better able to resist many of those diseases which carry off so many of our race. The habits of life too are formed, and where they have been habits favourable to health, they will be favourable to its continuance or to the recovery from disease.

The interests of the world, moreover, could not be sustained under a different character of dispensations, and the purposes of God, which, according to his arrangement, require human agency for their evolution, could not be accomplished. Thus, the order of nature evinces no less the wisdom than the goodness of God.

These facts have not failed to secure the attention of men, and they form the ground of their calculations in reference to life. They have passed through the scenes of childhood, been exposed to a thousand snares, been environed by as many changes. Many have been cut down on their right hand and their left, but they have escaped unharmed, and begin to feel as though they had a lease of life. Familiarity with danger blunts our apprehensions. If we have escaped evil and death in circumstances of great exposure, we think we shall escape again; and after having passed the point where our danger was the greatest, because the point previous to which death usually secures the greatest number of its victims, we feel as though we were, for a time, at least, delivered from his power.

Now, I repeat it, putting all these considerations together, it is not surprising that men in "the midst of their days" should think so little of death, and be so callous to its impressive influence; but it is dreadful that it should be so, because we are forced to another thought, viz.: of all men, they who are "in the midst of their days," are least prepared to die. There are exceptions, unquestionably, to this statement; but as a general remark, its truth must be perfectly apparent to any one of observation and discernment. You will find its illustration as well among the professed disciples of Christ as among those who make no pretensions whatever to spirituality of mind. Many a one, who in his early days appeared well as a Christian, as he has advanced in years and become gradually more and more involved in the cares and perplexities of life, has lost his fervor in religion and found his spirituality declining, simply because the engrossing occupations of earth have drawn away his attention from things appertaining to the kingdom of God. Of this change many a one is himself distinctly conscious. He is aware that in a spiritual point of view matters are not with him as they formerly were; if death should approach, he should have much to adjust, many questions to settle, many fears, many anxieties, many doubts to solve; in short, he knows his preparation for death is not what it should be, because he has not been looking for it. My Christian brother, let me appeal to you upon this point in a single question. Had your earthly history terminated with the winding up of the last year, should you have known in your experience the blessedness of that servant whom his Lord when he cometh finds watching? Take that question home, and justify me in the position I have assumed.

If the truth of my remark is evident, even in the cases of the professed disciples of Christ, much more apparent must it be in reference to those who know nothing of the spiritual influence of the gospel. If my unconverted hearers in middle life will look into their own hearts and observe their emotions and feelings, they will not judge me uncharitable in the remark, that the world never had such a hold upon their affections, never to such a degree controlled their purposes and movements, never so completely shut out all spiritual light from the mind, never rendered them so dead to the claims and appeals of the gospel, and so insensible to the enforcement of heavenly things, as at the present moment.

There is one fact which speaks volumes upon this general subject, going to show the prevalent state of mind belonging to the persons of whom we speak. That fact is this, that the legitimate effects of the Gospel are very rarely seen for the first time in persons who are passing through the meridian of life. This seems to be a period in human existence, when the Spirit of God, I will not say seldom strives with men, but when he seldom achieves any signal victories. For the most part, men are brought into the kingdom of God before they reach manhood, while a few after they have passed their prime are awakened by some providential dispensation, and hasten to secure an interest in Christ. The young have ears to hear the truth, consciences to respond to its claims, and hearts susceptible to its impressive power; but the ears of others are closed against us, and their minds are too full of earth to entertain the truth of God, and their hearts too much under the influence of the world, to be susceptible of impressions from spiritual realities. All the means of grace seem to be powerless, and it is looked upon as a signal manifestation of the grace of God, when one of their class is brought to submit himself to Christ.

I speak that which I do know, and testify that which I have seen; and if these thoughts are correct, it follows of necessity, that they to whom they appertain are of all men least prepared to die.

And O! how such thoughts should arouse to feeling, awaken to anxiety, and prompt to enquiry, all to whom they have reference. My beloved brethren, security is not safety, insensibility to danger is no guard against its approach. You may mingle in any scenes, you may engage in wide-spread business, you may form extensive associations, and assume weighty responsibilities,—you have no protection against death, in any or all of these combined. Others who have gone from the stage have told you so, they have fallen from your side, from amid the scenes in which you are now engaged, and the associations amid which you are now moving; and as they fell, their fall was Providence teaching you the worthlessness of all your confidences. Put all the grounds of your security together, they are valueless, they are worse, they serve only to render one's end the more terrible when he reaches it.

We may, my brethren, wrap ourselves up in unconcern about this matter, but we cannot put away from us a dying hour by closing our eyes against it, neither can we, by any insensibility, detract from the magnitude of eternal realities. The scene of our departure from this world is not to be delayed by any unconcern of ours about it, or any unfitness on our part to meet its issues ; and if, when it comes, it shall find us in a state of indifference and security, how inexpressibly fearful will be its approach. Let death come at any time, in any circumstance, under any form, but let it not come upon man when he thinks least of it, and is consequently least prepared to meet it, when, perhaps, it is the last event which he dreamed of as at all probable. Here it has associations, the sorrows of which no tongue can describe, because no mind can conceive them. Defeated plans, disappointed hopes, blasted joys, form but few, and those the least bitter of the ingredients of the cup which it puts to the lips. Now, in an unexpected hour, eternal things come before him, in such a light that he can doubt neither their reality nor their magnitude, and now he must prepare to meet them with a mind surprised, alarmed, harassed ; and too often self-reflection triumphs over every other feeling, and the unhappy man, amid his convictions and reproaches, his self-reflections and his fears, finds the ties which bind him to this world parting, and his surprised and unprepared spirit winging its flight to the presence of a forgotten God.

These are not strange and unusual scenes ; they have been, they are common. The history of the last year keeps the record of many of them, and the year upon which we have entered, will but repeat them. I look back over the past year, and I find that death, in the circle of our companionship, death in the midst of us as a congregation, has been very impressive in the lessons it has taught us, however slow we may be to learn them. Yet it is ours to ponder them, and turn them to a practical account. During the past year, nine who were with us at its commencement, have closed their earthly career. As I cast my eye over this assembly, I miss the youth who occupied his seat here on the first Sabbath of the last year, and who little thought that the warning which then we uttered was meant for him. I miss our aged friends who had filled up the measure of their days. And there have been those who were carried away in the midst of their days, whom no effort could deliver, no prayer save from the power of death.

And that which has been shall be. This year will bring about like events; some of my youthful hearers will be gone; of our fathers we shall say, where are they? and ye who are in the vigour of your days, secure against danger, ye too must pay your tribute to the king of terrors, by yielding some of your members a sacrifice to his claims.

But while thus I utter my warning, I feel that it is in vain. In respect to death, nothing but the influence of God's spirit can teach us to apply our hearts unto wisdom. The coffin will not teach us wisdom here, the grave will not teach it, pestilence will not teach it. Thou, O God, and thou alone canst make us feel that we are mortal, so that we shall live like the immortal, and, therefore, while we feel that argument is in vain, and exhortation is in vain, and appeal is in vain, we turn from reasoning, and expostulation, and pleading, to prayer as our only hope. Now as we enter upon another year, not knowing what is before us, we turn to thee, O Lord God of the spirits of all flesh. The young are before thee, the middle-aged are before thee, our fathers are before thee, pastor and people alike are before thee: "God of the spirit of all flesh, so teach us to number our days that we may apply our hearts unto wisdom."

THE NATURE AND DESIGN OF THE CRUCIFIXION SCENE.

"And when Jesus had cried with a loud voice, he said, Father into thy hands I commend my spirit, and having said this, he gave up the ghost."—St. Luke xxiii. 16.

"My God, my God, why hast thou forsaken me."—St. Matthew xxvii. 46.

The words of the text carry us directly to Calvary, a spot which we can never too frequently visit, and where the Christian loves to linger, especially when called upon, as we are this day, to remember the scenes which were there presented. In the description which they give us of the remarkable, and to many, mysterious close of the life of Jesus Christ, they suggest lessons, which, often as we have pondered them, we have never yet fully learned, and open sources of influence, the extent and power of which we have yet to measure. Indeed there is scarcely a line in the history of Jesus Christ which is not as instructive as it is wonderful. The annals of the universe will not furnish a parallel to the story of "the man of sorrows and acquainted with grief." He presents himself first to our view as one, who though he was "in the form of God," emptied himself "and took upon him" the form of man, and thus is introduced to our attention in an act of humiliation which is beyond the power of human thought to understand. As we cannot ascend to the throne, measure its height, or form any conceptions of its grandeur, we cannot tell how great was the humiliation of Christ Jesus, when he descended to the level of his creatures; as his previous glory is inaccessible to our soarings, it must always remain a prodigy too large for anything but faith to grasp, that he who was "in the form of God took upon him the form of man."

And yet this fact, surprizing as it is, does not constitute the wonder of Christ's humiliation; the marvel is not merely that he became man, but that having become man, he should put himself in man's most forbidding circumstances, clothe himself with human nature in its greatest meanness, submit to its greatest hardships, endure its heaviest trials, and submit, both in life and death, to its greatest ignominy. The scene of his earthly course, is, in its commencement, contempt and privation; in its progress, toil and shame; in its end, agony and degradation. The changes in his experience, were not, as is customary even with the most wretched of our race, alternations of joy and sorrow, but changes from sorrow to sorrow, each succeeding one deeper in its shades than the former, and as we look at the map of his life, we perceive the plot thickening and the darkness increasing daily and hourly around him. His whole course betokens a dreadful consummation; all the lines of conduct pursued by himself, and by those who surround him, seem to converge towards one fearful catastrophe, which when reached, surpasses in wonderfulness everything which preceded it. We can understand in view of his objects and his course, why he should be persecuted by the men of his generation; our knowledge of human nature may serve to explain to us, why in the hour of his trial he should be abandoned by his professed friends; but why, why, when he most needed Heaven's sympathy and Heaven's help, why, when heart and flesh fainted and failed, why, when all the resources of human comfort and human strength were exhausted, and he was sinking under a burden too heavy for him to bear, why in such an hour, he should be forsaken of God, this forms the great wonder of a Redeemer's humiliation.

Not one of us, my brethren, has ever pondered this event, without feeling that there is a mystery here which needs an explanation. It is not that a person from whose lips dropped words of unutterable tenderness, who rarely spoke but to bless the sorrow-stricken, or acted but to relieve the distressed, should be selected as an object upon which to wreak the fury of a spirit which, for cool, cruel and devilish barbarity, has never yet found its parallel; this is not the mystery; but it is that he who did no sin, and in whose mouth no guile was found, whose meat it was to do the will of his

Heavenly Father, who by "signs and wonders, and diverse miracles" had been accredited as the messenger of God, and by an audible voice had been announced as his only begotten and well-beloved Son, should at last die under a cloud, and utter in his last words a lamentation over his spiritual abandonment; this is the mystery of that event which to-day we commemorate, and to which in this exercise I shall call your attention.

My subject, I am aware, has not about it any of the attractive charms of novelty. We have often pondered it; and we all have its outlines, at least, distinctly before the mind, and yet I am persuaded that the views with which many fill up this outline, are at best exceedingly vague, if they are not often palpably erroneous, and that, consequently, the influence of the scene is in a great measure lost. To a certain extent, perhaps, our views must be limited and indistinct; inquiries may be started which can be fully answered only when the light of a better world shall disclose all the mysteries of redemption; and yet, without attempting to be wise above what is written, we may learn something by a patient examination; something which, even if it does not add to our stores of knowledge, may at least serve to set the event before us in a different light and put upon it a different aspect from that in which many minds are wont to look at it.

With these views, then, we approach our subject to ascertain, if possible, something of the Redeemer's state of mind, when upon the cross he cried out with a loud voice, and which certainly has an air of mystery about it. When we look at the record, we find that, previous to the moment of our Saviour's history now under consideration, there were exhibitions of feeling which plainly evinced that his mind was filled and crushed by painful premonitions of the experience before him. The garden scene shows us his spirit wrestling and agonizing with these dire apprehensions, which by their influence drove his life-blood from its wonted channels, and extorted from him his earnest prayer for deliverance.

It is, indeed, by no means difficult to imagine circumstances when a man may be convulsed and tremble greatly in view of the hour and scene of his dissolution. When the future is all dark, and the sepulchre looks like one's final resting-place, when one feels that the winding-sheet is to be his eternal habiliment, that light is never to break in upon his grave, and no voice is ever to be heard disturbing the silence of his resting-place, I can easily understand how one may shrink back; for nature, as such, never can be reconciled to the thought of an eternal extinction of being. Man may, indeed, prefer annihilation to a state of perpetual, hopeless misery, because the fear of the future may triumph over and paralyze even the instinctive laws of our being; but nature, as such, must shrink back with horror from the prospect of ceasing to be. So, likewise, when conscience, armed with the stings of a guilty life, lashes its victim, and heralds an approaching storm of fire and blood; when the undying worm begins to prey upon the mind, and the poison cup of the wrath of God is put to the lips, and the first taste of its bitter ingredients is perceived, there is room for the heavings of the stoutest spirit, and the convulsive agonies of the strongest frame. He who is entirely in the dark as to the future, he whose conscience having never been pacified by the peace-speaking influence of atoning blood, cannot be mastered, may well shrink back and cry in agony when his feet touch the first cold wave of that boisterous flood which rolls between time and the judgment-seat. Here we have sufficient sources of fear and agony in view of approaching dissolution. I allude to these, merely for the purpose of showing that they cannot be introduced as adequate or even appropriate exponents of the scene we are called to-day to study. There could be nothing in the darkness of the future, or the gloom of the sepulchre, to terrify the spirit of Him who brought life and immortality to light. No fears of a coming retribution could trouble Him who was "holy, harmless, and undefiled;" nor could there be any anticipations to appal him, who, "in the view of the joy set before him, endured the cross, despising its shame."

There is a wonderful difference—you must have often been struck by it—between the dying scene of our Saviour and that of many of his followers; in the one case, there is a crushing agony and the wail of seeming despair; in other cases, there are emotions of joy and shouts of triumph. What a contrast between the language of an apostle, "I have a desire to depart, I am now ready to be offered;"

and the prayer of Jesus Christ, "Father, save me from this hour;" between the Saviour's lamentation on the cross and the experience of the culprit crucified with him, whose troubled spirit that Saviour's promise calmed, and whose sinking soul that Saviour's strength sustained; a contrast, which, as we examine it, forces upon us the conclusion, that no ordinary principles of explanation meet the case, and compels us to find a solution in something which does not strike the eye.

There is a struggle going on in that sufferer's mind of which neither you nor I can form any adequate conception; and when we say that his experiences, so sad, so overwhelming, were of a mental nature, independent of visible scenes and circumstances, we seem to many to have reached a point beyond which we cannot go, without launching upon an ocean of vain and unsatisfying conjecture. True it is, that we cannot determine the precise nature of our Saviour's experiences in the hour of his conflict, for we can form no just idea of experiences of which we ourselves have not to some degree been the subjects; but if we cannot tell all the ingredients which were mingled in that bitter cup which was given him to drink, we can at least say what was not stirred into the bitter draught, and thus detect the fallacy of some views, which, I apprehend, are sources of painful feeling to many, because I remember well how once they troubled my own mind, as detracting greatly from the character of the Redeemer. Let me ask your attention to a thought or two.

The scene of the cross was the crisis of our Saviour's sorrow. The sufferings of his life had been many and bitter, as he had gone on from pain to pain, and anguish to anguish; yet they were but the sprinklings which heralded the coming tempest. It was on Calvary that the storm burst upon him in its tremendousness; and if you look carefully at his language during this crisis, you will find him overwhelmed and crushed, mainly by the consciousness of this fact, that he *was abandoned by God.*

Now, what did he mean by this? Is it true; can it be true, as many have often said, and as we ourselves have often thought, that God in this hour of his Son's extremity, withdrew from him the light of his countenance and threw over him the cloud of his displeasure? Was it any manifestation of wrath toward him personally which so distressed his mind and drank up his spirit? His language does indeed appear at first sight to suggest such a thought; but in view of this supposition, the scene of Calvary, is to my mind, wrapped in greater mystery than before. If, indeed, the mediation of Christ consisted in such an exchange of position between Himself and those for whom he suffered, that their guilt, as well as legal obligation to suffering, was transferred to Him, it should be perfectly consistent to speak of His enduring the wrath of God; but who can reconcile his views of the character of the Redeemer with the idea that punishment, in any proper sense, entered into His sufferings? Whose feelings will allow him to introduce the thought of punishment as an exponent of the dying agonies of Jesus Christ? Can we have in the same person a being innocent, yet guilty? one upon whom God looks in wrath, and yet with great complacency? one who is visited with punishment at the time when he is performing his highest act of obedience? it cannot be. Jesus Christ was God's beloved Son, in whom he was well pleased; and never was he more pleased with him than when he reached the extremity of his woe. If this supposition is inadmissible; is there any room for another, which has often been advanced, that Jesus Christ lost sight of his Father's countenance, or at least apprehended such a loss? How is such a thought to be reconciled with the facts, that in the moment of his bitterest experience his language is that of filial and affectionate confidence? that at this very moment, he had distinctly in view "the joy set before him;" that he had an interest in Heaven, as evinced by the assurance given to the thief at his side; that he could with perfect confidence commit his spirit to his Father, and act the part of intercessor as he prayed for those who nailed him to the tree. There is nothing in all this which looks like spiritual abandonment or a loss of the light of God's countenance. In view of such facts, I can never admit the common exposition of our Redeemer's suffering as consisting in anything like darkness or momentary despair. There is not a thought like this upon any page of the Bible; there is nothing in any recorded circumstance of a Saviour's passion which can furnish the least ground for such a supposition.

And yet there must be a sense in which Christ was forsaken of God, or he never would have used the language—what then, we repeat the question, are we to understand by it? He was given up to suffering. If you look at the pages of the Bible, you find that there was given unto the Redeemer a particular work to do. "For this purpose was the Son of God manifested, that he might destroy the works of the devil." To do it, he must show how iniquity can be forgiven, while at the same time, he breaks the power of him who had triumphed over man. It was a work at once of wisdom and of power. Under a perfect government, the connection between sin and suffering must be seen to be indissoluble. If you can conceive of any circumstances in which these two ideas can be dissociated, you can conceive of circumstances, in which the securities of righteousness and happiness, are not perfect. If Christ then is to accomplish his work, he must be made perfect through suffering, and his suffering, to answer its end, must be as intense as sin is malignant. He must therefore so identify himself with sinful man, that his sufferings shall be seen in connection with their sin as the ground of its forgiveness, or in other words its expiation. Thus it was that the curse of a broken law might be traced in his mighty pangs, and every line of the writing of agony, might be a lesson, as to the evil and magnitude of the curse. In this sense he could be given up by God to sorrow, and at one and the same time he might sink under the fearful pressure which was put upon him, while he yet had continually the light of his Father's countenance.

If you look again attentively at the record of the Redeemer's sufferings, you will discover in almost every line, intimations of some hidden, mysterious strife. The scene of Calvary was distinctly anticipated by him, as "the hour of the power of darkness." What was open and palpable in these tragic occurrences, was but part of the doings of the same agency which was working, still more terribly, unseen. In all that was visible the prince of darkness was using the influence of men, while in the spiritual and invisible world he was using other agencies far more mighty. Christ had voluntarily assumed the work of captain of our salvation, and as such he must carry it through single-handed and alone. It was necessary to the perfection of his character, as the great Mediator, that he should himself be seen to be the conqueror of death and hell, so as to be able to give assurance to all who put their confidence in him of his ability to secure to them ultimate victory by means of the same power, by virtue of which, he himself triumphed so gloriously. His language upon the cross, therefore, seemingly so mysterious, was, as I apprehend, but the expression of his feelings, as he found himself solitary in this last desperate strife. He had never uttered such language before—as never before had he been placed in precisely similar circumstances, never before had he been conscious, of being left to manage alone, and master alone the powers of darkness with whom he was called to contend. During his previous history, amid all the scenes through which he passed, and under all the difficulties he was called to encounter, and all the trials he had been summoned to endure, it never was true of him, that he stood alone. In the hour of his temptation he had succours from on high; in his conflict in the garden angels ministered to him. Very different is it with him now, and it is not surprising that when he reached the crisis and heat of the struggle, and the last great onset was to be made upon him, when about to receive the fulness of the cup which had been mingled for him, and his overwrought and overtasked human spirit was taxed to the utmost of its powers of action and endurance, he should give vent to his feelings in the language of dereliction. I look upon his words, therefore, in these circumstances, as conveying the same meaning with like words uttered in olden time by the Church, and on one occasion by the Psalmist, "The Lord hath forsaken me." At that very moment they were dear to him as the apple of his eye, and he never forgot them for an instant; but for the time, they were left under the power of affliction, without any visible means of relief but such as they themselves could furnish. So it was with Jesus Christ, and his language, so far from conveying the idea that he was suffering the wrath of God, or was a subject of spiritual dereliction, is but expressive of his feelings, as he entered single-handed into his last desperate conflict with his greatest enemy.

I give this interpretation of our Saviour's experience upon the cross, as the only one in which my own mind can rest, as relieving the subject from difficulties, not only upon any other supposition insurmountable, but as painful to every Christian heart.

And yet the scene which is here presented to our attention, even when relieved of its difficulties, is truly wonderful; and the end which it contemplated must be as extraordinary as wonderful. What that end was is an appropriate enquiry, because in the end as illustrated by the means, is found the power of the cross.

My first remark here is, that the trials and sufferings of Jesus Christ were essential to the perfection of his character as our great example. "To this end," we are told, that "he suffered for us, leaving us an example." There have been in our world examples of patience and submission and resignation to the will of God, but there have been none like that of Jesus Christ. To answer this great end, he must learn obedience from his suffering, and learn it too in the most painful circumstances; he must endure the heaviest trials which can weigh down a human spirit, and become acquainted with sorrow, not merely in its varied, but in its heaviest forms, and having thus learned obedience, by going through the perfection of suffering, he has become a perfect example. So, likewise, to qualify him for his office, as "the captain of salvation to all them who obey him," it was necessary for him to pass through the very scenes of trial and conflict which marked his history; he must meet the powers of darkness at the moment when they gained their greatest ascendancy, and overcome them, when they put on their severest forms of malice, and put forth the mightiest efforts of their strength. This he did upon the cross, and having there made a show of his enemies openly, he is manifested to the world "as able to save unto the uttermost all who come unto God by him." In the midst of such thoughts, however, important as they are, and essential as they may be to a correct view of our Redeemer's position and work, we must not overlook what seems to us to have been the main design of the crucifixion scene.

The grand theme which constitutes the burden of this revelation, is reconciliation between man and God, and this reconciliation is uniformly spoken of as effected only by the cross of Christ. The forgiveness of human transgression—that is the point to be compassed—and to be compassed in a way as honourable to God as it is safe for man. The integrity of the divine character, no more than man's own sense of right, preclude the idea of forgiveness and reconciliation separate from something which taking the place of our punishment, shall answer the same end, and make an equal or a better impression. Something there must be, upon which the human conscience can roll the burden of its guilt, something which can inspire confidence in God; otherwise there is a barrier between the soul and its Creator, high as heaven, and enduring as the Eternal throne; and upon this intricate and perplexing question, the cross of Christ has thrown its unequivocal and satisfactory light, demonstrating no less clearly God's justice than his grace in forgiveness.

I am not wrong in speaking of the wondrous impression, which the sufferings of a Redeemer as a substitute for man, have made upon the human mind. Since the world began, no transaction like it has ever taken place—no expedient like it has ever been found to influence the human heart or stay the swelling tide of human corruption. The flood swept away a guilty world, and the impression made by that dread manifestation of divine displeasure was soon forgotten. Fire from heaven destroyed the cities of the plain, and the impression was soon forgotten, and they who stood around the cross of Christ, thought that the impression of the crucifixion scene would be soon forgotten. But it was not so; the blood of Gethsemane and Calvary was scarcely dry, ere this event attracted the attention, affected the hearts, and changed the character of thousands. Its influence spread with the rapidity of fire; wealth and power were insufficient to stay its progress, or prevent its effect; at the present day, it holds an ascendancy over more hearts than ever; you feel it, I feel it, every where we cannot escape it, if we would; and its influence is extending and widening, and deepening, promising to reach every nation, every family, every human being upon our globe. The impression moreover, which it makes is of the very character needed; an impression not more distinct of God's readiness to forgive sin than of His displeasure against sin. Can any of us doubt its impressive power? Is there one who does not feel it? One, some of the movements of whose mind it does not control? I take the man who imagines that the question of his immortality can be very easily disposed of; the man who finds shelter from his fears under the influence of some vague notions of the mercy of God, and carry him to the scene of the crucifixion, and bid him study it, to look at his reasonings and his hopes in the light of the cross. If there is anything which will disturb a man in his unconcern about futurity; if there is anything which will shake the foundation of false hopes, the cross of Christ will do it. You think yourself safe, uninterested in the blood of atonement. See what God thinks of your confidence and hope. Your reasonings upon the subject come in too late. God has answered them already, in the expression of his views of sin, given in the death of His Son. Every movement of that sufferer as he prays in his agony; every drop of blood which he sheds, testifies to the worthlessness of your hope. Your most serious misgivings, your most anxious thoughts, your most harassing fears, your most unhappy anticipations, called into being as they are by the study of the cross, are the honest testimony of your own spirit to its impressive power and the demonstration of the wisdom of God in his plan of reconciliation.

No less mighty is it in its action upon the mind of the humble and contrite, than it is upon the conscience of the presumptuous and unsubdued. The impression which in this case it makes, as to one's safety, is as deep and effective, as the impression which it makes in the other case of one's peril. Christians there may be, whose claims to the character and name, I should be slow to dispute, who have very little confidence in the value of their hopes, and sometimes even pride themselves upon their doubts, as evidences of a sensitive and enlightened conscience; but what right have you or I to compliment ourselves at the expense of the cross of Christ? If the ground of our dependence was in ourselves, we might well doubt; but what room is there for doubt in view of him who magnified the law and made it honorable? My iniquities may be so many that I cannot number them, and so great that I cannot measure their enormity. My ill-desert may be so vast, as to be beyond my power of calculation, but I cannot go to the cross and study its meaning without learning that the blood of Christ cleanseth from all sin. Many and strong may be my temptations, and sometimes I fear that I may be borne down and carried away by their power. But my fears vanish when I remember that I walk under the protection of Him who having been in all points tempted like myself, and having learned obedience from the things which he suffered, is exalted to be a high priest, enabled from his experience to sympathize with me, and by his power to succour me in every exigency of my being. I may be called to wrestle, not simply with flesh and blood, but with principalities and powers likewise, yet the captain of my salvation is one who has made a show of them openly upon his cross; and where, or who is he that condemneth, since "it is Christ who died, yea, rather who is risen again?"

The impression then of the crucifixion scene upon the Christian's mind, assuring him of his safety, is no less distinct, than its impression upon the sinner's mind assuring him of his danger; the fears of the former and the hopes of the latter, can exist only as the garden, the cross, and the sepulchre are shut out from the view—if the one dare not hope, the other dare not fear, as he thinks of the Redeemer's work.

Oh! there is something in this cross, we know it and feel it, which has a wonderous power to arrest, awaken, and convince; and a power no less wonderous to soothe, to rest the anxious spirit, to charm to quietness the troubled conscience, and wake to hope the desponding soul. They who are careless have but to look to tremble, they who are sinking under a load of conscious guilt, have but to look to live, and they who are harassed by fears, have but to look to put on new forms of strength.

I have one more thought: the cross of Christ is a demonstration of love, a warrant for confidence, an appeal to everything noble and generous about human nature. I question not that the Redeemer's work took its peculiar form, as much to meet the feelings of the human hearts as to meet the requirements of God's justice and truth. Our feelings, my brethren, towards God, are naturally those of distrust and opposition, and that simply because we are sinners; and these feelings must be mastered before we can be saved; and they must be mastered by an unequivocal overwhelming demonstration of love; and we have it in the cross, for there "God is in Christ, reconciling man unto Himself." The Redeemer was not compelled to suffer; at any moment he might have turned back from the path upon which he had entered; he might have taken refuge in his own purity and thrown from him the oppressive curse, which seemed every moment to grow longer and broader, and deeper and higher. And why did he not do it? We have no other answer than this. His suffering to him was a continual lesson of the extent and magnitude of the curse, as it taught him how much he had to endure; it taught him how much man must endure if he gave him up; and because he loved man so much the thickening darkness of the curse only bound him the faster to his work; the increasing weight of the curse only urged him onward; its growing immensity only animated him to throw every nerve into the effort for its annihilation; the principle which controlled became more energetic and active as the suffering became more intense; he saw, he endured, he triumphed under the influence of love to man; and now he not only shows us that we may trust him, but he addresses his appeal to these hearts.

And I know, my hearer, that there are hearts which respond to this appeal, if yours does not. I know that there are those who will here and elsewhere, gather to-day around the memorial of a Saviour's love, and under the subduing influence of the cross, will give themselves away to him, who on their account shrank not from the curse. Theirs will be strong emotions as well of confidence as of gratitude. What shall yours be? What tale shall be told of you, and what record made of your feelings and purposes? A tale which will sound strange in heaven, and be read by you hereafter with an aching, sinking heart. The tale of one who could study a Redeemer's agony and sympathize with the spirit which caused it; of one who could go to his master in Gethsemane and wring into the cup from which he drinks some of its drops of bitterness; who could go with him to Calvary, and join with the unseen powers who distracted his holy soul. Sin forced from him his cry of agony, as it gave horrors to the curse which overwhelmed him, and you will not forsake sin! Sin, your sin, explains this dread catastrophe, and solves all its mysteries, and you will be a sinner still! You do not fully comprehend this matter, or you could not think, and feel, and act as you do. If you do, if you can remain a sinner, unsubdued by the cross, understanding its meaning and its mysteries, I would not occupy your position for ten thousand worlds. I would rather be one of those who nailed him to the tree and pierced his side, for of them could our Saviour say, as he cannot say of you, "They know not what they do."

My guilty, unhappy hearer, a dying Saviour speaks to you to-day; his bitter passion and his prayer of agony, his atoning blood, and his dying exclamation, these are the arguments of the sinner's friend. An archangel could not speak to you in strains so sweet, nor yet in tones so awful, as does the cross of Christ. Under the influence of that cross I would put myself, in strong confidence, and a spirit of devotion; under the influence of its arguments and appeals I would leave you. If you cannot admit its claims and yield to its power, if you cannot give yourself to your Master as he speaks to you to-day, go write, I know you must do it with a trembling hand, go write your decision upon his cross.

"THE LAMB SLAIN IN THE MIDST OF THE THRONE."

"And, I beheld, and lo! in the midst of the throne, and of the four beasts, and in the midst of the elders, stood a Lamb as it had been slain, having seven horns, and seven eyes, which are the seven spirits of God, sent forth into all the earth."—REVELATIONS v. 6.

FROM the splendid vision which was vouchsafed to the beloved disciple, on the isle of Patmos, we select that part contained in our text, as furnishing an appropriate theme for our meditation this morning. It is not upon the throne, circled though it was with a rainbow of emerald, nor yet upon him who sat upon it, gorgeous though he was with jasper and sardine stone, nor yet upon the living creatures, crowned though they were with gold, that we wish to fix your attention, but rather upon what at first sight appears to be out of place, because incongruous to what is so majestic and magnificent, a Lamb slain, a being, in the midst of this glory, clothed with the symbols of sadness, and exhibiting the marks of humiliation, and suffering and death.

The design of the vision must be apparent to every one who will give a careful attention to the context. It is to exhibit the dominion of God, and his unrestrained and controlling agency in managing the affairs of the world. In the hands of *him* who sat upon the throne, was a sealed, mysterious volume, full of the secrets of the future; and of all the hosts of heaven, not one was able to break the seals, and throw open the book, but one who was designated by the august title of "the Lion of the tribe Judah, the Root of David;" and surely, these notes of preparation, this wonderful and splendid preliminary process would lead us to anticipate in the person of Him who alone was able to open the book, the appearance at least of surpassing glory; and yet, while the apostle looks with admiring expectation for the coming of one who had been thus hailed and announced, he beholds not a being wearing an aspect of resistless power, not a being arrayed with thunder, and seemingly able to trample upon principalities and powers, but "a Lamb as it had been slain," a being, wearing amid all the grandeur by which he was surrounded, if I may speak so, the imagery of death. It was the glorified humanity of Jesus Christ upon which he gazed, bearing yet the evidences of a cruel and languishing death, to which it had submitted; the print of the nails was there, the gash of the spear was there. Exalted though he was, the evidences of his humiliation had not been effaced; there amid all his glory were the traces of his previous infamy and suffering: this is the being, with "the seven horns," emblems of power and "the seven eyes," emblems of wisdom, "which are the seven spirits of God sent forth into all the earth."

Now, can we mistake the doctrine inculcated? The government of this world rests with Jesus Christ, as a once crucified Saviour, and he is invested as such, with all the power, and all the wisdom, necessary to break the seals of God's book of Providence, and bring out the wondrous secrets contained within its mysterious leaves.

There are then two thoughts embodied in this exhibition. The appearance of Jesus Christ in heaven, "as a Lamb slain," bearing the evidence of his conflict and suffering; and the government which as such he exercises over this world. The reasons for this peculiar manifestation, the lessons which we are taught by it, and the fact, that all the events in the world, all the developments of God's providence are made subservient to the Redeemer's purposes, are to furnish us with topics of remark.

1. My first thought is, the sacrificial offering of Jesus Christ is recognized in heaven. Think as men may of the theme of redemption through atoning blood, it is acknowledged in its reality and perceived in its glory by the dwellers in a higher and purer sphere than our own. If the thrones of heaven bow to the Lamb slain, if its lamps burn around him, its laurels garland, its harps celebrate, and its incense enshrines him, what care we for the names and opinions and suffrages of men? You cannot by any possibility explain this peculiar appellation given to Jesus Christ, without bringing

into view the idea of his sacrificial work. "The Lamb," "the Lamb of God," "the Lamb of God slain." You must go back to Jewish history to find a key to unlock the mystery of these remarkable designations; you must go back to the dark stillness of that night when the destroying angel was commissioned to traverse the land of Egypt in its length and breadth, dealing out death to the first born of the people, and covering the country with a saddened and terrified population. On that night were the children of Israel required to slay a lamb for every house, and take the blood and sprinkle it on the side-posts and doors of their dwellings, that when the destroying angel went through the land, he might pass by, and leave unharmed the houses upon whose thresholds appeared the commanded memorial. It was a type, as the apostle tells us, of "the blood of sprinkling;" and if Christ is presented to us, as "a lamb," and "a lamb slain," if his blood is called "the blood of sprinkling," it must be so, because it is the mark of deliverance set upon those who are saved from the ruins of the apostacy; and as in the night of Egypt's dismay the destroying angel knew from the blood spots on the dwellings where to strike and where to forbear, so, in the last day, when the wheels of the universe stand still, and begin to break, when the year of the redeemed shall have come, and the day of vengeance shall have arrived, the angels of God shall be guided, by a like designation, as they go forth to sever between the wicked and the righteous, and they only shall be delivered from the terrors of the final catastrophe, who have been sprinkled with that blood which "cleanseth from all sin."

But while the correspondence between the ancient paschal lamb and the Redeemer, explains the peculiar appellation given to the latter, it goes no farther in unfolding the mysteries of our text. We can easily understand that Jesus Christ, as the anti-type of the ancient sacrifices, must himself be a sacrifice, and as the blood of the offered lamb was the only security to the Israelites in the night of Egypt's desolation, so in the day of this world's ruin, the only pledge of protection and passport to safety must be found in the blood and death of the crucified one. But why after the Redeemer has passed through and accomplished his work, and risen to his glory and his throne, should he be represented as wearing still, amid his splendour, the mementoes and badges of his former humiliation and suffering?

In the appearances of sanctified spirits in the other world, as they were made to the beloved disciple, there was nothing like sadness or suffering. They are, indeed, represented as those "who had come out of great tribulation;" but then all tears had been washed from their eyes, and all sorrow and sighing had fled away for ever. We feel that it would be incongruous to represent a glorified saint in heaven as one who bore the marks of suffering. It would give an aspect of melancholy and gloom to the whole scenery of the skies if the ransomed bore the marks of trial and suffering, because they would be mementoes, not of trials only, but of sins likewise; signs not of sorrow simply, but of a guilty apostacy. It is not so, however, with Christ. His sufferings were indeed connected with sin, but not his own. He sorrowed, but not for himself. He agonized, but the iniquity of others drove him to the garden and the cross. The imagery of suffering and death, which would appear exceedingly painful, and even reproachful, if woven into the raiment of one who died because he had sinned, may appear beautiful and glorious as the garb of one who died only that he might atone and save from sin. The scar of a felon's brand is the perpetual mark of his infamy, but the scars of a warrior's wound proclaim his courage and publish his glory.

There is, I imagine, a design in this representation to exhibit to us that glory of the Redeemer which is peculiar to Him only, "as a Lamb that had been slain." He has a glory independent of any of his achievements for man; a glory to which nothing could be added, and from which nothing can be withdrawn, whose shining can neither be brightened nor dimmed by the obedience or disobedience of his creatures, the glory of his essential Deity. There is a glory, moreover, belonging to him as the One Mediator between God and man, who, without ceasing to be what he was, yet took upon him mysteriously the form of a servant, and thus gathered into one the creature and the Creator, lighting up the humanity with Deity, and clothing Deity with humanity, and becoming a form for the manifestation of the invisible God.

But the peculiar glory of the Redeemer resulted from his work as Mediator. To accomplish this work he assumed humanity. The nature which had sinned was the nature to be redeemed, and it could be redeemed only by that which was effected in the nature which had sinned. Divinity alone could not be a Mediator; humanity alone could not be. The nature of the office, implying two parties, supposes of necessity a sympathy with both; and as God and man are the parties, none but the God-man can possibly be the Mediator. Hence it is that Christ took upon him the form of a servant. Hence it is that " the Word was made flesh." By sorrowing and obeying in the nature which had rebelled; by keeping it undefiled, and then offering it through the Eternal Spirit a sacrifice unto God, Christ accomplished the end of his office; and now I would have you distinctly to observe, as the illustration of the point before us, that he accomplished his work through suffering. The " Captain of our Salvation was made perfect, or exalted to glory by his sufferings." " By death he destroyed him who had the power of death." He died, but not as sinners die; he fell, but not as falls the child of mortality. His wounds overcame his enemy; and death as it took hold upon Christ, did but paralyze itself. We often say of some earthly warrior, that " he fell in the moment of victory;" but Christ did more than this, he obtained his victory by falling; and if the military chieftain returning a conqueror from the conflict manifests his energy, and prowess, and bravery by the wounds which he bears away with him from the battle-field, why can we not understand how the appearance of Jesus Christ on high, "as a Lamb that had been slain," is the brightest illustration of his grandeur. If his wounds were the arms by which he conquered, and his death the engine by which he shook to pieces the despotism of Satan, what attire can be so glorious a covering to his humanity, as the print of the nails and the gash of the spear? Under what aspect can he show himself more beautiful than that of a lamb slain? Where is the incongruity, the want of strict keeping between the scenery of heaven and this imagery of woe? These signs of death are the emblems of victory worn by the conqueror; the banner which floats over him is emblazoned with his enterprize: the covering which enwraps him is written all over with his successes; and if the marks of death are thus the tokens of triumph, we wonder not that he wears them; we wonder not that the cros sshould be near him, and the garment in which he bled should be thrown around him, and that the burning cherubim and seraphim, when they would sing his praise, take their harps and sweep them to the chorus, "Worthy is the Lamb that was slain."

2. Now, if we have gone so far in our remarks, as to shew that this peculiar appearance of Christ in heaven was the best and brightest illustration of his glory as a Redeemer, let us essay to go one

step farther, that we may ascertain whether there is not that about it which administers to our own personal comfort, security, and hope.

" Christ was once offered," we are told in the Scriptures, " to bear the sins of many;" and in reliance upon the statements of the same Scriptures, we believe, that " by the one offering of himself, he hath perfected forever them that are sanctified." In that one oblation there was such a virtue, that no amount of iniquity, however aggravated, can call for a new atonement. Under the law the sacrifices were continually offered; with the dawn of the morning and the shades of the evening victims must die for the offences of the congregation. But Christ having appeared as the great anti-type of the ancient offerings, has by one sacrifice made a full and complete atonement. But while we cling to this one sacrifice, believing that no sin ever has been, no sin ever will be committed, for which this will not suffice, we believe also that Christ is " the same yesterday, to-day, and forever." And what do we mean by this sameness? Am I wrong when I say he is the same, so that there is no such thing as age in his sacrifice? that centuries cannot give antiquity to his atonement, time cannot wear out its virtues; that his blood is as precious now as when first it was shed, and the fountain for sin and uncleanness flows with a stream as full and purifying as when first it was opened? And how? Simply because by his intercession he perpetuates his sacrifice; and his offering, though not repeated on earth, is incessantly presented in heaven. It was enough that he should once die to make atonement, seeing he ever lives to make intercession.

Now, when we read that Jesus Christ, in heaven, appears as "the Lamb that had been slain," you will not consider me as wresting the inspired language or drawing a conclusion any broader than my premises, when I infer that he is now carrying on in heaven the very office and work which he commenced when upon earth; and though there is no visible altar, and no literal sacrifice, no endurance of anguish, and no shedding of blood; yet still he presents vividly and energetically the marks of his passion, and the effect is the same as though he died daily, and acted over again and again the scene of his tremendous conflict with "the powers of darkness."

We can hardly imagine a figure which can more clearly than that of our text, express the idea that Jesus Christ on high presents himself as a mighty intercessor, an intercessor, not because he pleads with the plaintiveness of entreaty, or the eloquence of tears; but because he covers the defenceless with the shadow of his wing; because, whatever may be our necessities, however great the things we may need, however unworthy we may be of one of them, he has secured by his death a supply for our every want; and now by presenting the merits of that death, he asks and secures the abundant outgoings of heavenly influence for the meanest of his disciples.

There are sins daily committed, in thought, word and deed; how could they be pardoned, were it not for "the Lamb slain in the midst of the throne." Why do we look for the descent of the Comforter, the aids of that Holy Spirt, without whom nothing is strong, nothing is holy, if not because Christ intercedes? Why do we cherish such magnificent hopes? Hopes, whose objects, because of their grandeur, are symbolized to us under the images of eternal crowns and immortal sceptres. Why are we not visionaries for indulging such hopes, and supposing it not only probable but certain, that things so rich and radiant should be placed upon the brows, or given into the hands of beings, who, if measured by a standard of righteousness and truth, deserve nothing but a heritage of shame? Because we see in "the Lamb slain in the midst of the throne," marks which identify him with one, who while upon the earth left these words to encourage his disciples' hearts, "I appoint unto you a kingdom, as my Father hath appointed unto me." The intercession of Christ consists in his perpetual presentation of his one all-sufficient sacrifice, and as that intercession is essential to the life, the comfort, and the hope of his people, so is the assurance of its reality conveyed to their minds by the appearance, which he is represented as wearing in heaven, that of a lamb that had been slain, exhibiting constantly the marks of the sacrificial offering.

As we have already seen, therefore, that no aspect could be more honourable than this to Christ himself, and as we have now shewn how indispensable it is to his church that he should wear it, we are satisfied, that no nobler or more fitting description of him in glory, could be given than the one we have been calling you to study; and if myriads of exalted creatures should gather around him, and break out in a song, which should be echoed by every creature in heaven and earth, and under the earth, no richer, sweeter melody could be wafted to our ears, none more glorifying to the Redeemer, than that of praise to "the Lamb that had been slain."

Indulge me, if you please, in one more thought before I conclude my explanation of the symbol. There is no real, nor as we thus look at the subject, is there any apparent incongruity, between the magnificence and glory of the throne, as presented in vision to the apostle, and the marred aspect of the Redeemer as he is seen moving amid all this grandeur; so far from it, that the beauty and effect of the vision results from its combination of these, at first sight, apparently opposite exhibitions. There is the throne; it is a throne of majesty, but in the midst of it is a form, bearing the traces of anguish and of death; and surely if this teaches us anything, it teaches us that the crucified is not lost in the glorified; the diadem on his brow is the diadem of "the King of kings;" but the forehead, there are deep lines of sympathy traced there, which tell us that it is still that of "the man of sorrows." If we had been informed merely that the Redeemer had ascended on high, that angels had met him, and heaven rung with his praises, that he had risen to a dignity which we could never estimate, and a power which we could never calculate, and a happiness of which we could never form a conception; we should seem so far separated from him, there would be such a broad, deep gulf dividing us, there would in appearance be so little in common between us, that we could hardly apprehend the fact that Christ and his church make but one body, he being the Head and they the members. While he is in the midst of his splendours, and all this glory is thrown around him, where can be sympathy for the afflicted, where a fellow feeling for those who are still struggling with the trials and temptations of the flesh? At this point we go back to the fact, that he retains the marks of his sufferings; the crucified is not lost in the glorified; we cannot measure his power, his dignity, or his happiness, but whatever they may be, they have not removed Christ to a distance from his members; he is still linked with all "who sorrow in Zion;" for though he is in the midst of the throne, and surrounded by the praises of heaven, he is there, and is praised there, "a lamb as it had been slain;" and while he bears the marks of the scourge, the nails, and the spear, we are safe in believing that he can feel for us in trouble, and succour us in trial. It is precisely this combination of the emblems of grandeur, and the mementoes of his sorrow, which makes the exhibition so peculiarly beautiful and interesting to us; there are the traces of his sorrow to teach us his sympathy, there is the throne, to reveal to us his power; and thus who is the Lamb in the midst of the throne but our sympathizing and Almighty Saviour.

3. If we have thus explained the reason, and unfolded the lessons of this peculiar appearance of Christ in heaven, as presented in the text, let us look for a moment at the relations which he sustains, as possessed of infinite wisdom and unlimited power to govern the world, symbolized by "the seven eyes, and the seven horns, which are the seven spirits of God, sent forth into all the earth."

No doctrine, my brethren, is more plainly taught in the Bible than that Christ by his sufferings has been exalted to a throne of universal dominion, "given to be head over all things to the church;" so that Providence has brought all its resources, and all its instrumentalities, and laid them down at the foot of the cross, to be used in subserviency to, and in furtherance of, its grand design. The Redeemer has a kingdom and an end for which that kingdom exists peculiarly his own; and he must reign until his reign is universally acknowledged, and "all his enemies are put under his feet." It is as "the Lamb slain" that he is upon the throne; and, of course, his universal government is designed to illustrate the glory and execute the purposes of redemption. The time is coming when every tribe, every soul upon the earth shall bow to the cross; when the Redeemer's kingdom shall be reared upon the wreck of all opposing sovereignty, and all men shall call him blessed. Providence, as directed by Christ, has been, and is now engaged in bringing about this great consummation.

The world in which we live, with the influences which are at work, and the events and changes which are taking place in its different departments, varies in its aspect according to the medium through which we look at it. The politician watches events as serving to illustrate or contradict some particular political theory. The political economist studies "the signs of the times," as they have a bearing upon some favourite doctrine relative to the production of wealth; and each is waiting for, as he predicts, some grand demonstrations when all men shall have their rights, and the prosperity of the world shall be perfect, as the laws regulating the development of the world's resources shall be universally understood and obeyed. But to the Christian the world wears a very different aspect, and its events and changes have a very different meaning as he looks upon them in their relation to the triumphs of the Redeemer's cross. We speak in accordance with the teaching of inspiration and the sure word of prophecy, when we say that every occurrence is the herald of the Redeemer's triumph. We may not be able to show the connection of every thing with the general result, or the tendency of particular movements to hasten it; but we know that there is nothing in this world, in any department of human enterprize or action, nothing common or uncommon, melancholy or joyous, trivial or magnificent, which has not its own appropriate meaning and influence in relation to the success of the Redeemer's cause. The affairs of an individual and of a family, no less than the affairs of states and empires, are subservient to this grand issue. Whether an individual is preserved or stricken down in death, whether families are exalted or depressed, whether nations rise or fall, whether war convulses kingdoms, and famine and pestilence decimate the population of the earth, or peace waves its olive branch over the world, and health and prosperity prevail, and abundance is poured out from the treasury of heaven's bounty, whether the kings of the world join, and the rulers take counsel together against the Lord and his Anointed, or give their influence directly to the furtherance of the cause of Christ, whether he of the triple crown adopts a more liberal or a more contracted policy, and other potentates encourage or oppose his movements, nothing occurs which is not originated or permitted by him who is King in Zion, and head over all things to his church, nothing which is not directed or overruled to the furtherance of his grand designs. Thus to the eye which faith in the sure testimony of God has opened, this world, in all its transactions and events, wears an aspect of wondrous interest, because every one of them has some undoubted connection with the grand and final development of the system of redemption. We may not be able to see clearly the lines along which runs the influence of divine occurrences in this world; but to the eye of Him who sitteth upon the throne, they are lines of light, all converging to one point, that magnificent result upon which prophecy delights to pour all its splendid imagery, when the kingdoms of the world shall become the kingdoms of our Lord and of his Christ, and the whole human population shall bow at the name of the Redeemer. The days which are passing now, are the days of the Son of Man; and each successive one as it passes, heaving into being new and surprising events, is but an illustration of the wisdom and the might of Him who sits upon the throne, as they all mark the different stages of that grand revolution which is going on, and which in its issue shall show the earth converted into a noble temple, and that consecrated to Christ; and whose melody, issuing simultaneously from every dwelling-place, shall be but the echo of the anthem long since raised in heaven, the anthem of praise to the " Lamb that has been slain."

Take this thought then, and throw its light upon the world in which we live, and what a different aspect is worn by every thing. What before appeared small, now looms into importance, and is seen in its magnificence and grandeur; what before appeared great, now dwindles down into its own appropriate insignificance. The great and the noble, and the proud of earth, lose their importance; their mighty enterprizes, and their grand exploits, sink down into the petty strifes of an ephemeral ambition to the eye of one who sees the Lamb slain moving amid them all, directing them all, and using them all to fulfil the purposes of his redeeming mercy. Nothing, my brethren, is great in this world, but the kingdom of Jesus Christ; nothing but that, to a spiritual eye, has an air of permanency. The history of the past; has been but a history of the rise and fall of individuals and of nations; but amid all the changes and overturnings which have thus far gone to fill up the annals of time, the kingdom of Christ has remained, and under the protection of Him whose wisdom and power are symbolized by the seven spirits of God abroad in all the earth, it is steadily advancing, enlarging its boundaries on every side, and going on to fill the earth. Happy the man who can look at things with an eye of faith, and attaches himself to the only interest which is abiding, and gives his influence to the only cause which is destined to triumph. The man who takes his place by the side of the Redeemer, and identifies himself with his kingdom, consecrating his influence to the cause for which the Lamb slain has been raised to the throne, occupies the only position worthy of a rational being, especially one whom Christ died to save, and the only position in which a single hope that an immortal spirit deems worth the cherishing, can ever be fulfilled.

My brethren, allow me to ask, in view of the subject which I have endeavoured, though I am conscious with very little success, to set before you, what relation do you sustain to the Lamb slain; what part are you taking in the great drama which is now acting upon the theatre of our world? If we are Christ's, then we know that the mark of deliverance is upon us, and in the night of tumult, and confusion, and death, God's messengers of judgment shall pass over and leave us unharmed. If we are Christ's, then amid all the toil and trial which we may be called to endure, as we look up to the throne, and see the marks of the crucifixion on him who occupies it, we have the pledge of succour and safety. If we are Christ's, then his wisdom and his power, pervading all the earth, and regulating all its scenes, give conclusive evidence that not one hope which he has taught us to cherish shall fail. If we are Christ's, then the very act which seals our covenant, secures our triumph; for he who is our helper reigns, and our intercessor sits upon the throne. Is it so then with us, that we are safe under the covering of this great intercessor, and can we believe that he is now interposing on our behalf the all-prevailing plea of his wondrous sacrifice? Is it so, that we are indeed among the number of those for whom his wisdom plans and his power executes, the loss of one of whom would demonstrate the worthlessness of his atonement and rob his diadem of its glory? You cannot imagine a question which, in point of interest and importance, can for a moment be compared with this! Your all is wrapped up in it. It may not be long ere the symbols of Egypt's dark night of destruction shall be fulfilled in the still deeper darkness which shall gather around us. Is the blood upon our door-posts, so that if this very night God should pass through the land, he should see the mark, and leave us unharmed?

Very much do I fear concerning some of us, that the peace-speaking and life-giving blood has not yet been sprinkled upon the heart and the conscience. Very much do I fear for some, that, though nominally Christian, their hearts are upon their goods, their honours, and their pleasures, rather than upon

Christ. They feel no need of a Redeemer, see no beauty in him, have no sympathy with him, give no influence to his cause. Is it so with you, my brethren? Then lose sight, I pray you, of your speaker a moment, and let the Lamb slain be your preacher to-day; the cross is his pulpit, anguish his argument, his eloquence is blood. Oh! hear him, and let not your hearts by hearing him unmoved prove themselves harder than the rocks which were rent asunder. He preaches of sin; that forgetfulness of God and neglect of his laws, which you think a trifle, and bids you estimate it in view of his agony and blood, which as its only expiation, can alone be the true revealers of its nature and the just measures of its enormity. He preaches of perdition; deep, dark, and dreadful must it be, when the terrors of the crucifixion are its most fitting symbols. He preaches of compassion; his language glows with love; it is rich, inexhaustibly rich in encouragement. "I have found a ransom." "Look unto me and be ye saved."

But we have not been satisfied with taking you to Calvary; we have endeavoured to carry you within the veil, that you might hear the same truths which were delivered under a darkened sun, and upon a trembling earth, woven into the anthem of angels and archangels. Ye who are ashamed of Christ, listen, I pray you, to the notes of the crucifixion, as swept from the golden harps of principalities and powers, and borne upon a tide of melody, whose sound is as the sound of many waters. Among the voices which the apostle heard tuned to the praises of the Lamb, were the voices of those in whose behalf the Word never was made flesh, for whom he did not die, and whom he did not redeem. And if angels and archangels admire and adore the Lamb that was slain; if they discover the wonders of the atonement; if they understand the greatness of the achievement which wrought out our salvation, shall any of us, the very objects of this wondrous interposition, shall we for whom the Saviour left his throne, we for whom he was betrayed into the hands of wicked men, crucified and slain, be ashamed of giving him our homage, and swearing to him our allegiance?

God have mercy on the man who can give to this question an affirmative answer! Woe unto him who can practically judge the Lamb of God to be unworthy of his obedience, unworthy of his confidence, unworthy of his love. What is this but arraying one's self against all that is gentle, all that is tender, all that is meek, all that is forbearing in the Saviour of sinners? And when that which is gentle is roused to anger, and that which is meek into fierce indignation; what are they? and *who* can stand before them? Look ye, my brethren, upon Christ in his tenderness, and provoke not the wrath of the Lamb. Behold him as he taketh away the sins of the world, lest ye be crushed beneath his feet, when he treadeth the wine press of his fierce indignation. The voices of the blest as they follow him whithersoever he goeth, no less than the voices of the lost from their heritage of shame, bid you to "Behold the Lamb of God which taketh away the sin of the world." Hear them, and hear them speedily, that ye may be able now and hereafter more fully to enter into the spirit of the anthem—" Worthy is the Lamb which was slain;" for oh, be ye sure of this, my dear brethren, if with uplifted heads and joyful voices, we mingle not at last in that wondrous, mighty song, which is to be pealed forth from a renewed and purified universe, another cry shall be forced from us by our deep consternation and terror. " Hide us from the face of him who sitteth upon the throne, and from the wrath of the Lamb."

REASONS FOR EMBRACING THE GOSPEL.

"Come, for all things are now ready."—St. Luke xiv. 17.

It is not so much upon the nature of the invitation presented in the text, as upon the reasons for embracing it, that we design to insist this morning. We take it for granted, as a point not now in dispute, that the offer of the Gospel is full, free, universal—no terms could be used to express it more general and unrestricted. Whatever the Gospel may be, whatever it may involve, it is a message for all—"Go, preach my Gospel to every creature," is the commission under which it is announced to the world. It is meant for man whereever he may be, in whatever circumstances placed, whatever may be his character, his experiences, his hopes, or his fears—for man, as man—for man as a creature of time—for man as an heir of immortality—for man as a sinner, who needs forgiveness—for man as lost, who needs recovering and renewing influences. If there is a human being who has never sinned, the Gospel is not for him.

If there is one who is perfectly satisfied with himself, who has no trials, no weaknesses, no wants, the Gospel is not for him. It goes upon the presumption that we are a race of fallen creatures, who have sinned against God, and have forsaken the fountain of living waters, and makes a provision for us as such, and it is our want which brings us within its scope and under its blessed influence; and among those to whom its message has come, the first human being is yet to be found who is excluded from its offers. "Whosoever will, may come and take of the waters of life freely," is the free and untrammelled invitation we are commissioned to utter. It is worthy of remark, moreover, that the Gospel deals with men, not in the mass, but as individuals. It is a message for the world, only as it is a message for each and every man in the world—it is a provision for you and for me, as truly as though there were no other beings in existence to whom it could have any reference, and then only do we understand it, when we look upon it and listen to it as an invitation addressed to us individually. These positions I take to be incontrovertible. If I had doubts here, I should be at a loss how to preach the Gospel. If it was not certain to my mind, that its provisions were meant for each and every one of you, and were tendered to each and every one of you, I should not dare to preach it to any of you, for in saying "Come, for all things are now ready," I might be uttering an untruth.

It is upon the ground then of this doctrine, that I come this morning to speak to you, my hearer, as an individual, and I wish you to isolate yourself from all others, and listen to my text, as addressed to you personally. Sinful, weary, dissatisfied, unhappy man, Christ says, there is pardon, and rest, and fulness of joy for you. "All things are ready;" come, embrace his offer, and receive his blessings. To urge this invitation upon your acceptance is my present design, by simply setting before you some of the reasons by which it is enforced. If the Gospel is true, if it is what it proclaims itself to be, if you are what it represents you to be, if you must be what it commands you to be, then you have in the Gospel itself, in the principles which it unfolds, in the provisions which it makes, in the stern necessity of obedience which it imposes, overwhelming reasons for embracing it. Nothing, I care not what it is, commends itself so strongly to your mind—almost any thing else you can dispense with—fix your mind upon any thing, I care not what it is, however strong your attachments to it may be, you can do without it; but you cannot do without the gospel. If the Bible is true, you cannot do without an interest in Jesus Christ; and this is the great reason why you should embrace it.

Now, in unfolding this reason, it is no part of my design to enter upon an extended argument to prove the truth of the gospel, nor upon an extended illustration of its principles, its provisions, and its claims. I shall find the materials of my appeal to-day in your own clearly settled views and convictions upon these points, in your experiences, in your conscious need of something which you do not now possess, and which you are satisfied you can find in the gospel.

1. First, then, you believe that the gospel is true; perhaps upon no one point are your convictions so full, and clear, and decided. You avow yourself a believer in the Bible; you could not, with your present views and feelings, bring yourself to take the position of the Atheist, or the Infidel, or to "sit in the seat of the scornful;" you would not wish that your nearest friend should suspect even that your sympathies might have such a tendency. It would injure your reputation in the world; it would still more injure your feelings. We do not know how this conviction of the truth of the gospel has been reached; it may perhaps have been the result of a lengthened and careful examination of the testimonies which have been gathered around Christianity; it may have resulted from a self-evidencing power in the word of God itself; for one, we believe that the Scriptures carry along with them their own best credentials; its disclosures bear the evidence of their truth upon their very face; and no man can sit down with an honest mind to the perusal of the inspired page, and rise up from it with the conviction that he has been studying an ingenious fable—there may be difficulties here which the sincere inquirer may be unable to remove; a great variety of questions may start up, which he cannot answer, but even while he is grappling with those very difficulties, and endeavoring to work out answers to these puzzling questions, his conviction of the truth of

this written testimony will be continually growing stronger and deeper. This much is certain that there is something in every human bosom, which wakes responsive to the general spirit and teaching of the gospel. You have no feelings in reference to any other book like those which belong to you when you approach the Bible; and that simply because you think that God is speaking to you; and the thoughts here recorded find their way into your inmost soul. Even the man who has worked himself up to skepticism has certain undefinable emotions when he comes to commune with this book of God; because, amid all his doubts, which he has carefully been nursing, he cannot keep down the fear that in every one of his doubts he may be wrong.

The general force of public opinion, moreover, in every Christianized community, is in favour of the gospel; the men who think but little upon the subject cannot in view of the effects of the gospel upon the public mind, doubt its truth. A system which has done so much; done what no human wisdom, no human influence have ever yet availed to do, cannot be a deception; nothing would so shock generally the public mind, as a system of education upon avowedly infidel principles; and you would not trust your children to its influence for an hour. In fact, my brethren, the conviction of the truth of the gospel, whether resulting from examination of its evidence, from a knowledge of its effects, or from the influence of education, is well nigh universal. Some unbelievers there are, but they are comparatively few, and even these have reached their scepticism for the most part by artificial means; it is not the result of the natural and unfettered actings of their own minds in view of the testimony of God; it is an exotic, which requires careful nursing to keep it alive.

It matters not, however, whence this conviction has been derived; we have the fact, which is all we need upon this present occasion; you believe the gospel to be true, and here we take our stand and make our appeal. Why not embrace it? Produce your cause, bring forth your strong reasons. Why not embrace the truth? You are a sinner and need pardon; you believe it—God offers you pardon for Christ's sake—you believe it—you have not to go into an examination of its evidences; the reality of the Gospel, as a system of pardoning and recovering mercy, is past all question in your mind; why not receive it into your heart and submit to it. Its terms, perhaps, you say are exclusive; but it says "there is none other name given under heaven among men whereby they may be saved," but the name of Jesus; and you believe it; and what though they may be exclusive, they are true. It says "Come, for all things are ready," "Whosoever comes to me, I will in no wise cast out." "If ye believe not that I am he, ye shall die in your sins." And it is all true, and what more than truth does a man need to determine him? If it is true, it cannot be evaded; if it is true it will stand eternally; if it is true, no man can say why he should not embrace it. If upon this point you had any question in your own mind, if you feared the adoption of a falsehood, if you suspected even that there might be danger of error in embracing the Gospel, then there might be a reason why you should not become a Christian till all doubts were removed; but there is nothing of the kind; and we appeal to-day to your own convictions, while we say, "Come, for all things are now ready." You cannot get away from this direct home appeal, except as you throw suspicion on the gospel itself, and then you must be driven over upon the ground of the skeptic, upon which you are afraid to tread; and gather around you, and submit yourself to influences which you feel to be blighting to the soul, withering to all its richest joys and destructive to its most precious hopes.

2. While you admit the Gospel record to be true, you at the same time approve of the entire subject matter of its testimony. The human mind, unclouded by prejudice, and unperverted by sophistry, is always in favour of the Gospel. It is not until a man has been schooled and disciplined by desires contrary to the will of God, that he is able to cavil at any of the declarations of the inspired volume, or find fault with any of its disclosures, as inconsistent. Nay, it is the entire reasonableness of the subject matter of this communication from heaven which furnishes one of the most convincing arguments of its truth. We are not speaking now of the man who by reason of long familiarity with wrong principles has benumbed or destroyed his power of moral perception and discrimination. It is quite possible for one to bring himself to that state, in

which he cannot distinguish between right and wrong, between truth and error, as it is possible to damage the eye so that it cannot distinguish between colours; or pervert the taste, so that what was once nauseous may become pleasant; or injure the ear, so that there shall be no difference between a harmony and a discord; but in each of these cases the organ is in a diseased or unnatural state, and no more proves that all colours, all tastes, all sounds, are alike, than a vitiated moral sense proves any of God's communications to be unreasonable. I am not now, however, speaking of what a skeptic may think of the word of God, or of what a man who wishes the gospel were false, may say of any of its declarations; but I am speaking of the posture of your own mind, in reference to the subject matter of this revelation; and I say, that there is not a principle here unfolded, nor a claim here enforced, that does not approve itself to you as being what it ought to be. There are times, I admit, when you might, perhaps, wish that some of the features of the gospel system were different from what they are; when you would like to take somewhat off from the exclusiveness of its claims; when it would suit you better, if it were a little more accommodating, a little more uncompromising; but mark, these are the dictates of feeling, and not of reason; reason accords with the principles and claims of the gospel precisely as God has given them; it sees that if they were different, less exclusive than they are, they would be unworthy of God's wisdom, and undeserving of man's attention. You feel that as a creature of God, you ought to serve him, and serve him precisely in the way in which he declares he wishes to be served. If you have sinned against him, you ought to repent; if he has provided a way for your forgiveness, which he declares to be the only possible way for forgiveness, it is but reasonable to embrace it; if the Son of God has interfered in your behalf, and by his own death secured you the offer and means of everlasting life, you owe him a debt of gratitude which cannot be repaid, except by your intelligent, and cordial, and undivided service. If the principles of the Gospel are true, and you admit their truth, the propriety of the claims of the gospel follows of necessity. Who feels that it is wrong to serve God? Who looks upon obedience to Jesus Christ as a question of doubtful expediency? Not one whom I am now addressing. I should like to find the man who thinks it would degrade him as a rational creature and an heir of immortality to be a Christian. I should like to find the man who admits himself to be a sinner, who feels that he is a sinner, who is at all alive to the importance of eternal life, who would not, as his only rational course, come to this Bible to learn what he must believe and what he must do, in order to be saved.

On the other hand, not one of my hearers intelligently and heartily approves of an irreligious course. Forgetfulness of God, ingratitude in view of his mercies, rebellion against his authority, a practical disregard of his claims, never commend themselves to your minds as reasonable. It matters little upon what ground you put away from you the obligations of religion, it matters little how plausible the aspect which a sinful heart may throw over the excuses which are urged for a neglect of the great salvation, they are never such as you are willing, permanently, to rest upon, or always to abide by. So far from it, that you expect to give up, sooner or later, all these reasonings, and apologies, and to become, what you are not now prepared to be, a Christian. You could not sit down to construct an argument in favour of atheism, or infidelity; you would not know where to find the materials of such an argument; every thing upon which you could fix your mind would seem to be contrary to your purpose. I am not speaking of what has been done, or of what some men might do now; but of what you could do with your present views and feelings. You consider these systems of unbelief, in all their different forms, to be unreasonable in view of the testimony which crowds from every direction around the Bible, which springs from its own pages, or which is returned to you from the effects it has produced, whereever its influence has been felt; at least, they seem to be so to your convictions; and yet, my hearer, it is far more reasonable for a man to sit down, and dispute the evidences of Christianity, clear and conclusive as they may appear to your mind, than it is, after admitting the evidences of Christianity, to disregard its claims. I mean, if you will allow me to express myself in other words to render my sentiment, if possible, more plain, it is more reasonable to doubt whether God has spoken to us in these sacred oracles, than admitting this to be his word, to doubt whether we should believe his declarations, and obey his commandments. We have reached then another stage in our illustration. If the gospel is not only true, but if in all its principles and claims it is precisely what you feel it ought to be; if it commends itself to your understanding as good; if you can find no arguments against it; if you are sure that you will never have reason to reflect upon yourself for acting in accordance with its claims; nay, if you mean, and certainly expect, sooner or later, to come upon the ground where it would put you, and to be what it requires you to be, why, we ask, in view of all that is intelligible in your convictions of its truth and reasonableness, why not embrace it? If you cannot come and be a Christian, give some reason for a refusal, which will wear the appearance, at least, of consistency with your acknowledged views and impressions.

3. I make another point here, which I ask you to ponder. In my preceding remarks upon the reasonableness of the gospel, it has been my object to shew that you owe it to yourself to be a Christian; that in no other way can you honour your own convictions of truth and propriety; but I now add, that you owe something to God. You feel that there are influences thrown around you, which bind you to the eternal throne; do what you may, you cannot reason out of existence all sense of the divine claims upon you; they press you on every

side; they sometimes come down with an oppressive weight upon your spirit, and the fact that you have neglected them, or forgotten them, or postponed them to a thousand other things, is overwhelming to the mind in view of its certain future connections; you know that you must do right in order to be at peace; a consciousness of wrong-doing mars all your joy; you must in some way get rid of it, or be an unhappy man. Precisely, at this point then, I meet you; and this is my appeal. You are perfectly satisfied that it would be right for you to be a Christian; you have no fears that you would be breaking any of God's commandments, or be doing violence to your own conscience were you to embrace the offers of the gospel, and be a disciple of Jesus Christ. You never yet saw a man in your state of mind who had any misgivings upon this point; you have seen skeptical men who pretended to question the propriety of becoming Christians—they cannot be otherwise than sincere in their doubts if they are sincere in their skepticism—and yet among all those who profess to glory in their skepticism, there are very few, if any, who really think they would be committing a sin against God, whose consciences would upbraid or torment them with the apprehension of judgment in the event of their becoming the servants of Jesus Christ. The reason is, they are doubtful about their doubts. But no man who is convinced of the truth and reasonableness of Christianity, as you are, ever fears that he shall go wrong in becoming a Christian. Your conscience, my hearer, would not reprove you as taking a doubtful step, one of questionable propriety, were you to embrace Jesus Christ, and enter upon his service. On the contrary, conscience, enlightened by the truth, requires you to do it, reproves you for not doing it, and heralds a painful retribution for neglecting or refusing to do it. In whatever part of my appeal I may fail to-day, I do not fail in the case of any of my hearers when I address myself directly to his conscience; this is with me, and I can hold it; there is not a single claim of Jesus Christ, which, when it is laid plainly and fully before the conscience is not felt to be right. Every man knows that he must be a Christian, it is a matter of stern necessity with him; he is troubled because he is not a Christian; he is troubled whenever he thinks of his present relations to God, because he knows that whatever he has, he has not God's blessing; that whatever he does, so far as God's requirements are concerned, he is not doing right; he is troubled when he thinks of the future, for he is afraid to meet God, except as a Christian; and nothing gives him any peace of mind except as he can think it at least probable, that sooner or later he will be a Christian; and if all this is true of a man, he is in his present position not because his conscience is against the gospel, but because it is perverted or seared. It may be stupid sometimes, and not speak, but its voice, whenever heard, is clearly, decidedly, uniformly in favour of practical spiritual religion. This then, is my threefold argument to-day. In urging you to embrace the gospel, we are but urging you to receive that which you believe to be true, to submit to that which you apprehend to be reasonable, and to do that which you know to be right. If there was a doubt upon any of these points ; if you felt that there was room to question the truth of gospel principles, if its claims seemed inconsistent to you, or you had any reason to fear that you might go wrong in becoming a Christian, we should say to you, pause ; do not commit yourself to any course of questionable propriety ; but if you are satisfied of the truth of the gospel, if your mind approves of it, and conscience accords with its claims, why not embrace it ? Take my appeal, I pray you, as it is thus set before you, and dispose of it in a manner which will meet the approval of your understanding and your conscience.

4. I have another point to urge. It is this : You feel that the gospel of Jesus Christ is the very thing you need ; that is, as you look at it carefully, study it in its different aspects, and examine closely its provisions, it is precisely adapted to all those wants which, as unsatisfied, are the causes of your disquietude and pain.

The sorrows of human life are referable to three sources ; a sense of sin, difficulties and trials of life, and the prospect of the future. Dry up these sources of uneasiness, let there be no sense of responsibility for past transgression, let every man have that which will comfort and support him under the varied ills to which he is subject on earth, let there be no apprehension of the future to disturb him, and human life would wear an entirely changed aspect, and the page of man's history would reveal scarcely a single sorrow.

1. Upon one point human experience is uniform. Every man feels himself to be a sinner. To this statement there are no exceptions; it is true of the savage and of the civilized; of all men in all their varieties of feeling, thought, or circumstance. However conflicting may be men's theories of religion; however widely separated they may be from each other in the principles they adopt and the paths upon which they travel, whether they are skeptics or believers, men of religion or no religion, they are one in this feeling, that they are not what they ought to be. Whatever explanation they may give of their condition in this respect, however they may reason upon the subject of their accountability to God, they feel that they are accountable, and that their obligations have not been discharged. Call it by what name you please, it is after all a sense of sin against God which troubles the human spirit universally, and man cannot get rid of it. He has tried ere this to reason God out of existence, and after he has done his best in the way of argument he has the evidence that his effort is a failure, in this sense of sin, which remains to disturb and oppress him.

You feel, my hearer, that you have sinned against God; you do not need any of my arguments to demonstrate that fact to you. You carry the evidence of it constantly within you. Sometimes this sense of sin is overwhelming, crushing to the spirit, and every thing is dark to the vision, every thing palls upon the taste; and so completely in some cases does this feeling swallow up every other feeling, that men choose strangling and death rather than life; sometimes it is little more than a settled feeling of uneasiness, an undefined apprehension that all is not right, rendering one dissatisfied with every thing around him. Its subject may be unwilling to own it even to a bosom friend; he may perhaps be unwilling to acknowledge it to himself, but it is there, and he knows it, and it troubles him. *Now* its evidences are seen in a pensive sadness which comes over his spirit; there is no alarm, no agitation, no deep and agonizing remorse, but a gloominess of temper, as though every thing was wrong around him; *again* it is seen in an irritated state of the passions, when strong feelings are excited, and the bitterest enmity is developed against the friend who seeks his good and most faithfully reveals the truth. In some form or other this consciousness of having done wrong, coupled with a fear more or less distinct of God's displeasure, belongs to every man. It may not always be a present object of attention, for one may studiously avoid every thing which is calculated to excite it, but it is like a festering wound, which, carefully guarded, may not occasion any very intense pain, but which is constantly liable to be brought into contact with irritating causes, which, as they act upon it, produce the greatest anguish.

You feel that you need something; you need deliverance from this pressure upon the spirit, something which will put your mind at rest; and when I come to you, as I do now, and preach to you the gospel; when I tell you that Christ has borne our sins in his own body on the tree; that there is forgiveness with God; when I speak to you in the strains of the evangelical prophet, and say, "let the wicked man forsake his way and the unrighteous man his thoughts, and let him return unto the Lord, and he will have mercy upon him, and to our God, for he will abundantly pardon;" or when I say, "there is therefore now no condemnation to them who are in Christ Jesus," you feel that this is precisely what you need. Forgiveness, that is the charm which soothes to quietness the disquieted spirit; it is like oil poured on the troubled waters, producing an undisturbed calm. What a different man would you be, my hearer, were a sense of forgiveness, full and free, to take the place of that sense of unforgiven sin which now oppresses you and darkens your prospect. What a load would be lifted off from that now oft overtasked spirit, what a new light would be shed upon every thing. God would appear different; the world, life, death, every thing would wear a totally different aspect. You need forgiveness to make you a happy man; and the gospel, as it says, "Come, for all things are now ready," addresses itself to your very necessities, and urges you to embrace it by the pardon which it offers.

2. But this is not all. Every human being in this world feels his dependence; he cannot go alone; he must have resources other than those

which are hidden in his own bosom. Perhaps, in a scene of sunshine and of calm, man does not feel it; but the ocean of human life has its storms as well as calms; its adverse tempests as well as prosperous breezes. No man has ever yet passed through life; no man has yet advanced any distance in the journey of life, without encountering trials. We cannot escape them; it is idle to think of it; come they will, and sometimes with a crushing force, and when they come, man feels the need of something out of himself upon which to lean. Talk as you please about the manly independence of the human mind, which enables its subject to rise superior to the trials of life, and to triumph over them; it is all a dream. In such circumstances, man always goes out of himself for help; one goes in one direction, and another in another; sometimes the child of sorrow flies to the cares and troubles of business, to drive away distressing thoughts; sometimes he flies to scenes of gayety and worldly pleasure, where excited passion leads on the giddy dance, to find amid the refined, or it may be the boisterous, in either case the unsanctified revelries of earth, something to amuse the spirit, and wean it from grief. That wretched victim of the intoxicating bowl was once your man of lofty independence; of, perhaps, great resources, and strength of endurance; but trials came, disasters overtook him, and he felt his strength giving way, and he sought relief in the cup of the inebriate. Man must have something upon which to lean; he can no more go alone through the trials of life, than a child who has just learned to walk can travel safely, unsupported, amid the rocks and the precipices of the desert; and here, child of sorrow and of want, the gospel appeals to you again, to this sense of dependence, as it presents before you Jesus Christ, your sympathizing Saviour, able to feel for you, and to help you, and says "come."

3. And yet again, it approaches you as an heir of immortality; it meets your wants for this life, and it tells you and assures you of "the life which is to come;" you know that you are a dying creature; you dread the thought of dying, and yet you fear to live for ever; annihilation has no charms for the human spirit, except as a protection from an apprehended curse; and now I speak what I know, if you have never embraced the gospel, you will not deny that you are afraid of dying, that you cannot reconcile yourself to the thought of it; you shrink from it; you banish it from your minds, because it embitters life; and yet you know that it is coming, slowly, perhaps; quickly, perhaps; but surely; you know that in a very little while, at farthest, that dread hour will be here, the hour when experience will teach you what death is; and you dread it, because you are not prepared for it. All is dark beyond it; you must have something which you do not now possess, before you can be prepared for death, or think of it with any degree of composure; and that something is simply *hope*, a *good* hope, an *intelligent* hope, a *well-founded* hope, a hope which *will not make ashamed*. Oh! for this hope. How that anxious and troubled

spirit sighs whenever it thinks of death; how it looks around and within for something upon which it may hang its hope! What a different world this would be to you, my hearer, if you had such a hope of heaven! How you envy that Christian disciple, mean though his outward circumstances may be, who can say, "I know that when my earthly house of this tabernacle is dissolved, I have a building of God, a house not made with hands, eternal in the heavens;" "Lord, now lettest thou thy servant depart in peace according to thy word, for mine eyes have seen thy salvation;" you feel that you must have such a hope before you can die, and now see how you are urged to embrace the gospel by the appeals which it makes to this very feeling. "He that believeth hath everlasting life; he that believeth in me, though he were dead, yet shall he live; and he that liveth, and believeth in me, shall never die." The gospel comes to you with its provisions for the future. You see and feel that this is the very hope your troubled spirit needs. You have no doubt that it is a good hope, a well-founded hope, a hope that will not make ashamed. Child of sin and sorrow, subject all your life-time to bondage through fear of death, the gospel offers its hope to you; why not embrace it, and let your emancipated spirit go free?

This then, my hearer, is my appeal to you to-day in behalf of the religion of Jesus Christ. You could not have one more direct or more powerful; it is an appeal to your faith, to your reason, to your conscience, to your wants; and as the gospel says "come," its language is echoed back by your own deep and sincere convictions, by every sensibility of your nature, by all your wants and woes, by all your hopes and fears; and under the pressure of this appeal, can you give yourself a reason why you should not embrace the gospel, one which your convictions will honour, which your sensibilities will approve, and which your wants and your fears will justify? Is there an object worth possessing, or an interest worth preserving, or a hope, or a joy worth the cherishing, which says that you are wise, or right in rejecting this offer of the gospel which is now pressed upon your acceptance? If there is, we have done. If there is a good reason why you should not be a Christian, this mind shall cease to arrange arguments for you, and cease to plead with you; but while we know there is none, we can continue to press this matter home upon you, and say "all things are ready, come." Nor is it our argument alone which presses you. It is the voice of God which speaks to you to-day, and says, "Turn ye, turn ye, for why will ye die?" It is the Son of God who bore your infirmities and carried your sorrows, and put away sin by the sacrifice of himself, who addresses you to-day, and says, "Behold, I stand at the door and knock; if any man hear my voice, and open the door, I will come in to him and sup with him, and he with me." It is God the Spirit, who moves with his gentle influence over that breast, or who whispers with his still small voice into your ear, "come," and all those around you who have embraced the gospel say, "come," and all who have gone before you in the faith of this gospel, and have reached its rewards, take up the message, and send it back to you with all the strength which experience can give it; and from that bright world above, from among those "blest voices uttering joy," there is one, it may be of an aged Christian father, whose grave you bedewed with your tears, or of a mother, who often spoke to you of Jesus Christ, or of that child whom God took from you in infancy, and whose smile is yet fresh in your memory, which, as it stretches out its arms, says, "come." Come, ere these voices all are hushed, and the darkness of a spiritual night gathers thick over your soul. While God, and Christ, and the Holy Ghost, and every voice in the universe are speaking to you.

"Come, trembling sinner, in whose breast
A thousand thoughts revolve,
Come with your guilt and fear oppressed,
And make this last resolve.

"I'll go to Jesus, though my sin
Hath like a mountain rose,
I know his courts, I'll enter in,
Whatever may oppose.

"I can but perish if I go,
I am resolved to try,
For if I stay away, I know
I shall forever die."

THE GUILT OF UNBELIEF.

"He that believeth not is condemned already, because he hath not believed in the name of the only begotten Son of God."—St. John iii. 18.

The peculiarity of the text which I have just placed before you, is found, as every one perceives, in the prominence which it gives to unbelief in Christ as man's greatest guilt, and the only ground of his condemnation under the gospel. It seems to turn away our attention from every other position he may occupy, and direct it exclusively to the relation he sustains to the Saviour, making the question of his life or death, his acceptance or condemnation under the divine government, hinge entirely upon the attitude he occupies as a believer, or an unbeliever, in "the record which God has given of his Son."

I am not mistaken in supposing that there is something here, not only aside from men's usual trains of thought, but contrary to their ordinary apprehensions. They can perceive how human character may be determined, and human destiny fixed from man's relation to the simple code of the ten commandments, because they can see the righteousness, and feel the binding force of the moral law. They can understand that idolatry is a sin, that blasphemy is a sin, that the violation of any of the statutes which define our social duties is a sin, and that a man may be justly condemned for every or any one of them. They may apprehend, moreover, how a man who has sinned may be saved through the acceptance of an offered pardon; there are sufficient analogies in human things to illustrate this point. But here comes the gospel of Jesus Christ; and it loses sight, apparently, of all other sins, however numerous they may have been, however great they may have been, in view of the greater, the more monstrous, the overwhelming guilt of unbelief. With regard to all other sins, its language is, "Though they be as scarlet they shall be white as snow, though they be red as crimson they shall be as wool;" but the sin of unbelief persisted in knows no forgiveness, and entails consequences from which there is no redemption. It would be perfectly intelligible to say, that it is merely negative in its destructive influence, as shutting its subject out from all interest in the promised pardon, and leaving him precisely where he should have been had no offer of forgiveness ever been made; but vastly different from this is the representation given upon the sacred page. Here unbelief in Christ is represented as a positive crime, a crime with which, in point of enormity, no other form of human sinfulness can be compared; a crime which not only fastens upon its subject the guilt, and binds him over to the penalty of all his other sins; but which is itself the most striking and fullest development of enmity against God and opposition to his government, which can possibly be presented.

Sure I am that men do not feel, if indeed they apprehend this truth. To other forms of criminality, conscience may be sensitive, and administer its painful and forceful rebukes, in view of the transgression of any precept of the decalogue; but how many of the hearers of the truth, think you, my brethren, feel when they go away from an offer of eternal life through Jesus Christ, which has been presented to them, and from an appeal of the gospel, which has been ministered to the conscience and the heart, refusing the one and resisting the other, or careless and indifferent about either, that they are then and there presenting to the eye of God, and of every being who understands their spiritual relations, an exhibition of character, to be exceeded by none in the insult which it puts upon the authority and the contempt it pours upon the love of God; an exhibition, which concentrates in itself the elements of all sin, and which justifies the heaviest sentence recorded in the book of God against human transgression. How few believe it; and yet this truth is written in lines of light upon every page of the Bible. Of this it is the especial province of the Holy Spirit to convince men, when according to the promise and in the words of the Saviour, he comes to "reprove the world of sin, because they believe not on me." And this truth every one must understand and feel, before he is brought into the life, and light, and liberty of the gospel. Be it mine then to-day, to put the doctrine in such a light, and to give of it such illustrations as shall commend it to the mind and conscience of every one who hears me.

And here, possibly, I may in the very beginning divest the subject of not a little of its mysteriousness, by calling attention to the new circumstances and position in which the gospel of Christ places every one of its subjects. We are here, my brethren, upon trial for an eternal world—the question of life or death, the blessing or the curse is before us, and it is as yet with those who are out of Christ an unsettled question. It is not however to be settled upon principles of law. The event is not now to be determined, our destinies are not now to be fixed from our relation to this precept, or that precept, or all the precepts of the decalogue. For in this relation, every man has had his trial and reached the issue. In the eye of the law of God, every man is a sinner, has been pronounced such, and as such has been condemned. He needs no other trial here, he can have none, for already has it been settled and proclaimed as a universal truth growing out of the nature of his case, as a sinner, that "By deeds of law, no flesh living can be justified in the sight of God."

If then there is any hope for him, it must be under another dispensation, a dispensation of grace, a dispensation under which the question of eternal life or eternal death will turn, not upon his own personal righteousness or unrighteousness, but upon the acceptance, or rejection of the righteousness of another. This is the peculiar feature of the gospel. "Christ is the end of the law for righteousness to every one that believeth." Pardon is offered as a free gift through him who has "magnified the law and made it honourable," and every thing turns now upon simple faith in Jesus Christ; upon an accordance with God's plan of forgiveness; a cordial acquiescence in the principles upon which that forgiveness is offered. Now, the language addressed to us is, not "He that doeth these things shall live by them," and "Cursed is every one who continueth not in all things written in the book of the law, to do them," but "He that believeth shall be saved," and "He that believeth not shall be damned."

I wish you, at this point, to call up to your minds the illustration of the last Sabbath, which referred faith and unbelief to their source in the feelings and affections of the heart. They are something more than an intellectual assent to, or dissent from a proposition, according as the evidence may appear sufficient, or insufficient to sustain it. The faith of the gospel is a cordial admission of all the principles upon which the atonement of Christ proceeds, and all the claims which that atonement involves; unbelief is a rejection of Jesus Christ, as an offered Saviour, and an intelligent resistance to all the principles which the gospel involves, and all the claims which the gospel enforces. The feeling of the heart towards Jesus Christ which it embodies, and to which it gives expression is, "We will not have this man to reign over us." The state of mind which it denotes is not that of the avowed skeptic, who turns away from the gospel because of an alleged insufficiency of evidence to authenticate it, as a revelation from God; but it is a state of mind which is common, and which respects the subject matter of the gospel, where its truth as a communication from heaven is never called in question. It is a rejection of offered mercy; a dissonance of spirit from the God who made us; a direct resistance to his government; an insult put upon his authority; a contempt of his wisdom, a despite done to his love and grace. I would that men could see themselves as God sees them; and there would then be no need of my illustration this morning, to convince them of the deep, and dreadful, and dangerous criminality of their unbelief, in remaining unsubmissive to, and estranged from Jesus Christ.

In endeavouring to shed down light upon their position, I come to those of you, my brethren, who admit the divine origin of these wondrous communications; "God has spoken to us in these last days," and through these inspired pages, "by his Son." This, I take for granted; and thus far, my hearers and their speaker stand upon common ground. This word is truth. The message which we bring to you comes from the lips of the Infinite and Eternal God. He speaks to you from his high and holy throne; and this is his commandment, "That ye believe on him whom he hath sent." Were we reasoning with skeptics to-day, we should be obliged to go one step farther back in our argument, and array before you those varied testimonies which combine to authenticate this sacred volume as a revelation from God; but we need not do it, for we are not battling with speculative skepticism, but with a practical disregard of God's acknowledged commandments. Unbeliever in the Lord Jesus Christ, knowing your Master's will, yet doing it not, we are constructing a mirror in which you may see reflected the lineaments of your moral image. Turn not away from the mirrored likeness true to the life, however painful and humiliating the spectacle may be, but study and ponder it well, if perchance the proud heart may be humbled and the rebellious spirit bow and yield before Almighty God. It is not a trifling circumstance that which defines your character and fixes your position; that you are uninterested in the blessings of the gospel. It is not a step which reflects only upon yourself as it demonstrates your folly when you turn away from him who offers you eternal life upon condition of your faith, but a step which demonstrates your guilt as it reflects upon God, by whose authority this offer is pressed upon your acceptance. He who has a right to control man; he, in whose hands his breath is, requires that he should believe on him whom he hath sent, and the creature of a day turns his back upon the God who made him, and says, "Who is the Lord that I should obey his voice?" Nothing short of this, nothing less criminal than this, nothing less fraught with peril to the immortal spirit, is unbelief in Jesus Christ. It is contempt put upon the authority of God, and a rejection of his claims, kindly yet firmly asserted,—" I have set my king upon my holy hill of Zion." " Kiss ye the Son," is the message which has gone forth from the throne, and has fallen upon our ears. The unbeliever knows the voice, understands the message, then looks upon God's Anointed One, and says to the world, and to every looker on in the universe, " Let others do as they may, I will not have this man to reign over me." His pride of reason rejects the statements which place the movements of the Infinite God beyond his comprehension; his pride of heart nauseates the doctrines of the cross, because they are so humiliating; and his independence of spirit turns away from its salvation, because it is so perfectly gratuitous. Thus unbelief is human littleness cavilling at the Unsearchable One; human pride denying the statements of him who cannot lie; and human independence refusing a gratuity from the Creator, from whom day by day man receives the very breath in his nostrils, and the very powers which he arrays in hostility against the throne.

It goes not a little way to aggravate the guilt of the unbeliever, that God has been pleased in his gospel not only to state the plan through which he forgives sin, but to show also the indispensable necessity of that plan as growing out of his justice as God, and his uprightness as a moral governor. He tells us, in language too plain to be misunderstood, that he can save us in no other way than through faith in his Son. In no other way could he make glory to God in the highest harmonize with peace on earth and good will to men. The sacrifice of Jesus Christ was a method of infinite wisdom to pay a tribute to justice, while it threw the mantle of mercy over the lost. Christ is the great propitiation to declare God's righteousness in the forgiveness of sin. God can save in no other way, because in no other way would it be just to save; but the unbeliever rejects the offers of mercy coming through Jesus Christ, and challenges the approbation of God upon some other ground, than the propitiation of his Son. He thus stands out against his Maker upon a point, in reference to which God's character is committed against him. He thus enters into a controversy with all the plans of heavenly wisdom, and all the claims of heavenly righteousness; throws an insult upon the justice of his Maker, as he had already poured contempt upon his authority, and assumes the fearful position of one who demands the favour of God, upon grounds upon which he knows God's justice will never let him grant it, and declines it peremptorily and entirely upon the only ground upon which it can be made to harmonize with the holy and inviolable glories of the Godhead. To be a sinner against God is dreadful—it is to resist his authority and put one's self in a position where all the high and unutterable sanctions of the eternal throne are arrayed against him; but to be an unbelieving sinner in the circumstances in which we, my brethren, are placed, and in view of the reasonings which God addresses to our understanding, and which we can fully comprehend, is more dreadful still, for it is supposing that God may look kindly on that which his soul abhors, and pass by with impunity that against which he has pledged all the attributes of his nature and all the truth and righteousness and power of his throne. Unbeliever in Jesus Christ! —mark, study, and inwardly digest this painful, this appalling truth. God offers to save you through his Son—he tells you he can save you in no other way. You perceive that it is so; you understand how his righteousness stands in the way of any other mode of forgiveness; you turn away from his offer, and challenge forgiveness upon some other ground, as though you would bid the Almighty to sacrifice his righteousness to your pride, and put all that is dear to him in the holiness of his nature and the interests of his kingdom upon the altar of your peace.

I must add to this exhibition, that the gospel of Jesus Christ, which unbelief rejects, is the highest expression which God could give us of his grace. The burden of his message to you, and to me, is, "God is love." The plan of redemption through Jesus Christ, had its origin in compassions as wonderful and incomprehensible as is the unsearchable nature of God. To angels, gifted with powers far larger and stronger than our own, it is a mystery whose depths they have never yet been able to fathom. Inspired men, who spake as they were moved by the Holy Spirit, enlarging their conceptions, and inditing their utterances, never yet attempted to describe the height, and depth, and length, and breadth of redeeming love. They bid us to take our measures of its greatness from the modes of its expression which God has adopted. Cast your eye over the inspired record, and what do you see, upon its every page, but "God manifest in the flesh," "full of grace and truth." Look upon the countenance of him who is to us the revelation of the infinite One, and you trace tenderness in every line, and see compassion in every aspect. How much God loves us, an angel tongue could never tell, because an angel's mind could never estimate the value of the sacrifice to which that love has led. The cross upon which hangs an expiring Redeemer, and where he breathes away his life, is to us, at one and the same time, the expression of the greatness of that sin of ours which brought about so dire a catastrophe, and of the love of God, which could consent to its occurrence in order to our deliverance from a penalty which could not otherwise have been avoided. "Herein is love, not that we loved God, but that God loved us, and gave his Son to be a propitiation of our sins."

There is a tasteful sentimentalism, my brethren, which descants, with wonderful fluency, upon the goodness of God, as seen in the works of his hand, and the dealings of his Providence. There is an admitted, felt obligation to gratitude at least, in view of the evidences of kindness seen in the adaptation of all God's arrangements to the good of his creatures. The unwearied Providence which sleeplessly watches over human interests, and interferes at particular crises, to warn and protect against danger, throwing its shield over the defenceless, and the arm of its strength around the feeble, demands at least the thankfulness of the human spirit. He who never regards the works of the Lord, nor the operations of his hand, the responses of whose heart to the evidences of kindness which they present, are kept back by the pride of a selfish or haughty spirit, is a being upon whom nature frowns as a deformity upon her works, and from whom humanity shrinks, as an outcast she will scarcely own.

Unbeliever in Jesus Christ! go ransack the universe and find among all the works of God anything at all comparable with God's gift of his Son to you. What day that passes over you, rehearsing, as it goes, the goodness of your Maker, can tell a tale like that of the crucifixion, or present a spectacle so expressive of love, and which appeals so strongly to the heart? If the claims to gratitude and affection rise in number and strength according to the greatness of the benevolence which originates them, there are then no claims like those of a redeeming Saviour, and no ingratitude like that which lightly esteems them. Compass, if you can, the mighty dimensions of the theme upon which now we speak—the measure thereof is longer than the earth and broader than the sea; it is the measure at once of the love of God and the guilt of unbelief. The scene of the cross is not an unreal thing to you. We have not to demonstrate the fact, that "God so loved the world as to give his only begotten Son, that whosoever believeth upon him might not perish, but have everlasting life." The testimonials which authenticate the fact are before you; you have admitted their sufficiency; you wonder how any one can suspect them; and yet, when God appeals to you, by such a mighty demonstration, you can turn away with a listless heart as though there were nothing in such wondrous love to demand a response from the spirit before which it lays its claims. My unbelieving brother, it is a God of truth whose words you doubt; a God of love, whose offers you slight. Unbelief in Jesus Christ, disguise it as men may—it is the darkest form which human depravity can assume—it is an impeachment of the truth of God; for he who believeth not the testimony he has given of his Son, has made him a liar. It is a contempt put upon his authority, whose voice was heard from the excellent glory, "this is my beloved Son, hear ye him." It is an insult to the character of God, who declares that he can be just only as he pardons the believer—it is despite done to his love, since he "has given his Son to be the propitiation for our sins." There is nothing in God, nothing in his truth; nothing in his wisdom; nothing in his holiness; nothing in his justice; nothing in his mercy, which unbelief does not array against its subject, because it puts him in a position of direct resistance to his Maker, and leads him in a course, in the pursuit of which he must fly in the face of every attribute of the eternal God.

Such, my brethren, is unbelief in its own intrinsic nature, altogether independent of the circumstances in which it is manifested, and irrespective of the influences which are used to overcome it. Do you wonder at the language of my text? "He that believeth not is condemned already, because he hath not believed upon the name of the only begotten Son of God." If there is not guilt here, where is there guilt? If this is not a righteous ground of condemnation, what can be? If you cannot understand the justice of the principle, point me, if you please, to anything which God ought to punish, or any circumstances in which man is without excuse. Shew me anything that man can do, which, in respect to the affront it puts upon God, and the rebelliousness of spirit against his authority, his truth, and his grace, can for a moment compare with unbelief in or a rejection of Jesus Christ; and I yield at once the point, and cease to vindicate the judgment of God.

It is, however, an acknowledged principle, and one which we cannot overlook in illustration of the present subject, that a man's character, so far as the degree of its excellence or demerit is concerned, must be determined in a great measure by the circumstances in which he is placed, and the influences which are brought to act upon him. The restraints which are thrown over transgression, and the motives to uprightness of life, enter largely into that standard of judgment by which we measure the character of him with whom they are ineffectual; the guilt of the same action as performed by different persons, though attended by precisely the same results, varies with the ignorance or knowledge of its authors, and with the peculiar influences which acted upon them, as they tended to further or prevent the perpetration of the crime in question. According to this very obvious and obviously just standard of judgment, unbelief in the Son of God, or a rejection of the claims of the gospel, stands by itself, perfectly isolated in the features of enormity which mark it, as least allowing of an apology, or admitting of defence. It is not a sin of ignorance. for every man under the light of truth knows it to be wrong. Conscience does not slumber over the slighted claims of infinite mercy and eternal truth. The sinner who throws off from him the obligations of an atoning Saviour, does not carry within him a mind at ease in view of those manifestations of grace which a Redeemer has made to him, and those appeals of the cross which have been ministered to his heart. The convictions of his own spirit, clear, numerous, and irrepressible, often testify against him, as one who sins against light and knowledge. The thousand extenuating pleas which he conjures up to satisfy his wakeful conscience, are so many witnesses of his guilt, witnesses whose testimony he cannot set aside, because he has summoned them himself; they are evidences clear and palpable of guilt, great indeed, which demands so many and such mighty efforts to hide it from the view, or sustain the burden it imposes.

I can see, my brethren, how a man who disbelieves the existence of God, can put forth an argument wearing the semblance, at least, of reason, in defence of his strange and anomalous position; for we cannot say, that there might not be clearer and stronger evidences of a first great cause, than those which are engraven upon the creation which we behold around us. True, we can say, that these evidences are sufficient to secure a rational faith; we can say, and say with truth, that the man, who in view of every thing he beholds, can maintain his disbelief in the divine existence, could not be brought to its acknowledgment by any additional accumulation of evidence. But then, we cannot say, that there might not be other and stronger testimonies to the being of a God than those which we have in our possession; we can conceive of others, we could, perhaps, if it were necessary, mention others. But, as it is, we cannot come down upon the atheist, and say to him that there can be no other nor stronger proofs of the divine existence than those which God has furnished, and thus demonstrate his folly and his guilt in view of the fact that he remains unconvinced, notwithstanding that God has done the utmost to satisfy his mind. No, he might answer, and you could not meet him here, that God might do much more; he might have other and more striking evidences. I grant you his argument is pitiful, it is evasive; but such as it is, it is better than the practical unbeliever in Jesus Christ can urge in excuse for his rejection of offered mercy. If a man admits this Bible to be a record of truth; if so far from cavilling at its communications, he admits that this is a veritable record of facts; then he admits that God has done as much as he can do to commend himself to his affections. When you study the handiwork of God there is room for the play of fancy; we can conceive of a more glorious creation than this which our eyes behold; or, we can conceive how there might be such an influence exerted upon our faculties, that every thing should, in our vision, teem with more wonderful testimonies in behalf of God. But it is not so with the work of redeeming love which has been set before us upon these sacred pages; you cannot conceive of a more wonderful, a brighter, a grander display of God, than that which is made upon the cross; there cannot be a more striking proof of the love of the Almighty, or more stirring motives to repentance and obedience. God, in the gift of his Son, has not fallen short of, but gone beyond the power of all human imagination. Angels themselves bow down before the mystery of redeeming love, unable to compass its mighty dimensions, to tell its heighth and depth, its length, and breadth. Unbeliever in the Son of God, is it so?—that in commending himself to your heart your Maker has done his utmost; is it so, that the divine nature in all its attributes of wisdom and justice, and power and love, seems to have exhausted itself in the mode of your deliverance; that God could not have shewn himself more mighty, to overwhelm, to deter you from disobedience, more compassionate and able to save, to allure you to himself than he has done in the cross of his beloved Son. Come then to that cross, and ponder it well; study it in its amazing dimensions, in its mysteries of wisdom, and power, and justice, and truth, and love; let these be to you the measures of your guilt in rejecting the offered atonement, and cease, oh, cease, forever, to wonder at the words of Christ, "He that believeth not is condemned already, because he hath not believed in the name of the only begotten Son of God."

In order to complete our illustration, you must add to what God has done without us in the way of commending himself to our affections; what God has been and is doing within us to call our attention to, and secure our acceptance of his proffered mercy.

If it is a remarkable feature in the great plan of human redemption, that he who "was in the beginning with God," should come down and tabernacle among men, and go through his experience of humiliation, and sorrow, and death, in order to execute God's designs of mercy, it is, I apprehend, a feature quite as remarkable, that after the plan has been executed, God himself should come down in a manner inexplicable and mysterious indeed, yet really, and busy himself with these hearts of ours to commend that plan to our affections. For one, I shall not undertake to compare in point of wonderfulness the different parts of this great scheme of redeeming love. In fact, it is perfectly wonderful throughout; from its conception in the divine mind down through the mode, and every step of its execution and application, to its final result, when the crown is put upon the head of the

7

redeemed sinner. Throughout, God acts like himself, "wonderful in counsel and mighty in working." But now I fix your thoughts upon the fact, that he who is busy every where through his universe, upholding and directing and controlling all things, regulating the movements of unnumbered systems, sustaining alike the life of an insect and an archangel, should be no less really and constantly engaged with men, throwing over their spirits the influence of the cross, bringing out of its treasury of motives the dissuasives from sin, and the inducements to faith in Christ Jesus. The peculiarity of our position, my brethren, which gives so much interest to our circumstances, adding to our hopefulness, while at the same time it increases our peril is, that the truths of the gospel to which our attention and faith are demanded, are ministered to the conscience and the heart by the influence of the Holy Ghost. We live under "the ministration of the Spirit," and though his agency, like that of the mind, is not palpable to the senses, yet every man carries about with him the evidences of its power and reality, in the effects it produces within him. We should like to find among the hearers of a preached gospel the wonderful anomaly of a human being, whose experience does not demonstrate the fulfillment of a Saviour's promise, when he said to his disciples that he would send the Holy Spirit to convince the world of sin. We know that this blessed agent has been and is now abroad in our world. We know that he has left his testimony in behalf of

God and his gospel, in the mind of each one of our hearers. We are not afraid, upon this point, to summon the experience of all before us. The youth who gives up his reins to his passions, and lives for the pleasurable excitement of the world, has he not,—bear me witness, my youthful hearer,—oftentimes his painful misgivings, when he passes by the Redeemer's cross, and hears its solemn and affecting warning? The man of middle life, who is grasping after the good things of this world, feels,—I appeal to you, my brethren, who are engaged in the plans and activities, and business of life,—that he is after all but a spiritual bankrupt, destitute of an interest in Christ, and without any rational or well-founded hope in God's pardoning mercy; and the man who has placed himself in a condition of spiritual insensibility, where he is neither alarmed by the terrors, nor won by the mercies of the cross, will testify—I appeal to you, my brethren, to whom I have so long and so fruitlessly ministered the motives of eternal truth—will testify, if he will allow himself to speak out his distinct remembrances, that he has fought his way to his present position against powerfully opposing influences, and has been compelled, at times, in order to hold on his course, to crush with a desperate effort, pleadings of almost irresistible energy. I charge upon a rejection of the gospel, not only a contempt cast upon every attribute of the divine name—not only an insensibility to the mightiest demonstration which God could make of his love, but a resistance to the strivings and suggestions of the Holy Ghost. Unbeliever in the Son of God! I summon you to-day, to testify against yourself, before your Saviour's cross. I would bring your experiences to the light of day, and wring out from them a reluctant but convincing evidence of your guilt, as you have been obliged, in order to put away from you the offers of a Redeemer's mercy; to cast a slight upon the truth of the ever living God, to question as well his justice as his love, in view of their highest possible demonstrations, and to do violence to some secret influence within you, and even to some of the noblest attributes of your own nature, as you have turned away from him who pleaded with you from his cross, and invited you in strains of love to peace and hope.

And yet, in the minds of many, unbelief is nothing; nothing but a want of faith; nothing but a want of love; nothing but the absence of obedience. Let the man who doubts or contradicts your word, truly and solemnly given, wonder that you should resent such a negative thing as a want of faith; let the being who ruthlessly tramples upon a benefactor, who has saved his life at the risk of his own, talk only of his want of gratitude; let the man who utterly disallows your admitted, righteous, and unalienable claims, talk of his want of obedience; but let not the unbeliever in Jesus Christ talk thus; rather let him look at the means and inducements to faith, and as he sees how the gospel brings before him the glory and beauty of "Immanuel," "God with us," let him learn that unbelief is human nature shutting closely her eyes lest she should perceive and love; as the voice from heaven speaks to the ruined sinner, with all the earnestness of truth, and all the tenderness of pity, let him learn that unbelief is human nature making her ears heavy lest she should hear and be saved. Man, ruined, wretched, complaining, dying man, is haughty and unbending, still clinging to his own miseries, aggravating his own sufferings, provoking the doom which he sincerely dreads, and refusing to "Come to Christ, that he might have life." Heaven urges by all its joys, and hell by all its terrors; the cross of Christ pleads by all its wonders of justice and of grace, and unbelief replies to every commandment, "We will not have this man to reign over us;" and to every gracious overture, "Depart from us, for we desire not the knowledge of thy ways."

I question whether there is in any part of the universe of God, another being like the unbeliever in Jesus Christ. If there is not among the unredeemed in heaven, one who can compare with him who lives by the faith of the Son of God on earth, one who so much honours God, and who shall stand so high at the last; where among the ranks of those who kept not their first estate, will you find one who carries upon his conscience such a load of guilt to press him down for ever, as that which weighs upon, and will for ever crush the spirit of him who rejects the great salvation? Say what you please of those who first made war upon the throne and monarchy of God, and who sank into the darkness of everlasting midnight; you must say more of him who rejects as his ground of hope the blood of the everlasting covenant. Over those lost spirits God never spread the bow of hope. For them no Saviour died. Into their dark habitation no messenger of mercy ever found his way, coming from the cross of Christ, to bid them live. Upon their minds and hearts the spirit of grace and truth never moved, to wake them to life and righteousness. Upon their consciences rest not the deep and damning guilt of unbelief in an offered Saviour. But, my beloved hearers, my dying fellow travellers to the retributions of an eternal world, can all of you say as much? Have we, has any one of us, the nerve to meet, the heart to bear the issues of unbelief in Jesus Christ? Oh! ye for whom a Saviour has died—ye to whom a Saviour has been offered—ye who have been plied so oft and so strongly by the touching, and powerful, and impressive motives of the gospel—ye subjects of the Spirit's influences, "How"—ponder the question, it is one of life or death to the undying spirit —"How can ye escape, if ye neglect so great salvation?"

PEACE IN BELIEVING.

"Now the God of hope fill you with all joy, and peace in believing."—Romans xv. 13.

"Peace in believing," is the thought to which I call your attention this morning. It is a very simple thought, and yet one which to the majority of minds is exceedingly difficult of comprehension. It is so contrary to man's ordinary modes of thinking, it so conflicts with his prejudices, as to the sources of human good, it withal, is in such seeming conflict with the laws of our nature, as creatures of sense, that I question whether any thing but actual experience can bring a man to appreciate its meaning, or to admit its truth. Certain it is, that to a carnal mind, it presents the most unintelligible mystery with which it is called to grapple. Whatever views it may take of the spiritual religion of the New Testament, the element of which is faith, it never regards it as in itself a source of positive enjoyment. Its importance may be admitted, its indispensableness may be felt, but so far from being regarded as desirable, it is looked upon as something which must be submitted to in obedience to the law of stern necessity, or as the only alternative to an experience more intolerable than itself.

It is not at all surprising that it should be so. As the scenery by which we are surrounded takes its colouring from the medium through which we look at it, so do the objects which are presented to us wear a pleasing or displeasing aspect, according to their relation to, as in harmony, or at war with, our desires. The sources of enjoyment which faith brings nigh unto the soul, must seem unreal to a man whose vision is bounded by sense, while the submission which faith requires contravenes all the natural passions of the heart, and conflicts with the plans and purposes in which the carnal mind finds its highest enjoyment. The objects of faith must, therefore, wear a visionary aspect, while a submission to its control must be as undesirable as the plans and purposes with which it conflicts are dear to the heart. I speak in accordance with the consciousness of every man who is out of Christ. The highest attainment which a carnal mind reaches upon the subject of religion is a simple conviction of its necessity; its necessity, as something which, however unpleasant and even painful, must be submitted to as an alternative to greater evils. I repeat, I do not wonder that such a mind looks upon religion with distaste, and postpones attention to it, and endeavours to evade the necessity which is forced upon it, by pushing forward the decisive question of submission to the extremest verge of safety.

And yet, my brethren, there is "peace in believing;" the purest, the most rational, and solid and satisfying peace of which the mind can form any conception. Nay, we take higher ground than this, there is peace in nothing else. The human spirit can find nothing upon which it can rest securely, but that testimony of God upon which faith fastens; the human conscience can find no where, but in this testimony, any thing which can compose it to quiet; the human heart can discover only in the revelations of a spiritual and eternal world, that which can satisfy its cravings, and meet all its desires. Man never can be at peace, but as a believer in Jesus Christ. Indeed, ever since the days of the original apostacy, when he threw away his confidence in God, he has thought differently; and while the history of the world is a history of experiments upon this subject, it is a history of their failures likewise. Not a single instance of a practical contradiction of this great truth has yet been furnished; while every man who has submitted to "the truth, as it is in Jesus," has found what none of the discoveries of human reason, what none of the costly sacrifices and painful austerities of superstition, what neither the wealth, nor the honours, nor pleasures of the world can furnish—"*rest for his soul.*" Now, upon this general point, though I may not be able to secure a sympathy of feeling from many of my hearers, I think I can secure a sympathy of conviction from all. I can show that this must be so, though I may not awaken the feeling that it is so.

If you ask me here what I mean by "*believing*," my answer is this—it is that state of mind in which a man receives as true the entire testimony of God, as given to us upon these sacred pages. Every principle which is here laid down is considered as firmly settled, past all dispute; as infallible a rule of human action, as any which have resulted from the discoveries of human reason—the objects of the spiritual world which it reveals are as real, as are any of those of which we have the evidence of sense, and the promises which it unfolds are as certain of their fulfilment as is the regularity ot any of the movements of nature. This testimony of God covers the entire length and breadth of our being—its truths appertain "to the life which now is," as well as "that which is to come;" to our spiritual no more than to our temporal relations, to all the circumstances and exigencies of our being—so that not only in respect to the higher and more enduring interests which belong to us as spiritual and undying creatures, but also in reference to all those interests which grow out of our temporal relations, the man, and he alone, who receives this testimony and rests upon it as true, may be at peace at all times, and amid all the chances and changes of earthly things.

To make good this doctrine, I submit in illustration several thoughts, which I ask my hearers carefully to ponder.

1. Nothing but the testimony of God gives a man clear and settled views upon those points in reference to which his peace of mind demands fixed conclusions. No one can be satisfied with himself in reference to any subject, if his views concerning

it are confused, obscure, or uncertain; a region of shadows and darkness, will always be peopled by the spectres of an excited imagination, and our path through it never can be trodden with an unhesitating, firm and elastic step. We must have, or at least think we have, some evidence of the truth of our principles before we can act freely in accordance with them; and of the certainty of the end which we contemplate before we can put forth any energetic efforts to reach it. In philosophy and the systems of human science, the days of theorizing and speculation have gone by, and no system can secure our confidence, which does not appeal to the evidence of facts.

The same thing must be true in our spiritual relations. If we sustain any such relations, the interests belonging to them must be paramount to all others; nay, there is not a question which takes a stronger hold upon the human mind, or is more disturbing in its influence, and for which our peace demands more imperatively a rational answer than this one: What am I in my nature, my relations, my destiny? I must have satisfaction here; every mind must have it. To be in this matter at the sport of conjecture—now adopting one principle, and then being compelled to suspect its correctness, is torture—a world of suspense is a world of agony, especially when the interests involved are of such amazing magnitude. I carry the assent of all my hearers along with me in this matter; an unsettled mind never can be at peace; and then I go a step farther, and say that an unbelieving mind must, from the very nature of the case, be an unsettled mind. I can appeal with the utmost fearlessness to the experience of every man who does not rest with implicit confidence upon this testimony of God, and govern himself by it, that he has no views upon the subject of his spiritual relations so settled that he is willing to abide by them, and that he never has been able, though he has often made the attempt, to satisfy himself as to his position or course. It is immaterial what principles he may adopt, or to what system he may adhere, so long as they are not the principles and the system of this written word. He may call himself an atheist, or a skeptic, if you please, and if it were possible for a man to bring himself to that state of mind in which he believed nothing, it would be a state, of all others, most unhappy. The unbelieving world is a world in which there is nothing fixed; there is no truth, no certainty, any where; and of course there is nothing upon which the mind can rest. If, perchance, there is no God, perchance there is a God—if this Bible may be false, this Bible may be true—the unbeliever can reach no other point but this. With all his boasted convictions there will be mixed up the most harassing doubts; at the very moment, perhaps, when he has reached the persuasion that it is immaterial what his feelings and course may be, because all the teachings of the Bible concerning God and human accountability are vanity, various apprehensions will rise up in conflict with his conclusions, and an irrepressible, uncontrollable suspicion, that things may not be as he supposes, will overbear all his arguments, all his subtlety, and all his wit. The reason is obvious. Such a man's conclusions are at war with the promptings of his own nature. There is a something in our very being, as God made it, I care not what you call or how you explain it, a something which binds us to the throne. Man can never, do what he may, break that mysterious chain which fastens him to God; rivers do not more certainly in accordance with their fixed laws, roll onward to the ocean; the fire does not more certainly ascend, than do our minds, by virtue of their own inherent laws, tend heavenward; and always when the film of prejudice is withdrawn, and the excitement of the passions subsides, we revert to our natural apprehensions. Hence, in the season of calamity, in the hour of danger, in the prospect of death, the unbeliever loses all his courage, because his nature compels him to distrust and question his own principles.

It is no better, nay, it is worse with the man who intellectually honours this testimony of God and yet does not admit its principles to control his heart and shape his course. Many a man is there in our world who would seek his peace of mind in a compromise between the convictions of his judgment and the feelings of his heart. Admitting the truth of the gospel testimony, and unsubmissive to its requirements, he finds his source of mental trouble, not in a doubtfulness as to the propriety of his course, but in a clear, settled conviction of his error; he knows, he feels that he is not what he ought to be. He may, as he often does, weave an ingenious system of religion, comprising some truth, but so mingled with error that its power is completely neutralized, by means of which he may endeavour to satisfy his mind. He may rest upon an outward conformity to the requirements of the truth, or upon a submission to the external ceremonial of religion, and thus try to smother his convictions and fears, but he can never destroy them. There is a meaning, and he feels it, which he has never mastered, in language like this,—" Except ye repent, ye shall perish;" " Except a man be born again, he cannot see the kingdom of God." There is, after all that may be said to the contrary, a spirituality in the religion of the New Testament; there is such a thing as a new creation in Christ Jesus to which he is a stranger; and as he ponders such thoughts, he cannot but feel that he has never approached in his experience the standard of God's testimony; and the foundation of his peace is broken up, and his confidence is cast to the winds, for he finds that his heart is not in unison with the spirit of those requirements, which, at the same time, his conscience pronounces to be just and good. The unbeliever must be at war with himself.

I must advance no argument upon this point, for man is an argument to himself. The human heart, laid bare to view, would reveal this inward conflict of which I have been speaking. The emotions which often are wakened in the bosom, if gifted with a voice and speech, would but utter a language responsive to my illustration. There is no peace where there is no believing. Man is not satisfied with himself. He is afraid, if he is not sure that he is wrong. He is not contented with his position, his relations, or his course. His fears, his convictions, his hopes, his resolutions, his purposes of a change, each and all, constitute the evidence which human experience furnishes of the truth of my doctrine, that there is no tranquillity separate from confidence in Christ.

But there is "peace in believing." To the man of intelligent, heartfelt, yet childlike faith in the testimony of Jesus Christ, the principles and promises of that testimony are what the facts of nature are to the philosopher—*absolute certainties*, in which the mind may rest. He never is the subject of doubt, while his views of things are conformed to the disclosures of this testimony, and his feeling and course, are in harmony with its requirements. In resting upon this word as the ultimate ground of certainty, in taking from it his ends, his rules, his motives, his encouragements—all the powers and elements of his nature work in harmony with each other; his conscience, his intellect, and his heart, draw together. What the mind perceives to be taught here as true, conscience approves as right, and the heart loves as good. The man has never yet been found, who felt that he was doing wrong in submitting himself in a spirit of implicit faith to the truth of Jesus Christ. His submission has always been the source of his peace; a peace as deep, and refreshing and satisfying as his faith has been strong and decided.

I mean, however, by this "peace in believing," something more than a mere freedom from anxiety and doubt; it is a peace inseparable from an intelligent conviction of truth and right. I suppose a man by indulging certain processes of thought and feeling may reach that state of mental and moral insensibility in which it will be a question of indifference to him whether this word is true or false; precisely as a man may so vitiate his taste as to be unable to distinguish between bitter and sweet, between wholesome nutriment and the most deadly poisons. There is a vast difference, however, between the composure produced by artificial means which deaden the sensibilities to the action of painful causes, and that which belongs to man upon whom no such causes act, and who in a state of perfect health sinks to repose. The believer is at peace not because he is stupified and insensible, but because he is satisfied that he is right. We all feel that there are some obligations resting upon ns; there are some feelings, there are some actions which are right, and there are some which are wrong. This consciousness of obligation is something altogether independent of our feelings. It rises above the reach of every argument which would disprove it, and triumphs over the strongest passions of our being. So deeply is this consciousness inwrought among the elements of our being, that every man, not even the atheist excepted, in his modes of speech proves himself its subject; and there can be no rational peace for the human spirit unless this consciousness and our feelings harmonize; and this is the peace of believing in Jesus Christ. Its subject, when in view of the testimony of God he repents of his sins; when in view of the work of Christ he casts himself upon him as a redeeming Saviour; when in view of the promises which are here recorded, he commits all his interests in a spirit of trustful reliance to his Lord and master; when in view of the requirements of these written oracles, he marks out his path of duty and goes forward without hesitation or reserve, feels that he is doing precisely what he ought to do; whatever he may be in other respects, in these he is right, and he knows it; and this consciousness of right doing is a possession which worlds are too poor to purchase. There is something in a sense of right doing which is satisfying to the mind; in any relation to our fellow man, there is something exceedingly sweet and greatly refreshing in the thought that we have done precisely what we ought to have done; and it is an analogous experience in the relation between man's soul and the God who made, who controls, and who will judge it, to which we refer, when we speak of "peace in believing." It may indeed be so, that the experience of the Christian is not unfrequently an experience of anxiety, and that because his confidence in the word and promise of this testimony is shaken. There may be doubting Christians. and therefore unhappy Christians; but there can be no such thing as a doubting faith. If God has spoken in this sacred volume, if these principles which are here unfolded have his sanction, if these commandments have his authority, if these promises have been uttered by him, then as they are the disclosures and commandments and promises of one who is infallible truth, there can be no room for doubt. The objects of Christian faith are something more than mere human notions, speculations, conjectures, or opinions; they are ascertained virtues, because they are confirmed by the testimony of one who cannot lie. Let me be persuaded that God has spoken here, and in embracing these principles, I am sure I am embracing truth; in obeying these commandments, I am sure I am doing right; in trusting these promises, I am sure of the results they contemplate. Faith in God's testimony necessarily excludes every thing like doubt; and if I am harassed by anxieties as to my principles, my course, or my ends, I do but show myself to be under the influence of "an evil heart of unbelief."

2. My second thought in illustration of our general doctrine, has been, to some extent, involved in my first, and yet it demands a distinct consideration; it refers to the testimony of God as furnishing the only source of intelligent peace to the human conscience. I do not think I am wrong, when I speak of a pressure of conscious guilt upon the spirit, as marking, to a greater or less degree, the experience of every man who is not a believer in Jesus Christ. We all acknowledge our sinfulness. However varied may be men's theories upon the subject of human sinfulness, their feelings always harmonize in this—that they are not what they

ought to be, and have not done what they ought to have done. We are, moreover, so constituted, that the conviction of wrong-doing is always connected with painful emotions; we cannot separate in our minds the idea of sin against God, from the idea of retribution; and the anticipations of the future, joined to the reflections of the past, must be a source of disquietude. Now, we can never reason these convictions out of existence. The human conscience is not to be argued down by the sophistries of a deceitful heart. Its voice may be drowned, its reproofs may be hushed, and if man's life was a monotony of health, and prosperity, and worldly joy, it might be a monotony of spiritual insensibility; but every change, (and changes are numerous,) gives conscience an opportunity to act. When any danger is near or any calamity approaches, this consciousness of wrong and these apprehensions of its consequences, wake at once within us, and fill us with agitation and alarm. Now, my doctrine is, that no where but in the testimony of God, which is here presented to our faith, can we find any thing which can give rational and abiding peace to an enlightened conscience. Men have adopted divers expedients upon this subject, without success. Some have resorted to philosophy and turned stoics, but they have failed; some have fled to the regions of literature, or tried to escape from the realities of things by living in the dreamy world of poetry and fiction, but they have failed. Some have entered upon a career of worldly ambition, chasing worldly glory as their end, or pursuing worldly wealth as their chief good. Some have sought relief in the witchery of song, or the mazes of the dance, and have endeavoured to crush and kill thought in the splendid circles where God is unknown, and amid the fascinations by means of which earth holds spell-bound its votaries. But this conscience finds man every where. It presents to him problems which his philosophy cannot master, it sheds around him a light in which earthly glory grows dim, it peoples the dreamy world which his imagination describes around him with spectres which he cannot lay; it heralds a future for which wealth makes no provision, and throws a gloomy haze over the brilliant scene of this world's revelries, so that he sickens in the midst of earthly joys, and in the midst of laughter his heart is made heavy.

But, my brethren, there is "peace in believing." There is that in this testimony of God, which satisfies conscience, as well as enlightens the mind. I do not mean to say that faith in "the record which God has given of his Son," will relieve the mind of all sense of past guilt; but it puts that guilt in new connections, and strips it of that fear which hath torment—the plan of forgiving mercy which the gospel reveals, sets this thought distinctly before the mind, that the work of Jesus Christ as an atoning Saviour has taken away the necessity of punishment; and the simple assurance that "the blood of Christ cleanseth us from all sin," becomes an effectual balm for the wounded spirit. The man who believes it, adds his testimony to that of thousands, whose experience has verified the sentiment of the apostle, "being justified by faith we have peace with God through our Lord Jesus Christ." Explain it as you may, here is the fact; a fact seen in no other circumstances and connections, that the man who casts himself in confidence upon this simple assurance of God is at rest—he can look at his transgressions, not indeed without repentance, not without humiliation of soul, but without alarm, and anticipate, (no one but he can do so) not only unappalled, but with calmness, with joy even, the day of irreversible decision, when God shall give unto every man according to his works. His peace is always in exact proportion to his confidence—if his faith is weak, his hope will be a trembling one; and as his confidence in the word of this testimony increases in strength, his deliverance from the painful apprehensions of conscious guilt is made perfect.

3. I must add another thought to complete the outline of my subject. Nothing but faith in this testimony can give the heart an object in which it can rest. Disquiet, dissatisfaction, restlessness have been the attributes of human experience ever since the days of the original apostacy, because then man threw away his confidence, and ever since has been endeavouring to fill with the creature the place which was intended for the Creator. What are the disappointments of this world, so many, so severe, so biting, so crushing, but the illustrations which Providence is every day working out, and the testimonies which human nature is every day

furnishing of the variety of human pursuits. Roving amid the objects of earth, we find nothing upon which we can rest with full satisfaction, because there is nothing created which can meet all the desires, and fill up all the capacities of our spirits. The laws of the mental and spiritual world are as fixed as those of the natural world; and the efforts after happiness of a human soul estranged from God are no less idle than would be those of a man who should essay to reverse the laws of gravitation, or blot out the sun from the system, or check the world in its revolutions. There is no human experience, whether recorded or unrecorded, which at all clashes with this general thought; ask the unbeliever, who has no God, no Saviour, if he is satisfied; ask the child of revelry and song, why he sickens amid all the excitements of the passions. If you are unreconciled to God, look into your own heart, and see if you could be contented under the full assurance that you should never be different from what you now are, and never possess but what now belongs to you. We must rest in God, my brethren, if we rest at all; and yet nothing but faith can bring us to this resting place. You may look at God as he reveals himself in the works of nature, or in the dealings of Providence, or in the movements of the human conscience; but in all these disclosures there is more to awaken distrust than to inspire confidence. It is God as revealed in this testimony that the heart can rest upon; and it is only as we embrace by faith this testimony, and see God in

Jesus Christ, that we can go to the throne, and say in the spirit of children, "Abba, Father." Under the influence of this faith, I can perceive that the perfections of God are not only not arrayed against me, but are actually enlisted in my favour; he is now my shield and my defence, my joy, and my portion, and the lifter up of my head; and no sooner do I see him thus than I say, "Return unto thy rest, O my soul."

I speak not the language of theory but of fact. When I speak of "peace in believing," I speak of the results of actual experiment—an experiment, too, which has been tried at all times and in all circumstances, and by all classes and conditions of men. It is a sad mistake which the men of the world commit, when they suppose that none but the wretched, the poor, the miserable, and they who have not the means of securing other enjoyment, testify to the reality of a "peace in believing." To a great extent it may be so, and then it is not an insignificant testimony to the value of religion, that it can do what the world has never done, give to the forlorn, the down-trodden, and the outcast, peace and joy. But not only they who have had no earthly cistern from which to drink, but they whose cisterns have been full, have forsaken them for this fountain of living waters. There have been men of royalty who have never known true peace till they have laid their crowns at the feet of Christ, and covered their princely robes with the garments of salvation; and they who have followed ambitious promptings, and they who have trodden the halls of splendour, have fled the camp, the cabinet, and the festive board to seek rest for their spirits at the foot of the cross. It is "a great cloud of witnesses," who attend at our summons to testify to the reality of "peace in believing;" from the poor man's cottage and from the rich man's palace, from the associations of haggard want and the ease and luxury of earthly abundance, from amid the subjects of earthly trials and those whose lives have been crowned with prosperity, from the circles of the gay and the frivolous, from the ball-room and the theatre, as well as from the chamber of sickness and afflictions, out of all classes, and ranks, and conditions of men, from Newton as he treads with lofty and majestic step the firmament, down to the humble shepherd who feeds his flock upon Salisbury plain, they come, each one uttering the strain,—

"People of the living God,
We have sought the world around,
Paths of sin and sorrow trod,
Peace and comfort no where found.
Now to you my spirit turns,
Turns, a fugitive unblest,
Brethren, when your altar burns,
O! receive me into rest;"

and when they have cast themselves in confidence upon the testimony of God, then has their language been, "Thou art my portion, O Lord." "As the heart panteth after the water brooks, so panteth my soul after thee, O God." "Whom have I in heaven but thee, and there is none upon earth whom I desire beside thee; my flesh and my heart faileth, but God is the strength of my heart, and my portion for ever." "As for me, I will behold thy face in righteousness, I shall be satisfied when I awaken in thy likeness." There is "peace and joy in believing."

Allow me here, my brethren, to arrest my subject, though my remarks have had reference only to our spiritual relations, and have left wholly untouched the influence of faith in God's testimony upon our experience amid the varied and changing scenes and circumstances of the present life. I claim your attention for but one moment longer to two very simple thoughts.

I do not think that I have been wandering from the point which should properly engage a Christian's mind upon a sacramental Sabbath. We come to-day to commemorate the death of Jesus Christ, a death which sets a seal upon the truth of his testimony. We have here then a means of strengthening our faith, and bringing us to the enjoyment of our privileges. If ever a Christian's mind should be at peace, it should be at a communion table, where, by means of striking symbols, the evidence of the truth of this testimony is vividly presented to him. Here those doubts, which so often disturb our peace, that unbelief which cripples us and mars our enjoyments, are out of place. Here, as we profess at the foot of the cross to set to our seal that God is true, let us give our fears to the winds, and bid all our doubts to be gone; and in the exercise of that confidence which Christ's work is calculated to inspire, learn to say, "We know in whom we have believed." We are at the source of these comforts which faith ministers to the spirit, because we are in communion with the great fact—a Saviour's death—which forms the burden of the inspired testimony. May the God of peace then fill our minds with all peace and joy in believing.

Then, for my last thought, I address it to the wanderer from his God. I call him an unhappy man, only that I may echo his own sincerest sentiments. It may be a strange thought which I bring you, but it is a true one. You cannot do without confidence in God. There is no peace for that sin-stricken, weary spirit, but the peace of believing upon Jesus Christ. Nothing but this can fix that wavering, uncertain, doubting mind; nothing but this will minister peace to that uneasy conscience, nothing but this will give rest to that dissatisfied and unquiet heart. You are a wanderer from home, and must return to your father's house. Where you are, nothing can give you peace; neither business, nor wealth, nor fame, nor pleasure; nothing can give you peace, estranged from God. No portion which earth can give can to the human spirit be a substitute for its Creator. You may be false to yourself and false to heaven, but conscience and the world will be true to the God who made them; the one will not allow you to be at peace divorced from him, the other will never furnish you with happiness, except as he permits it; you may doubt it, but your experience will demonstrate it; and if you ever have peace or joy, you will find it only in believing upon Jesus Christ. We would summon you away from your wanderings, and call you back to God. Here is the fountain of living water; and the Spirit and the Bride say, come; and let him that heareth say, come; and let him that is athirst, come; and whosoever will let him take of the water of life freely. Come then, and rest upon Christ, and be at peace; come and drink of this fountain, and live for ever.

PEACE IN BELIEVING.

"The Lord will perfect that which concerneth me."
—Psalm cxxxviii. 8.

"What time I am afraid, I will trust in thee."—Psalm lvi. 4.

"Lead me to the rock that is higher than I."—Psalm lxi. 2.

The language of the text is that of strong and intelligent confidence; and as an illustration of the nature and effects of such confidence, we have selected it as the basis of our remarks this morning. It is the picture of a human mind at rest, and at rest in view of the word and the character of the living God. It is the more interesting to us, because it is the exhibition of this confidence in the hour of its trial. The language we have set before you is not that of a man who theorizes in circumstances of outward prosperity and quiet—who is at rest because there is nothing in his present condition to annoy and disturb him, and nothing seen in the future to awaken painful apprehensions—but that of a man in the most depressing circumstances—uttered in an hour of peril, when the present was all disaster, and the future all gloom; when earthly confidences failed him, and the vanity of human help was demonstrated, and nothing was left upon which to stay his spirit, but simple confidence in God. We need not attempt to ascertain the precise posture of David's affairs at the time when he gave utterance to the words of my text—perhaps it is impossible to do so. It is enough for our present purpose to know that it was such as to show the utter uselessness of all human trust, and shut him up to simple faith in the word of God, as his only source of peace; and in the composure of his mind, as he strengthened himself in God, assured that he would perfect that which concerned him; he teaches us that there is that on which the human spirit can rest, and in which it can find strength to sustain it under present ills, and support it against the apprehensions of future woes.

We were permitted upon the last Sabbath to illustrate this thought in reference to man's spiritual relations, and to show how simple confidence in the character and testimony of God can give a man a rational and abiding peace; our purpose upon the present occasion is to carry out this thought, and show that there is a "promise for the life which now is," as well as "that which is to come; and that the peace which faith ministers to the spirit, appertains as well to the temporal as to the spiritual circumstances of our being.

I need hardly say, my brethren, that the life which we live in the flesh, is a chequered scene; monotonous prosperity is and can be no man's allotment. A world of probation must be a world of trial, and trial always painful, oftentimes excessively severe. Even where the outward condition generally is one of the greatest comfort and the brightest promise, there are nevertheless some scenes through which men are called to pass, in which their hearts fail them through fear, and anguish preys upon their spirits; scenes where we must have what earth can never give us, scenes where human fortitude is overborne, and even earthly sympathy will not sustain the spirit under the crushing weight which is thrown upon it. If you have never passed through such scenes, they await you yet. I cannot tell in what form these trials may come, nor when they will touch you, but come they will, and you never can pass through them in peace, except as your spirits cling in the exercise of a truthful, relying spirit to the word and testimony of God. "But the people that do know their God, shall be strong." Confidence always brings peace, and the man has never yet been found, in any circumstances, under any form of calamity, who as his faith fastens upon the word and promise of God, could not possess his soul in patience, and even "rejoice in tribulation."

Now in illustrating this thought let me be distinctly understood. I do not mean to take the position that a man may upon the ground of his faith calculate upon an exemption from trials. It does not follow if I believe in God that he will of course give me peace and quiet in all my external relations. It does not follow by any means that I shall be able to carry all my earthly purposes into execution, and that I shall be free from all disturbing causes; on the contrary, "peace in believing" is perfectly consistent with the most disastrous events in these outward relations; it is perfectly consistent with defeated plans, thwarted wishes, and blasted hopes. No such exemption from trial is ever contemplated in any word or promises of God upon which faith fastens; on the contrary, the assurance is that "in the world ye shall have tribulation." Nor do I mean to say, that nothing can be, strictly speaking, a trial to a man of faith. The peace of believing is not insensibility. It is as far removed from the apathy of the stoic, to whom good and evil are alike, to whom there is no such thing as pain and sorrow, as it is from the frenzy of the fanatic, who upon the strength ot a supposed relationship to God, claims and boasts of an exemption from all sorrow. I grant you, it is possible for a man to work up himself to a state of indifference, for the time being, to the painful scenes which are enacting around him; but in doing so, he is warring against his own nature, and contradicting the first lessons of the gospel of Christ. It is unnatural not to feel in the hour of sorrow; the smitten heart will bleed; the workings of human nature must have vent, and faith does not suppress them. God did not give us hearts to be petrified, sensibilities to be locked up in adamant. We are creatures of sympathy, and Jesus Christ, as he wept at the grave of a beloved friend, dignified, as well as vindicated, the sacred social feelings of our nature. Human philosophy may comfort us by blunting the fine sensibilities of our nature, and relieve us of our distresses by robbing us of some of the nobler attributes of our minds; but the religion of the gospel refines while it controls the susceptibilities of our nature. It does not forbid the heart to sigh or the tear to fall, but it sets before the mind that which administers to it a peace which will comfort and sustain and cheer the soul in the darkest hours, and amid the most troublous scenes of our earthly pilgrimage. I care not what may be the nature or severity of human trials, how withering their influence, how deep the wounds they may inflict, how thick the gloom in which they may enshroud one; faith in the character and word of God can do what nothing else can do, give light in darkness, joy in sorrow, hope in despondency, and even convert "the shadow of death into the morning." I will point out to you the elements and sources of its power, and give you some illustrations of its efficacy.

1. The hand of God is in every thing. No point is more distinct to a trustful, relying spirit, no truth is more settled than this. There are no fortuities in this world, there is not an event which has not its meaning, its connections, and its end. The confidence which gives peace, and fixedness, and strength to the mind, fastens upon the views which the Bible gives of God, his agency, and his purposes, as a God who is concerned with every thing, and who acts in every thing in reference to an end worthy of himself. It has no sympathy with that cold and heartless philosophy which separates between God and his creatures, or which

places any the most unimportant or minute of our interests beyond the range of divine inspection and control. There is nothing comforting, nothing staying to the mind in any such views; human reason, untaught by the word of inspired truth, can give us only conjectures when we need certainties; and the teachings which to it seem most truthful, are the most disturbing to the spirit. I confess when I go away from the region upon which revelation has shed down its light, I go where all is doubt, and darkness, and confusion. I can find no where but in the Bible those views of God in which I can rest with entire satisfaction, because no where else can I see God interesting himself in, and managing all my affairs as an individual. If I thought there was one event among the occurrences of my daily life which God did not regard; if I thought there was one emotion of this bosom which escaped his notice, one sigh which he did not hear, or one tear which he did not observe; if I supposed that a single hair could fall from my head without his ordering or permission, my confidence would be robbed of the main element of its strength. If a man is at peace in the exercise of a trustful confidence, it must be because he has something of the same spirit which Hagar had, when driven out into the wilderness and beyond the hope and the reach of human help, she said, "Thou God seest me;" something of the same spirit which David had when he said, "O Lord, thou hast searched me and known me; thou knowest my down sitting and uprising, thou understandest my thought afar off, thou compassest my path and my lying down, and art acquainted with all my ways." It is this God —always with us, directing all things, arranging all things, who is the object of that confidence which gives fixedness to the mind.

2. My second thought is, that the word of God in which faith rests, contemplates man in all the various circumstances of his being, in every possible or supposable condition in which he may be placed. My first thought had reference to the actual presence of God with us, and his ability as a present God to help and sustain us. My second has reference to his positive assurance of help. The revelation which God has given us upon the sacred pages is wonderful in this respect, that it is a revelation of a promise, and all its disclosures are regulated by, as they take their shape from the promise they are designed to unfold. That promise, I mean the promise of a Saviour, and of all good in him, covers all our interests; hence the word which is here given to us is full of promises, and they are "exceedingly great and precious;" great in their range, because there is no circumstance which they do not reach, precious in their character, because there is no exigency in our affairs to which they are not adapted. It is the beauty and the charm of these inspired oracles that there is not a human solicitude for which they do not contain a word in season; not a doubt which they leave without a message to disperse it; no anxiety which they pass by without a whisper to soothe it; not a sigh which they do not hush; not a tear which they do

not wipe away. If this is not so, I will give up my point and renounce my confidence. There is nothing, I apprehend, in which the wisdom and goodness of God is so apparent as in the exactness and precision with which his words of promise are adapted to the wants of those who trust him. It is wonderful indeed that God should be mindful of man, of every man; wonderful that he should attend to the wants of an insect, of every insect to which the leaf upon which it rests is a world. But when I remember what thought is, over what an unlimited range it can expatiate, and how many and varied are the materials of solicitude which it can gather in its wanderings, when I muse on the almost endless varieties of human sorrow, and the multiplicity of causes which may disquiet one, and then find that there is not a doubt or a sadness for which this record of truth does furnish a promise; when I know that the case has never yet occurred of a man turning in faith and prayer to the Bible whatever may have been his peculiar trial or sadness, who has not found some portion of it which seemed to have been written expressly for himself, so that there has been a power in its words which have spoken to his heart, I am overwhelmed; and the faith which takes hold upon these promises as real, can give fixedness to the mind, because there is not a wave of trouble which some promise may not repel; not a season of darkness where some promise does not shine; not a chamber of gloom where it does not light up the lamp of consolation; and here are the resources of comfort and strength for the confiding spirit. If God is near me, if he is engaged in all my affairs, it is God who speaks in the promises; and though I cannot see him, I can hear him,—sometimes it is when the waves of trouble roll around me, and he whispers, "Peace, be still;" sometimes when I am called to pass through the fires, and he says, "They shall not gather upon thee;" sometimes it is when a sore temptation tries my spirit, and his language is, "My grace shall be sufficient for thee." Always it is in words which meet my case, and which, by their wonderful adaptedness, prove that they come from one who knows my heart, and is perfectly acquainted with all my circumstances and wants.

3. My third thought is that all these promises are promises in Christ Jesus; and herein we have the evidence of their certainty, the assurance of their fulfilment. We can give you but an outline of this general idea, and yet it is too important to be omitted. I fix your minds then upon this fact: all the good which comes to this sinful world comes through Christ. If I speak of the promise of pardon to the penitent, of forgiveness to the prodigal; if I speak of the assurance that the sting shall be taken from death, that the dead shall be raised, that eternal life shall be secured, you associate all these promises and assurances with the work of Christ, as establishing the certainty of their fulfilment; but I put every assurance of God's word in the same connection, and in this connection alone I find ground for my faith in their certainty. The assurance that the sun shall rise upon the evil and the

good, that the fields shall be covered with abundance, as well as the promise that God will be a husband to the widow, and a father to the fatherless, I put in the same connection, and trace to the same source. They were uttered only by virtue of the covenant with Christ, they have been and yet are to be made good, only because Christ has fulfilled the conditions of that covenant. Thus it is that faith, fastening upon the promises of God as promises in Christ, anticipates all the objections to their fulfilment growing out of our unworthiness and ill-desert. It meets exactly a very common case in human experience; the case of a man who is staggered by the greatness of God's promises, by the excess of their blessings over our deserts, nay, over our wishes and our hopes; and to whose mind the question will be secretly proposed, "can these promises ever be fulfilled?" He does not, you will perceive, intend to question God's faithfulness, but he may fear, and he thinks with too good ground, that the promise will not, on account of his unworthiness, be fulfilled to himself. Ah! if the promise was made to me dependent upon my deserts, then, indeed, I might doubt and fear; and it is because men who call themselves believers look away from the covenant with Christ, and look to their own frames and feelings, that they lose the benefit of their faith, and become very much like barometers, which rise and fall with the changes of the surrounding atmosphere. If my worthiness is to determine the fulfilment of God's promises, I can be certain of none of them; but if my faith fastens upon Christ, and upon what he has done, as the ground of the certainty of God's promise, there can be nothing to shake it; while there might be room for a thousand fears and suspicions, were every thing dependent upon me, whose failures in obedience might remove me, so to speak, out of the sphere of the promise. There is room only for fixed confidence and full assurance, when every thing depends upon what Christ has done, who having in his humiliation and death fulfilled the conditions of the covenant, lives now in glory, exercising there a ministry which secures the fulfilment of the promise to every one who believes in him.

These are the elements and sources of that power which faith in the word of God's testimony has to give fixedness to the spirit, amid all changes, and a peace which rises superior to the influence of all the disturbing causes which may act upon the mind; and if this is a right view of God, if he is thus near us, cautiously engaged in all our concerns, acquainted with all our circumstances, if his promises meet us in all the conditions of our being, assuring us of his protection and care, and his determining to make all things work together for our good; if every one of these promises is thus certified, and put past all doubt, can it be otherwise than that there must be peace in believing; and may not a man, in any circumstances, be at rest in the full confidence that "God will perfect every thing concerning him."

In the remarks we have thus far thrown out, we have given you what may be called the theory of our subject, by exhibiting the elements or grounds of a Christian's confidence; we have shown that it ought to be a source of rational and abiding peace; we now advance a step farther and speak of it as something which has been actually tested by experiment and has never yet failed. In point of fact, this confidence in God always does minister peace and joy to the human spirit.

We have already remarked that the life of every man has its shades as well as its lights. There are hours of sadness as well as of joy—of fear as well as of hope—and it is in the seasons of gloom that human confidences are tried; and if we would know the value of a Christian's faith we must look at the influence it exerts over the mind in those circumstances in which naturally mens' hearts fail them through fear, and the character of their trials places them beyond the reach of all mere human consolation.

We admit that there are some of the calamities of human life under which natural fortitude can sustain a man, and earthly philosophy can cheer him; but they are invariably of that nature that time and diligence may repair the injury they have occasioned. A man may be stripped of his property, and yet if he sees how he can make his losses good, the hope of coming prosperity can sustain him, the prospect of future success may buoy up his spirit and give him energy, nay, the very efforts he puts forth to regain what he has lost, may almost make him forget that he has been a loser.

But there are other trials which do not admit of any such alleviation; there are losses which admit of no earthly reparation; there are griefs of the human spirit which are not to be assuaged by any earthly consolations, and sorrows to which no human philosophy can minister alleviation. We take you to the scene where the heart bleeds because of its ruptured ties, where death has been doing his work in the household, where his stroke has fallen so as to be most surely felt, because the fairest and loveliest of the family circle has become its prey. Here is a case upon which human philosophy may try its strength, and worldly consolation may exhaust its common-places, but the one is unmeaning, and the others are painful; and pleasure may touch the harp whose strains have often enchanted and seduced, but the worn and wearied spirit has no ear in the gloom for what sounded magically when a thousand lights were blazing. There never yet was a man placed in circumstances like these who did not feel that he needed something more than earth could give him; and these are precisely the scenes in which the confidence of which we speak is seen in its beauty and felt in its peace-speaking power. The writer, whose sentiment we have been illustrating, uttered not simply the language of theory but of experience; the confidence to which he gave expression had been tried. He remembered the hour when his city was destroyed and his family were carried away into captivity, how amid those who wept and wailed around him, and refused to be comforted, his heart was at rest because it was stayed upon God. We all know, moreover, that some of his sweetest songs were sung in the seasons of his deepest sorrow, and that in circumstances which would have unnerved any spirit destitute of his resources. When closely pursued by those who thirsted for his blood, he said, " I will both lay me down in peace and sleep, because thou Lord only makest me to dwell in safety." Nor is that upper chamber at Shunem without its meaning, where a mother has laid the body of her only son in death, and answers the inquiry of the people after her welfare, by saying, " It is well."

The illustrations of this character might be multiplied a thousand fold; we might summon up a weeping group, and as they passed before you, you should see orphans whom death had made solitary, parents to whom the world had become a desert, because some long-watched and cherished flower had withered and died; widows in their loneliness, whom death had reft of every friend but God; and if there are tears upon their faces, there are smiles also, and their testimony is, that they have never been deserted in their sorrows; they have had peace, but it has been "peace in believing," their best lessons of truth have been learned, their clearest views, their largest apprehensions of spiritual things have been gained in seasons of trouble; and never have they had such full proofs of the preciousness of Christ, never such abounding consolations, as when one joy after another has departed-

and wave upon wave of sorrow has rolled over them. While earth around them has seemed a desert, and while they were toiling painfully along, the arid sands have grown fertile, and fresh things and green things have sprung up around them ; and where it seemed as though nothing but the deadly nightshade could grow, the tree of life has sprung up with its twelve manner of fruits ; and never were its clusters so rich, never did so many hang within their reach. Such is the testimony of those who have put their trust in God ; and the experience which it sets before us, forms a striking contrast to that of others who know nothing of the value and efficiency of God's promises, upon whom in darkness no light arises, and who in the desert can find no green thing upon which the eye may rest. Nay, I think I may go farther than this, and I imagine that many a man's experience will bear me out in the seeming paradox, that the joys of the spirit which clings with an unwavering confidence to the promises of God, are greatest in the hours of the greatest trial, because faith then is strongest in its exercise. It is in moral as in natural things ; music sounds softer and sweeter by night than by day, because then all is still, and the notes are brought out more fully. It is in the hour of calamity that the ruptured heart-strings yield the sweetest melody, when touched by God, and the notes of praise are loudest and richest, because the promises of truth which alone can raise them, then seem most precious.

Now if these things be true with regard to what

may be termed the ordinary scenes of life, because trials and affliction are the common lot of humanity, if a man must have that strength which confidence in God alone can give him, to prevent him from being overborne by common calamities, if he cannot separate from faith in the promises, possess his soul in patience and peace, amid the every-day events of life, he cannot certainly in the hour of his greatest trial, when all earthly resources fail him, and all earthly supports sink beneath him.

There is an hour before us, my brethren, when nothing but confidence in God will help us; and herein we have an illustration of the value and glory of this confidence, that it can, and does sustain the spirit and give it in this hour perfect peace. We all feel that death is an evil, a terrible evil; and yet an evil which we must meet. Looking at it from a distance, we may talk very calmly about it, and indulge in very ingenious reasonings; but when we look at it as near at hand, it is a very different thing from what it appeared to be in the light of our philosophical speculations. We never passed through such a scene, or any thing like it—a scene where all that may have cheered us onward in the world is withdrawn—a scene where sense can teach us nothing—a scene where reason can give us no help, because it has no promises upon which to build an argument, or from which to draw an inference—a scene where these spirits must leave these bodies, and go forth, each one by itself in its solitariness, to tread a hitherto unexplored pathway, and to abide the searchings of judgment. That scene is just before us; it will not be long before we shall be passing through it. Happy is the man, I do but echo the sentiments of every heart when I say, "Happy is the man who can say with calmness and composure, in view of such a scene, "The Lord will perfect that which concerneth me." Faith, simple confidence in God through Christ, can give a man strength and peace in such a scene as this, and nothing else can do it. I do not enter upon an argument here; I might, if I were so disposed, show how this confidence secures to a man victory of death; I think I might make it perfectly apparent, that the man who believes in the word of this testimony, has in his possession, while he looks upon Christ as revealing immortality, as taking away the sting of death by his atonement, as himself triumphing over the grave, and giving to his followers an assurance of like victory, has in these views all the elements of peace, and a peace as full as his views are clear, and his confidence in them is strong. But I appeal now to facts. It cannot be denied then, as a simple matter of fact, that persons of every age and every rank in life, are continually meeting death with calmness and even joy. Though not insensible to the terrors of death, they have yet that which enables them to triumph over them—nay, with a full view of what death is, what it involves, and to what it leads, they can approach it with confidence, and even exult that the hour of their departure is at hand. If you ask me for an explanation of this fact; what it is which upholds the dying Christian, what throws over his wasted countenance such an air of serenity, what prompts his expressions of peace, his breathings of hope, which seem so illy to accord with his circumstances of decay and trouble, I answer it is some such simple word of promise as this, to which his faith clings: "Fear not, for I am with thee; be not dismayed, for I am thy God." That is the secret of the Christian's peace, and joy, and triumph. Confidence in the word and promise of his master; and that confidence assures of victory, that confidence brings heaven near to him, so that he is like one who already sees the glory, and hears the minstrelsy of the eternal city.

I have never witnessed such scenes in any other connection. I have never heard of such peace and joy as resulting from any other influence. The history of the world cannot produce a single case of a man dying in peace without simple faith in the promise of God. I have heard, indeed, and have seen men of the world, men who knew nothing of Christ and him crucified, utter strangers to faith in God's promises, go hence without betraying any particular emotion. The wicked, according to the teachings of the Bible, may have no bands in their death, they may sink into apathy, and some men may look upon their blighted energies and gross insensibility, as evidences of peace and victory. I have heard, too, of men who have gone the length of denying Christ and rejecting God's truth, dying in apparent unconcern. Hume and Gibbon could even trifle on their death-beds, and in trying to act the hero play the buffoon; but their very trifling betrayed a restlessness of spirit, and an anxiety to drown serious thought. These, however, are exceptions to the general rule. Most generally the last hours of skeptics have been like those of Paine and Voltaire, hours of horror; while the votaries of this world, who have passed through life unconcerned about spiritual things, have shown themselves the victims of agony and remorse, when they have approached the border line of eternity. But in the cases where such has not been the fact, cases like those to which we have alluded, while there may have been insensibility, there has been no peace; if they have not been aghast with terror, they have been void of any pleasing anticipations. There have been none of those beamings and flashings of hope and joy which faith kindles; there have been no boundings of a spirit elastic with immortality, no such thing as a palpable mastery over death, no such thing as a holy defiance of the terrors of dissolution, no such thing as a vivid anticipation of happiness, no whispered assurance when the voice is failing that all is well, nothing of the kind; oh! no, these are the fruits of believing on the testimony of God.

My brethren, there is a reality in the religion of faith, there is a power in it which is no where else to be found. There is a reality which we must all appreciate, a power which we must all know experimentally, if we would be at peace. With this conclusion, sustained as it is so fully by argument and fact, I come to my hearers to-day; I dedicate the thoughts I have thrown out to the tried and wearied spirit. There is peace in believing—there is peace in nothing else. Could I bring all who hear me to-day to the exercise of this simple confidence in God through Christ, what wondrous change would pass over their experience; how soon would that troubled conscience be soothed, how soon would that aching soul be relieved of its burden, that vacant heart be filled, that weary spirit be at rest, and those sighs for peace be lost in the joy of its attainment. Believe me, my brethren, you cannot do without confidence in God. Perhaps in an hour of earthly joy, when all is bright around you, my appeal may not come home with power to the spirit. But this sky will not always be bright—there is a storm cloud rising. The voice of joy will not always be heard in your dwelling, the bitter lamentation will be there. There are scenes before you which will try the spirit, and you must pass through them, and you never can be sustained except by confidence in God. Ten thousand withered hopes and as many broken hearts will tell you so; or if you could pass unharmed through all these scenes; if you could weather all these storms of life, there is yet another; it will come when perhaps you are least expecting it. It will be a dark, a dreary and oppressive night, when it gathers around you, that will try you as you have never been tried before; and then if you have no confidence in God to steady and fix you, all will be lost, and lost forever. Of that coming tempest I would warn you. Every thing may now be calm, but it is always still before the fiercest storm. Your firmament may seem clear, but yonder is the little cloud no bigger than a man's hand, which portends the tempest. As you watch, it approaches, it increases, it gathers blackness; if it finds you, without an interest in God's promises, it will sweep away all your confidences, overthrow all your towers of strength, and leave you a ruined thing over which others will say, Alas! Alas! this is the man who made not God his strength.

To Him who is a hiding place from the storm and a shelter from the tempest, I would commend my hearers, and to them I would commend his truth. "Come unto me and I will give you rest." "He that believeth on him shall never be confounded."

SUPPORTS OF FAITH AMID THE MYSTERIES OF PROVIDENCE.

"Thy righteousness is like the great mountains; thy judgments are a great deep. O Lord, thou preservest man and beast."—PSALM xxxvi. 6.

THERE is nothing very striking or remarkable in this text as it presents itself to the eye of the superficial reader, and yet a closer examination will show it to be full of the most interesting and consolatory instruction. It appears at first sight to be but a simple statement of three distinct, familiar, and indisputable propositions, without any close connection with, or dependence upon, each other. The first has reference to God's righteousness, that perfection of character which secures perfect equity and justice in all his procedures,—and its comparison with the great mountains is designed to show it fixed and immoveable; so high that it cannot well be lost sight of; so deep in its foundations that it cannot be overthrown or shaken. The other has reference to God's judgments, his dealings and dispensations towards men; and under the emblem of "a great deep," to which he likens them, it is affirmed of them that they are inscrutable, incomprehensible, not to be fathomed by us in our present state of being. The last refers to God's general providential care, as its evidences are presented daily to our observation; or more particularly to those common mercies which are shed down constantly upon the creatures of his hand, as intimating not more clearly the minuteness of God's inspection and care than the kindness by which they are uniformly marked. These are the three propositions before us. In bespeaking for them your attention, we do not feel ourselves called upon to enter upon an extended demonstration of their truth. We suppose them to be all admitted. No one who believes in the existence of God, and acknowledges his government, will pretend to call in question the equity of his administration,—"He is righteous in all his ways, and holy in all his works." The supposition that he can possibly commit a mistake, that he is liable, however remotely, to an error, either of judgment or of heart, involves an inconsistency which the intellect as well as the feelings of man at once repudiates. This is a fixed principle, an axiom in all our reasonings upon the divine dispensations which no rational man would think of questioning a moment; and under the full conviction of this truth it is that we so promptly resolve all the apparent inconsistencies or inequalities of the divine administration, not into any want of equity or justice upon the part of him who sits upon the throne, but to our own ignorance or short sightedness, which disqualifies us from taking those large and comprehensive views necessary to a clear perception of his dealings in their varied and often complicated relations.

Equally uncalled for is an argument to demonstrate the mystery of God's dispensations. No one can study or even slightly observe the divine dealings, whether in reference to individuals or communities, without perceiving much, the fitness and propriety of which are matters of faith, not of demonstration, calling not upon ingenuity to speculate, but upon reason to submit. God's "judgments are a great deep," which we have no line to fathom, and beneath the surface of which, if we dive, we are completely lost. While at the same time we cannot cast our eye abroad in any direction without observing traces of perpetually exercised skill and unceasing goodness; the universality of God's providential care can no more be questioned that the righteousness of his government or the mystery of his proceedings. It is as true that he "preserveth man and beast," as it is that his "righteousness is like the great mountains," or that his "judgments are a great deep." We have, then, on this occasion, nothing to do with argument going to demonstrate the correctness of either of these propositions; we assume them as granted, and proceed therefore to the main purpose of our discourse, which is to show the connection between them, and ascertain what, if any, great practical lessons may be learned from the manner in which they are combined by the inspired writer.

I. In order to bring out distinctly the idea I have in my mind, as suggested by the language of the text, I begin with the proposition relating to the unsearchable nature of the divine dispensations, the judgments of God, which the Psalmist compares to "a great deep." It is undoubtedly a fact that the grounds of God's procedures, and the methods of his action, are very often beyond our ability to discover and trace them. There is not one of us, perhaps, who has not been greatly perplexed by events in his own private history, events which have disarranged all his plans, and it may be blighted his most dearly and longest cherished hopes, and been baffled in his best efforts to explain them or unravel their intricacy. The surprise at these developments of Divine Providence is as unwarranted as is our dissatisfaction in view of them unreasonable; for, as we apprehend, there is nothing but what we ought to expect; nothing but what is unavoidable in the incomprehensibility of the divine judgments. If among ourselves the dealings of wise men, proceeding from a high degree of sagacity, appear unaccountable, because founded on maxims, or contemplating ends not understood or appreciated by the great mass of their fellows, it surely is not to be wondered at, that God, who in his wisdom is as far above us as the heavens are above the earth, should be inexplicable in his actings, often doing the very opposite to what in the same circumstances we should have done, and proceeding in a way to us apparently least likely to produce the desired end.

But if the inscrutableness of Providence did not result necessarily from God's superior wisdom, still there would be sufficient reasons to justify its propriety. It would be quite possible, we admit, for God so to arrange every thing that his judgments should not be a great deep, that his motives and ends of action should always appear upon the surface, palpable and obvious to every one; and yet there would be sufficient room to question the wisdom of such an arrangement, as there would be little or nothing to conciliate our reverence, or compel our submission. As things now are managed, while—

> "God moves in a mysterious way,
> His wonders to perform,"

we are constantly reminded by the fruitlessness of efforts to fathom the divine judgments, of our limited knowledge, and feeble penetration. Let Providence be divested of all its intricacies, so that there should be to us no obscurities, and our sense of the distance between the finite and the infinite would be very much diminished; we would feel that God was brought down to the level of our capacities, or what, practically, would be very much the same thing, we would feel ourselves exalted to his level. It is, we imagine, quite necessary, in order to inspire humility, awe, reverence, and discipline us to faith, that God in his ordinary operations should be hidden from us; that he should discover himself sufficiently to prove to us that he is at work, yet not so as admit us to his counsels, nor allow us to trace the steps of his progress. Submission to God is a virtue, as well as reverence; and if always able to discern the reasons of the divine dealings, to determine the end proposed, and the suitableness of the means used for its accomplishment, we would think God little wiser than one of ourselves, and find nothing any where to fill us with reverence. So in the hour of trial and sorrow there would be nothing to exercise patience, or teach us submission, if we saw distinctly the process by which God was accomplishing his purpose, or the benefit it was designed to secure.

God is mysterious. It is well, we see it, that he should be so; far more mysterious in the works of providence than of nature; and they who confess his authorship and superintendence of the objects around them, must admit the propriety of this characteristic of his movements, even though they should sometimes be staggered when reflecting on the course of human things, and be tempted to doubt whether the very being whom they recognize as presiding over the mechanism of the material universe, acting with such unfailing precision and uniformity, does, indeed, sit perpetually at the helm of human affairs. Though we may attempt, as we look over God's dealings, and observe the jostling and confusion which seem well nigh universal, and mark the unexpected turn which things often take, to assign a reason for one appointment and determine the possible use of another, yet we find it very hard to assure ourselves that all is for the best; that there is not a spring in motion which God does not regulate, nor a force in action which he does not control; still all this is precisely what we ought to expect. God's wisdom and knowledge, so far surpassing our own, teach us that his dealings must be founded on principles which we cannot discover, and influenced and guided by motives and maxims which we cannot understand; and, therefore, must be to us, who are but children in understanding, little else than a mass of mysteries. Working as he is with a view to various and distant events, involving, perhaps, the interests of a kingdom in those of an individual, having respect to a single family in the changes of an empire, how can he be otherwise than unsearchable in his Providence to us, who can apprehend nothing but the nearest design, our supposed knowledge of which may after all be but little more than conjecture; and when we add to this that "it is the glory of God to conceal a thing," that it is the very darkness in which he dwells which secures our reverence, and compels our submission; not with a feeling of surprise and discontent, but of admiration and praise, nay, with a confession of the greatness, the majesty, the wisdom, the goodness of the Creator, should we remember that his "judgments are a great deep."

II. The effect, however, upon us of the mysteries of the divine procedures, will be dependent almost entirely upon the position from which we view them, and the light in which we look at them. The mariner out upon the ocean at midnight is bewildered if he has no compass by which to steer, or if he loses sight of the fixed star by which he may direct his course. To plunge into the midst of a labyrinth, without any clew to its intricacies, is to perplex, and dishearten, and throw one's self into deep despondency; and so it will unnerve and prostrate any man to find himself in the midst of God's judgments or mysterious dealings without any previous preparation to meet them, or any light to throw upon their darkness.

It is not therefore without reason, that the Psalmist says, "Thy righteousness is like the great mountains," before he speaks of the great deep of God's judgments; for it is only upon the ground which his righteousness puts under us, that we can look calmly upon his judgments; only the intelligent and firm conviction of that righteousness which can balance and steady the mind amid his mysteries. As by the righteousness of God, already explained, we mean that perfection by which He is holy and just in himself, and observes the strictest rules of equity in his dealings with his creatures; to be convinced of his righteousness is to be satisfied that, whatever may be appearances, God is guided in his actions by the most unimpeachable principles, and has only to make known his reasons, to secure the approval of all his intelligent creatures. We cannot be satisfied of God's righteousness, without being thoroughly persuaded that even when his dealings are the darkest, they need only to be seen in the light of his wisdom to commend themselves as the best that could be devised; and the reason why the men who walk with God, and study well his character, are so little perplexed by the intricacies of his Providence, and so little disheartened by what is obscure, is, that they have settled it in their minds that God is righteous in all his ways; and holding fast this great truth in every hour of difficulty, and doubt, and trial, they are as thoroughly satisfied that what is unsearchable is right, as though it were all laid open, and they had the evidence of sense or reason for its goodness. Thus it was that the Psalmist fortified himself against the inscrutableness of the divine judgments, by assuring himself of the divine righteousness; and herein he teaches us a lesson we are very apt to overlook, but which our comfort requires us perfectly to learn. We cannot always walk in the light; sometimes God will throw darkness about us; prosperity cannot be our unfailing allotment; our life is a chequered scene, the bright spots of which are intermingled with shade. If we have our hours of ease, we must have hours of difficulty; if we have comforts, we must have trials likewise. At times we may feel that we are treading upon the solid earth, and again we are launched out upon the ocean of God's judgments. And nothing will give us light in darkness, or strength in weakness, or relief in perplexity; nothing will equip us for the hour of difficulty or trial but the conviction, intelligent and thorough, of this simple truth, God's "righteousness is like the great mountains." Fixed upon this ground, we should always be firm, calm, collected, never afraid of evil tidings, never dismayed by the divine dealings, because we would be stable, trusting in God.

One great practical mistake upon this subject, my brethren, is, that we wait till we are enveloped in darkness before we acquaint ourselves with God; and then when the hour of difficulty comes, we have to search for relief, instead of being provided beforehand; and when the storm bursts upon us, we have to look round for shelter, when the way into God's pavilion should have been perfectly familiar. We are driven out into the deep of God's judgments, with but very dim apprehensions of his righteousness; and then without any thing to which we may cling, we cry out as though God had forgotten to be gracious. Had we certified ourselves beforehand that God never can mean but what is right, that he never can swerve or be diverted from his purpose, we could not fail, when we found ourselves upon the dark waters, to see the star which is to teach us how to steer.

In the imagery of the Psalmist which has suggested these thoughts, there is beauty as well as truth. We have here a combination of the mountains and the depths, and there should be no difficulty in sketching upon canvass, as there is none in the conception of a picture which would distinctly symbolize the writer's idea. Here we have before us the deep of God's judgments, waters unfathomable by any human line; and here we have the mountains, whose foundations are washed by these unfathomable waters; they seem to be rising out of the waters, and girding them round upon every side. We know from the parts of the mountains which are visible, that there are lower parts concealed from us by the waters, and are just as confident that the lower parts form the basin out of which the waters flow; and thus, when we see the mountains all around us, we may be sure that the foundations beneath the waters are of the same materials with the summits above, which, though sometimes hidden in the mists, often glow in the sunlight. Such seems to be the conception of the Psalmist. It is truthful, and beautiful, and impressive. God's judgments are the deep which we cannot explore, but from this deep rise mountains, and these mountains are the righteousness of God; as they gird around the waters, so does the righteousness of God embrace all his dealings. As we doubt not, that their foundations are the same with their summits, so we cannot doubt that the righteousness of God is the same in what is dark as in what is clear. Nay, more than this, as the surface of the water often mirrors the tops of the surrounding mountains, so not infrequently can an attentive eye observe the image of God's righteousness upon the very front of his dispensations.

What then are we to do when upon this mysterious deep, but to look at the mountains which rise upon every side, and remember that under the waters, unseen by us, are their foundations? Though we cannot take the soundings of the mighty abyss, yet we should feel safe if we kept in mind the righteousness of God. We should never be at a loss or bewildered, if faith in the divine character were always in lively exercise; and it might be always kept in exercise, for there is always something upon which it may fasten and act. Driven and tossed as we may be, there is always some peak of these everlasting hills discernible, some eminence of the mountains to serve as a guide and assure us of our safety.

It is because practically we regard the righteousness of God as sand, which may be displayed or encroached upon by the waters, and not as mountains, which cannot be removed, that we are disturbed when thrown upon the sea of God's judgments. Only let us give the character of "mountains" to the righteousness; look upon it as unchangeable and immoveable, as girding round the whole economy of divine Providence, and it could hardly happen that we should be overwhelmed by the divine dealings, however unable we should be to fathom them. Thus fortified by God's righteousness, we might turn our attention to God's judgments, and then it would be as though we were standing upon earth's mountains, and throwing our gaze over the ocean; the heavings of the waves would cause us no solicitude, as we should feel certain of the solidity of that on which we stood, and have no fears that the waters, however agitated, would pass the boundaries appointed by the God of nature. So when we stand upon the righteousness of God, knowing it to be immoveable as a rock of adamant, what to us are the tossings and fluctuations of human affairs? There can be no overleaping the boundaries which the God of providence has appointed.

Thus it is that the divine righteousness can give us light in the midst of darkness, relief in the midst of perplexity, and fixedness in the midst of the changes which are taking place around us; thus it is that the consideration of what God is will always sustain us in view of what God does. He is "righteous in all his ways." He cannot fail to be righteous, righteous equally whether his doings are known or unknown, whether his ways are in the sunshine or the storm. His righteousness is not dependent upon our perception of it; it is a necessary property of his nature. He might as well cease to exist as cease to act upon the best principles, in the best mode and to the best end; and then what have we to do with murmuring at his dealings, as though their propriety could be suspected. What if we cannot fathom them? what if we cannot comprehend them? If we could, we would be no more sure of their righteousness than we ought to be now, on the testimony of his character. If we look on the mere dispensation, it seems a vast profound in which the mind may sink; but if we look at him whose dispensation it is, we might at once find a resting-place for our spirits. Be it so that his dealings are inexplicable; it is not ours to penetrate those dealings, but as they bear us along on their mighty deep, to keep looking, as the Psalmist elsewhere says, "to the hills whence cometh our help." There is not a billow on this deep from which we may not see land; though if we dive beneath the surface we shall find only darkness, and be presently overwhelmed. Never should we study God's dealings apart from God's attributes, but prepare ourselves to study his dealings by studying his character; for if we once settle it firmly in the mind "that his righteousness is like the great mountains," it will never be in fear, never in perplexity, much less will it be in fretfulness and impatience, that we shall say, "Thy judgments are a great deep."

III. The connection between the first and the second propositions of our text being thus established, we turn our attention for a moment to the last, that we may ascertain, if possible, its relation to those which preceded it. The transition, at first sight, we must admit, seems to be very abrupt; for what has the mysteriousness of God's dealings to do with his providential care? and yet we can easily understand, that if to muse on the righteousness of God be the best preparation for the consideration of God's judgments, the doubts and difficulties which this consideration may nevertheless excite, may be best dealt with by pondering the every day mercies which are showered upon the world. I can easily imagine the state of mind which the introduction of this idea, in this precise connection, is calculated, if not designed, to meet. I may have prepared myself for surveying what is inexplicable in God's dealings, by fortifying my belief in God's righteousness, and yet while my eyes are upon the great deep, it will oftentimes be hard to keep faith in full exercise. I shall be very apt to forget, while gazing upon the dark, unfathomable expanse, the truths of which I thought I had certified myself. I shall feel as though I needed some distinct, visible evidence of the goodness of God, which all this darkness and confusion seems to contradict; and here I remember that "God preserveth man and beast." I summon to my aid, in this emergency, the young and the old; the men of every age and every clime; I summon every beast of the field and every fowl of the air; I make the sea give up its multitudes; I make every flower, every leaf, every water drop, pour forth its insect population, and they all pass in review before me. I ask myself who feeds this innumerable throng? Who erects store-houses and keeps them supplied for all these tenants of earth, sea, and air? How happens it that morning after morning men go about their varied employments, that the forests echo with the warbling of birds, that thousands of creatures are active on every hill and in every valley, and yet that out of these countless multitudes of living beings, there is not the solitary one for whom abundant provision is not made in the arrangements of nature? Is this animation which is perpetually kept up in the universe, and this sustenance which is so liberally provided for its entire population, to be referred to the working of certain laws and properties, irrespective of the immediate agency of an ever present, ever actuating Divinity? Oh! this is an idolatry of second causes, little better than a denial of the First Cause—this is substituting that ideal, fabled thing, called Nature, for the God of nature—this is making the laws and processes by and through which God operates, omnipotent, intelligent, omnipresent agents. No! no! The hand that made, sustains; the breath that animated, continues in existence—"The Lord preserveth man and beast." He gave them being at first, and he is the fountain of their being at every subsequent moment; and there is not in this wide creation the single living thing which is not perpetually drawing upon God; so literally dependent upon his care and bounty, that an instant's suspension of his providential arrangements would suffice to quench the vital principle. Never let us for a moment indulge the atheistic thought, that though the universe could not have been made without God, it can nevertheless go on without God. Its wheels are not wheels, which once set in motion, may continue to revolve without fresh interference of the original agency. Its springs are not springs, which once touched, will vibrate for ever, without the hand of the contriver and architect. Its seeds are not seeds, which, when once sown, need no influence from above to secure their perpetual springing. Every planet, as it marches, is impelled by God; every star as it revolves, is turned by God; every flower as it opens, is unfolded by God; every blade of grass, as it springs, is reared by God. And if in place of suffering thought to wander along the spreadings of the universe,—though it could no where reach the spot where God is not busy, nor find the creature of which he is not the life,—if in place of this you tie it down to the inhabitants of this lower creation, what a picture is opened before us by the simple fact, that in every department God is momentarily engaged in ministering to the beings whom he has called into existence; and from the king on his throne to the beggar in his hovel; from the grey-headed veteran to the infant of a day; from the lordly lion to the most insignificant reptile; from the stately eagle to the animalcule, which we know only from the microscope, there is not to be found the solitary instance of a being overlooked by God—of life sustained independently of God, or which could last one second without his inspiration. And ought not this picture, upon which we may gaze daily and hourly, to have its effect upon the mind when we turn to the great deep of God's judgments, to refresh us in the midst of dark and intricate dispensations, and relieve us of those doubts which are often raised in view of the apparent want of goodness in the government of God? Why, my brethren, there is not a morsel of food which we eat, nor a drop which we drink, there is not a bird which cheers us by its wild music, there is not an insect which we see sporting in the sunbeam, which does not rebuke us when we mistrust God because sometimes he is "unsearchable in his ways." Can it be that he is unmindful of the world, that he is not studying in all his appointments and arrangements the good of his creatures, when every where he is showing himself attentive to the comforts and the wants of the meanest living thing; and while he is ordering the course of nature, and marshalling the ranks of cherubim and seraphim, he is yet bending down from his throne and applying as close a guardianship to the ephemera which floats in the breeze as though it were the only animated creature, or the only one requiring his providential care? This we apprehend to be the idea of the Psalmist; and there is thus seen to be a strong and beautiful, though it be only an implied reasoning, in our text; and I put all its propositions together, and show their mutual dependence upon, and relation to each other, *thus:*

We muse in the first place on the righteousness of God. He would not be God if he were not "righteous in all his ways and holy in all his works;" and, therefore, we may be perfectly confident of this, that whatsoever he does is the best that could be done, whether we do or do not perceive its excellence. Having gained this point; being fairly fixed in this conviction, that "his righteousness is like the great mountains," we turn to look at his judgments; and what an abyss of dark waters is here! How unsearchable, how unfathomable is God in many of his ways; and yet if satisfied of his righteousness, why should we be staggered by his judgments? There is no method of getting away from this argument as an argument, and yet the mind does not always rest perfectly satisfied with it, and that because, while it is adapted to convince the intellect, it does not address itself forcibly to the feelings. Well, then, let us pass from what is dark to what is clear in God's dealings, and see if we cannot find something which may bring the sensibilities to harmonize with the convictions of the judgment. "He is about our path, and about our bed continually;" "The eyes of all wait upon him;" "He openeth his hand and satisfieth the desire of every living thing." Is God, who is thus displaying himself to us, hourly and momentarily, a God of whom we may be suspicious? Do we honour the sensibilities of our nature which apprehend his goodness, any more than our judgments, which are convinced of his righteousness, when at any time, or in any circumstances, we mistrust him? If when brought to see that God's "righteousness is like the great mountains," we still have our fears, when looking upon the great deep of his judgments, oh, surely, as we cast our eyes around us, and find in every direction the evidence of sense to this fact, that "God preserveth man and beast," there is enough to quiet every alarm and hush every remaining suspicion.

In the expository remarks we have thus been enabled to present to you, this morning, we have, as we imagine, given you the spirit of our text, and set before you the lessons it may be used to inculcate. I do not know how I can leave my subject so that it shall make its most salutary impression, better than by winding up my remarks with a single thought which the subject seems to suggest—viz.: the importance of thinking much on our common mercies, in order to prepare ourselves for uncommon emergencies. My brethren, we live in eventful times. In various ways God is moving through the world, accomplishing his designs. His path is a path of mystery, and his footsteps are not known. Like the wind which bloweth where it listeth, we trace him only by his effects. His judgments are a great deep. Now we see him in the upheavings of empires, and the convulsions of nations; again we find him in the pestilence that walketh in darkness, and the destruction which wasteth at noonday; what the end is to be we cannot tell; how we are to be affected socially or personally we know not. We may be, as individuals, the subjects of very mysterious dispensations; we may be tried, perhaps some are now tried, tried severely; and we must have something upon which to stay our minds. The great difficulty, when the trial does come, is to maintain a sense of God's loving-kindness. He who is strong in the conviction that "God is love," can hardly fail to be patient, if he is not joyful in tribulation; and the reason, I apprehend, why we are not all of us strong in this conviction is that we overlook the incessant, momentary evidences of divine love, and think only of those which are vouchsafed in some great crisis or emergency. And yet our common mercies are the best; we should feel their value if they were more rare. God demonstrates his kindness more by keeping us in health than by raising us from a perilous sickness; more by warding off from us danger than by shielding and delivering us when it comes. And, oh! if we accustomed ourselves to think of our common mercies, to study God as an affectionate parent in his every-day dealings, if we thought of his love as sustaining us at night, and awakening us in the morning, and guarding us during the day time; if we saw his love in every thing; felt it in the beating of the pulse, heard it in the voices of friendship around us, it could hardly be that we should think it withdrawn from us the moment we were overtaken by any sorrow. We should have this truth then graven upon our minds; our common mercies are the best preparations for trials. We may have to go down into the deep, my brethren, the great deep of God's judgments; and our faith may be shaken, because we lose sight of the mountains of God's righteousness which are round about us, those attributes which guarantee the fitness of every dealing; but, oh! it will cheer us, it will sustain us, it will be to us like a rafter to a man sinking in the waters, if we have stored our minds with the tokens of God's unvaried loving-kindness, and have been in the habit of pondering our daily mercies. Then we can say, "Thou art good, and doest good continually." "Whatsoever time we are afraid, we will trust in thee."

MOSES ON THE MOUNT.

"And Moses rose up, and his minister Joshua, and Moses went up into the mount of God."—Exodus xxiv. 13.

The entire scene to which the text calls our attention, is doubtless familiar to all my hearers; and I am therefore absolved from the necessity of entering upon a detail of the circumstances, any farther than is needful to bring out distinctly the great practical truths upon which I design to insist. There is manifestly much in the occurrences here brought under our observation of a miraculous character, much that is to be explained by the peculiar genius of the institutions under which they took place, much that to us wears the aspect of mystery. There was, moreover, a specific purpose to be answered by this particular dispensation toward Moses, and consequently we are not now, under God's ordinary arrangements, to look for a repetition of scenes conformable in all their external aspects to the one which is here recorded. And yet these outward forms, which so strike the senses, embody a great fact to which we may expect something correspondent now, though nothing analogous, so far as its accompanying symbols are concerned. In reality, if we compare faithfully the Old Testament with the New, we shall be struck with the wonderful correspondence between them. Every type has its anti-type; every shadow its substance; every symbol its great truth; and to all the ancient manifestations of God, there is something answerable in man's spiritual experience now. Though the forms in which truth may have been conveyed are changed, the truth is the same; though symbols and signs may, in a great measure, have vanished, the things signified remain. Nay, more than this, the truths which were of old conveyed in these peculiar and oftentimes miraculous forms, are even more distinctly presented to us under the gospel; and the privileges to which we are now introduced are larger and fuller than were those vouchsafed in ancient times.

With these general remarks, designed to justify the train of thought I am about to set before you, and to relieve me from the necessity of an attempt to explain all the minute circumstances here recorded, I proceed at once to a consideration of the great subject suggested, in the lights in which this narrative presents it.

That subject is *communion with God*—as to its *reality*, as to the *principles* upon which it is secured and maintained, and as to *its effects;* upon all which points, I think, we shall find light shed by the history before us.

I. Our first remark then is, the fact that Moses went up to the mount and there held communion with God. It was a wonderful dispensation we say, and a privilege, we are apt to think, which growing out of his peculiar circumstances, we are not now to look for. This may, indeed, be so, if we refer exclusively to the outward visible preparatives and accompaniments; yet, as to the thing itself, there is not a little language in the New Testament which represents it as the common privilege of believers in Jesus Christ. "Our fellowship is with the Father and with his Son." "Ye are the temples of the Holy Ghost." "Know ye not that God dwelleth in you?" There is something in these expressions which convey the idea of a very close and intimate intercourse between the soul and God; and if we are told that the language is figurative, we reply that there must be a correspondence between the sign and the thing signified, and that the truth conveyed by a figure must be more wonderful than the figure itself. The fact itself of this communion is unquestionable, however difficult it may be to explain the manner in which it is enjoyed. Paul speaks of it as a matter which every Christian ought to understand. "Know ye not that ye are the temples of God, and that the Spirit of God dwelleth in you?" It is one of the earliest lessons in religion; you cannot have taken a single step in an enlightened Christianity, and yet be ignorant of this, that ye are sanctuaries of the most High God in which he dwells. Such a spiritual fellowship involves on our part a simplicity of faith in the Divine testimony, a coming unto God, "believing that he is, and that he is a rewarder of them that diligently seek him;" and on the part of God a manifestation of himself in a distinct manner to the believing, waiting soul, so that it has a conscious sense of the divine presence. I am perfectly aware of the aspect of mysticism which such a subject must wear to the inexperienced, and I do not know that it can be made intelligible in any other way than by experience; and yet so far as I can see, there is nothing irrational in a consciousness of the Divine presence. God is the omnipresent one, omnipresent in all his perfections. He is every where in his wisdom, his love, his power, and his purity; and surely he can make a soul who waits upon him conscious of his presence. It is, moreover, right to add here, that a spiritual mind is possessed of those susceptibilities, or is in that state which adapts it to receive impressions from God's character. There may be and doubtless is an analogy between the sensible and the spiritual world which will illustrate this thought. There is a relation between our senses and the objects by which we are surrounded. He who created the eye and the beautiful things which we behold in nature, created them so as to adapt them to each other. God, most assuredly, would not have thrown on the theatre of nature forms so lovely, and beauty so great as we perceive, unless in connection with them he had made a rational, thoughtful creature, and bestowed on him senses by means of which he might derive pleasure from these created beauties. So in the spiritual world, through faith in the divine testimony, the attributes of God, the great objects of religion touch (if I may speak so,) the soul at every point. The spiritual man has a perception of God, an understanding of truth, and an enjoyment of spiritual objects which the carnal man has not, and can pass through and beyond earthly and created things, and find his happiness in God himself. If it is folly for a blind man or a deaf man, to talk of the mysticism of him who speaks of the beauties and melodies of nature, no less folly is it for a man, a mere creature of sense, destitute of all those susceptibilities of spiritual impression which are inseparable from faith in the divine testimony, to talk of the mysticism and enthusiasm of the spiritual man, who speaks of his conscious sense of the divine presence. Why, my brethren, every religious act, every spiritual experience, implies this fellowship of which we speak. What is the Christian's trust but the simple dependence of the mind upon a present God? What is religious joy but a happy emotion of delight in God? What is love but the attraction of the heart's affections to the divine character, distinctly perceived? What is hope but the pleasing anticipation of the full possession of those spiritual objects with which now we partially commune, and which, though imperfectly exhibited, are so satisfying to the mind? Religion, spiritual religion, look at it in any aspect, what is it but the communion of the soul with its God; but the consciousness of an influence which binds us to the eternal throne; but contrition in view of God's mercy; confidence in view of God's truth, wisdom, and power; devotion, in view of God's claims upon us, all seen and felt to be true? There may be no literal mountain which man ascends; there may be no outward manifestations which strike the senses of beholders; but there is a communion between God and the soul, a conscious sense of the divine presence, as real and as effective now as that which belonged to Moses, when, at the bidding of God, he went up into the mountain. To deny it, is to rob the religion of the gospel of all its spirituality; to be ignorant of it, is to be destitute of the very first elements of Christian experience.

II. The second thought upon this subject, which the narrative before us suggests, relates to the mode in which this communion with God is attained and preserved. If you turn once more to the history, you will find that Moses, in every step he took in obedience to God's commands, conformed himself strictly to the provisions of the dispensation under which he lived. An altar was built at the foot of the mountain, victims were slain, sacrifices were presented, and after these rites were performed, Moses ascended the mountain and entered into the presence of God; and here you have a principle, which ever since the fall of man, has entered into true religion. The idea of atonement in some form is inseparable from that of fellowship with heaven. The ancient patriarchs never approached God but on the ground and through the medium of a sacrifice. The whole Jewish service and ritual rested upon the same principle. During that entire economy nothing was done in the shape of religious worship but what was done through the intervention of an atonement.

It was only by complying with provisions which recognized this great principle, that any man could hold communion with God. This same principle constitutes a distinctive feature of Christianity; but as this is a spiritual system, there must be in addition a recognition of spiritual influences. All communion with God supposes on our part an approach to God, on the ground of the sacrifice of Jesus Christ, and in dependence upon the Holy Ghost.

I surely need not say to my hearers that the work of the Redeemer is the standing medium of communication and fellowship between God and man; in all his transactions with us, God regards the sacrifice of the Saviour; this is a first element of Christian doctrine, the reception of which is essential to every thing like Christian experience. God never pardons a sinner but through the atonement; he never raises man to a state of grace but through the atonement; he never receives a returning prodigal and invests him with the privileges and immunities of a child, but through the atonement; he never meets man on earth, so as to make him one with himself, and admit him to the hopes and joys of eternal life, but through the atonement; and no man can offer prayer, no man can believe to the saving of the soul, no man can rest in a state of Christian liberty, or enjoy spiritual purity, but he must come to God through the atonement. The cross of Christ furnishes the only ground where God can meet man, or man successfully seek God; and it is a remarkable fact in the history of mind, illustrating this great feature of the evangelical system, that a recognition of the atonement and true Christian experience are inseparable. A stranger to the sacrifice of Jesus Christ is a stranger likewise to a sense of forgiven sin, to intelligent, spiritual peace and joy; and to speak to him of fellowship with the Father and his Son Jesus Christ, of a consciousness of the divine presence, of a resting of the soul with delight in God, is to speak to him in an unknown dialect.

The fact upon this subject, my brethren, is, that God is unknown except as God in Christ. It is not only that we cannot approach him, but we cannot understand him, we cannot appreciate him, except in the manifestation he has made of himself in his Son. The gospel, the burden of which is "Christ and him crucified," is God's grand plan of spiritual and providential government. Christ sits as "priest upon the throne," "the government is on his shoulders," every thing is in his hands. Nature, in all her departments, belongs to the Messiah. The world has an interest in his redemption. He planted his cross upon our soil, and adapted the provisions of his gospel to the ways of the world. But for the intervention of grace through Christ Jesus, we do not see but that upon the entrance of transgression, these heavens must have been wrapped together as a scroll, and have passed away with a terrible noise, and these elements must have melted with fervent heat. Upon no other principle can we understand how a kind Providence could shed down its favours upon individuals or nations. If justice had taken its unobstructed course originally, the world would not now have existed. But it does exist, it is preserved; and we can account for the preservation of a single man, only on this principle, that the government of the world is an administration of grace and mercy in the hands of Christ, embracing every thing. To talk of trusting in God, hoping in God, having communion with God, in any other way than upon the ground of a Redeemer's sacrifice, and through a Redeemer's mediation, is not simply to overlook one important article of Christian faith, but to overlook that which constitutes the foundation stone of the entire edifice, giving consistency, coherence, and value to all its different parts.

No less essential to communion with God, is, I imagine, a recognition of spiritual influence. Cast your eye over the New Testament, and see how it speaks of the office and operations of the Holy Ghost, and then determine, whether this influence is not part of Christianity itself. "I will send you the Comforter, who shall abide with you forever." "Who shall guide you into all truth." "Who shall take of mine, and shall show it unto you." "No man can say that Jesus is the Christ but by the Holy Ghost." "The Spirit of God dwelleth in you." There is, I am aware, sometimes in the minds even of Christians, a scepticism upon this point, when they pray for an outpouring of the Holy Spirit upon themselves and others, as if it were too much too expect it, or as if the gift were to be brought from some great distance; and yet spiritual influence is inseparably connected with the work of our Lord Jesus Christ. We might as well talk of Christianity without a Saviour, as of Christianity without the Holy Ghost. Wherever God's truth exists, there the Holy Ghost exists. Wherever the cross of Christ is proclaimed, there the dews of heavenly grace descend; and in the sanctuary of the Most High, where God has promised to meet his people, there is the presence of the Holy Spirit to sanctify and bless those who seek his influences. I do not mean by this remark to limit spiritual influence to the appointed ordinances of the sanctuary, for unquestionably it goes beyond them; but I mean to say that where the ordinances of Christianity exist, there is the Holy Ghost, to impart light, holiness and joy to those who thus wait upon God.

There is, then, my brethren, such a thing as ascending the mountain, in a spiritual sense, to hold communion with God; and it can be our privilege only as ours is the spirit of his ancient servant. We must go to the cross, we must acknowledge the atonement, take into our lips the name of Christ, and, in dependence upon the promised influences of the Holy Spirit, approach the Throne of Grace with confidence and boldness.

III. I proceed to a third remark. Moses ascended the mountain *alone*. If you turn to the narrative you will find that Joshua and some others were permitted to go partly up the hill, and then they were commanded to stop, and Moses singly proceeded, and by himself was admitted to this elevated intercourse with God. And here we have presented to us another principle of all spiritual religion and spiritual communion; they are strictly personal. Our devotional exercises are all of this nature. True it is, we meet, at this day, in public fellowship, but there is a sense in which the soul sits solitary and alone in the midst of a multitude. Here I stand, and there you sit. There may be one character, one faith, one love, one hope, one joy, but our several emotions are personal; they belong to ourselves, not as united in a particular association, but as individuals. You know not my feelings, I know not yours. Poetry may represent our praise and prayer as ascending to God like a cloud of incense; but though they may ascend intermingled, and in common language, yet when they reach the throne, we may be sure that God will separate the elements of which they are composed. We may join in the same service, sing the same hymn, unite in the same prayer, and yet there will be in the case of every individual a difference, and that difference is distinctly recognized by God.

So in the bestowment of good, on the part of God, the same principle obtains. He has, indeed, made a general, all-sufficient provision for the salvation of men, he has provided for the pardon of all; but then in the bestowment of the blessings of his grace, he deals with man as an individual. When the soul is converted, justified, sanctified, and the witness of the Spirit is bestowed, God deals with man as an individual. He raises him to the condition of one of his own children, by an act of sovereign grace and love, contemplating him in his personal character. If our salvation is personal, so also, must be the duties and privileges connected with it. No man can discharge duty; no man can enjoy privilege for another. Our communion with God must be personal.

But I may carry my idea still farther, and say that solitude, strictly speaking, is extremely favourable to the highest attainments and enjoyments of the Christian life. The closet of the Christian is analogous to the mountain ascended by Moses. There the Christian ascends, shut out from human observation, the carnal affections of life, the influence of human passion and desire; there he ascends, his mind fixed upon God as he reveals himself in Jesus Christ upon the pages of his holy word, and waits for the communications of his grace. There he stands like the traveller upon the mountain with the sun shining over and around him in his brightness, while clouds and darkness roll beneath him.

I may add, moreover, that solitude furnishes the best test of our religious enjoyment. There is always something suspicious about the character of our experience, when our happiness is connected only with public devotions. No man can join in the services of the sanctuary without having his feelings excited in one way or another. Our sentiments, in such circumstances, may, in their own nature, be happy, but if they subside when we leave the sanctuary, we have reason to doubt whether they are truly the result of divine influence; but when we enjoy ourselves alone; when alone we have communion with God; when alone we find joy in pouring out our hearts in prayer, we have a proof of the purity and genuineness of our Christian feelings. And this is a thought to which I imagine we cannot in our day give too much prominence. It is an age of externals—it is an age of action. I do not mean to say, that men pay too much regard to what is carnal and sensible in religion; but I fear they pay too little regard to that which is spiritual and truly sanctifying. I do not mean to say that there is too much activity among the professed disciples of Christ, but I fear there is too little retirement; and no man can be truly wise or holy, or spiritually great, unless he tears himself away from the bustle of life, and holds frequent communion with God in private.

IV. Another thought I have to offer upon this subject is suggested by the brilliant appearance of Moses, consequent upon his communion with God. An unusual light, beauty, and glory shone upon his countenance. We cannot give a satisfactory explanation of this appearance. It was undoubtedly typical and symbolical of a greater glory; and yet I think we are warranted in view of it to say that communion with God will cause his beauty to rest upon the soul. There may be no external brightness like that which beamed upon the face of Moses, but there will be a spiritual light beaming forth instead upon the mind. Joy, for example, will be a consequence of this communion. How can it be otherwise? When the Saviour first reveals himself to the heart, there is a consciousness of delight. No one can be admitted into the family of God, and have satisfactory evidence that he is delivered from the wrath to come, without knowing the joy which springs from the manifestations of the Saviour to the heart; and where there is the experience of the love of Christ in daily fellowship, there must be a peculiar happiness with which a stranger cannot intermeddle; of which the world knoweth nothing, and which it can neither give nor take away. I know when we indulge in such thoughts, and speak in such a strain of inward Christian experience, we seem to many to be moving very close on the confines of enthusiasm. Of this, I imagine, however, that we need have no apprehensions in our day. Surrounded and influenced as we are by earthly things, there is little or no danger of religious enthusiasm. The incrustations of the world so weigh down, and if I may speak so, sensualize our Christianity, that instead of prizing, we are apt to neglect the pleasures to which we are invited in communion with God; and yet the man who never received any happiness from such communion, or never in his experience resulting from it, found himself a subject of a deep and peaceful emotion, has never fully entered into the spirit of true Christianity. The impulses of vital religion, when they exist in the mind, and they will exist when there is communion with God, must animate the spirit.

Nor is joy the only fruit of this fellowship. There

must be in consequence of it an expansion of the capacity, an enlargement of the soul. Worldly men, sometimes designate Christians as *little* creatures; but the man who walks with God cannot possibly be a man of contracted, paltry views; there is that in divine truth, there is that in the spirit and habit of devotion, there is that in intercourse with God which must expand the mind; the soul which is stretched to the dimensions of Christianity must be the greatest soul on earth. The man of religion can enjoy every other form of truth and knowledge in common with the man of the world; he can traverse the pages of history, he can enter into all the sciences and philosophy, he can appreciate the productions of the poet, he can (like other men) transact the common, commercial business of life, he can comprehend with others the principles of political economy and legislative jurisprudence, he can go in intellectual attainment, all the lengths of the men of this world, and when he comes to the termination of all that earth can teach and earth can give, God opens the treasures of religion, and the boundless prospect of an eternal life. We cannot, my brethren, throw our minds fully into devotional duties without finding that our intercourse with God, and with spiritual and eternal things, must produce elevation of thought and purity of heart. Oh! if we constantly indulge in little petty passions, in worldly feelings, in insignificant doubts and fears, if we are troubled and thrown into consternation by the small interests of time, and the passing, ephemeral events which are occurring around us, we indicate too surely that we are living at the base, and not on the top of the mountain. Fellowship with God and with his Son Jesus Christ, while it will elevate man to the highest point attainable below, will produce a spirituality and a purity unknown in any other circumstances whatever.

Then we must add that there is always a correspondence between inward experience and outward manifestation; and he who holds communion with God, will be marked by an external beauty of character. Internal purity shows itself in outward conduct; if it belongs to us, the evidence of its reality and degree will be furnished in a spotless, holy life. Make the tree good, and its fruit will be good. As a man catches the spirit of his master from constant intercourse with him, the Christian will live the life of his Master upon earth, imitating Him, who in a spirit of love sought the glory of God and the good of others; and this it is which gives effectiveness to Christian character; it is this manifested spirit of Jesus Christ which is to save the world. The contest which is carried on between truth and error, between righteousness and sin, is more a contest of feeling, than of principle. Men, indeed, array themselves as disputants against the truth, and are prepared to oppose by argument every argument of Christianity; and yet the triumphs of the cross are not usually secured by disputation; it is not learning, it is not logic, it is not brilliancy of talent, which makes a man mighty to the pulling down of strongholds; it is the power of the manifested spirit of Christian love. The difficulty to be overcome lies back of the intellect, in the heart; and he who goes in the spirit of prayer, under the influence of the love of God and the love of man, does not meet directly the obstacles which sophistry and false reasoning oppose to the truth, but by the blandness of his character, the purity of his life, the plainly manifested spirit of his Master, forces his way through all difficulties to the heart, and by influencing that controls the mind. Communion with God, gives no less joy, and elevation, and purity to the soul, than it does energy to the character.

V. I have yet a final remark to make upon this general subject. It is suggested by the veil which Moses put upon his countenance when he came down from the mountain to hold fellowship with the people. The meaning of this we cannot, perhaps, thoroughly divine; it may have been designed to symbolize the darkness of the dispensation under which the Jews lived. But, whatever may have been the meaning, we have the fact, which, perhaps, may find something analogous to it in the circumstances of some Christians which veil their spiritual glory and obscure their grandeur. There is, for example, now, often a great contrast between the outward circumstances of a spiritual disciple, and his privileges and inward experience. You find a man occupying perhaps the lowest position in life, busied in the most menial services. These are his earthly relations. Who would think of such a man that he constitutes part of God's portion, an object of his highest delight; and yet follow that man in his retirement, and you will find him opening the sacred page, kneeling before the mercy seat, admitted to fellowship with God, drinking in streams of spiritual joy, and rejoicing in heavenly hope. What a contrast! How little the world, as it looks upon him, knows about him!

It is not an uncommon thing to find the highest style of spirituality concealed under an exterior far from prepossessing, and by circumstances oftentimes forbidding, on account of their painfulness. Who would think that that wretched, forsaken one for whom no friendly eye weeps, and with whom no friendly heart sympathises, is yet dear to God as the apple of his eye, is living under the light of God's countenance, and in the assured faith of joys to come.

Providence, too, how often it throws darkness around the Christian, contrasting strongly with his spiritual light. In his spiritual state he enjoys the richest blessings, while he is the sport of natural troubles, disappointment, and grief. Some men, and Christian men, seem as though they were born to trial. If they think they have escaped one wave of sorrow, another soon overtakes them. If they appear to gain one haven of repose they are soon driven out again to sea. If the wind and the tempest are hushed for a short time, they rise again in greater turbulence and darkness, and it is only when the last wave comes, which leaves them on the shore of immortality, that their troubles terminate.

Affliction often veils the state of Christians. What judgment, what strength of intellect, what mental resources, what deep-toned spirituality, marked the character of Richard Baxter; and what a contrast to all these, is furnished in the fact, that he scarcely enjoyed any temporal comforts from the time of his conversion till he put off mortality and went to his eternal home. Robert Hall, with a genius than which none more brilliant, a mind than which none more elevated, a taste than which none more refined, eloquence than which none more polished, public spirit and patriotism than which none greater ever belonged to a human being, a man withal deeply imbued with the love of God, and whose marked spirituality of character, formed his brightest adornment—Robert Hall did not recollect from his infancy the enjoyment of a moment's ease. And they are but instances of the kind. Good men in this world, are often misunderstood and mistaken. Sometimes they may appear morose; circumstances throw a veil over them, and though unobserved by the public eye, the impress of God's image is bright and beautiful upon the mind.

Permit me to add, in concluding these remarks, and as exhibiting the end upon which they are designed to bear, that communion with God is the privilege and duty of every professed disciple of Jesus Christ. We never can attain to Christian joy or Christian usefulness without it. The soul must converse much with herself and with God to be either very great or very happy. Our sources of happiness, our power for usefulness, are found in scenes of close communion with our Master. A stranger to such scenes cannot be a useful man. Natural talents, great learning, eminent reputation, and great wealth, may do much toward the external development of Christianity in the world; but it is only genuine Christianity in the heart which can win souls to Christ.

Go up into the mount, then, my fellow Christians, and there hold converse with God; and then and there, in your happiest moments, when faith is in its most lively exercise, and you have most power with God, remember the church of Christ,—remember your own church. They prosper who love Zion. Pray for the peace of Jerusalem; for the extension of Christ's kingdom; for the salvation of souls; and then the dews of heavenly grace will descend, and measures of divine influence be poured out, and our souls shall rejoice together in the loving kindness of God.

THE LIFE TO COME.

"The life that now is, and *that which is to come.*"—1 TIM. iv. 18.

"THE life which is to come," (the thought upon which I wish to fix your minds this morning) is to be looked upon in its connection with "the life which is," as being its full and perfect development. The one is the commencement, the other is the consummation of human existence, neither of which is rightly understood except as they are considered to be the successive stages of one and the same being. It is a very simple idea, apparently, —that I am to live hereafter—that in "the life which now is," I am standing upon the threshold of "the life which is to come," and preparing the elements of its character and experience—that through whatever scenes I am to pass, whatever may be the changes in the form and mode of my existence, I, the same conscious, thinking, feeling, active being, am to live hereafter, and live for ever. And yet, simple as is the idea, it is one of commanding power over the human mind. It gives us views of the present such as no other thought can impart to it, and stirs up emotions such as no other influence can excite, and gives birth to purposes, and prompts to action such as nothing else can originate. It is a mighty conception, that of "the life which is to come," one which grows upon us the longer we ponder it, and which whenever taken in by the mind, must be seen in corresponding effects upon the character. I am now a conscious being; what I am now in this respect I shall be for ever. As to the power of this thought we can imagine none which does not dwindle into insignificance when brought into the comparison. Doubtless all of my hearers are familiar with the story of the man who was arrested in a career of sensuality and crime, brought to think upon his ways, and turn his feet unto God's testimonies by simply reading the record of the deaths of the antediluvian patriarchs. The simple words, "he died," appended to each of their names, brought home in the most startling manner to his mind this thought, that the most protracted life on earth must come to an end. He could not banish the idea that his life on earth must close, and he was stirred up most effectually to prepare for its termination. But how much more startling should be the sentence, "he lives," written upon every man's tomb-stone, or appended to the record of every man's departure from this world. From the simple expression, "he died," taken by itself, we gather no other idea than that he has passed from this stage of being; but the expression, "he lives," indicates a futurity, and lets the imagination run wild in filling up that futurity with images of magnificence and terror; and it is because the thought of living hereafter has become associated somehow in our minds with the thought of dying here, that the latter thought exerts such an influence over us. It is an impressive thing, a genealogy of the generations who have gone before us; not because as we look over page after page we read the names of those who once were like ourselves instinct with life, who had their joys and sorrows, their hopes and fears, their plans and projects, which have all come to an end, but because we read the names of those who are now living, and whose present consciousness takes its character from the hopes and fears, the plans and projects which marked their earthly history. *The dead*—we speak of them as those who are not. But in this sense there are no dead in the universe; of the mighty catalogue written in heaven's book of men who have been, not one has passed into nothingness; of every human being, it is true, that when he began to be, he began to be immortal; he may have changed his place and his mode of existence, his dust may have returned to the earth as it was; but yet he lives as truly as he ever did, and will continue to live through ceaseless ages; and what is true of all before us is and will be true of each one of ourselves. There is a "life to come," and in a very short time we shall be mingling in its scenes with those who have preceded us. This then is my thought this morning, "The life to come;" *its certainty; the elements of its experience; the influence it should exert over our minds.* Give me your attention while I endeavour to set these thoughts in order before you.

I. Now, with regard to the first point—the *certainty* of "the life which is to come," I admit, that our storehouse of proofs is *here*, in the revelation of God. I do not suppose that the human mind could, as it never has done, reach absolute assurance upon this article, independently of some supernatural disclosures. It is here that life and immortality have been disclosed by the Great Teacher, who came down from heaven, and not only disclosed in his instructions, but set in a most vivid light, by the miracles he wrought, in bringing back men from the grave, and by his own resurrection, the type and pledge of the resurrection of the race. It is upon this proof, then, that we fall back, and we are not ashamed to avow our unshaken confidence in these disclosures, in the face of a gainsaying and skeptical world, in view of the evidence of truth which crowds itself upon the mind, from the facts of history, from the fulfilment of prophecy, from the performance of miracles, and from the internal fitnesses and proprieties of the disclosures themselves; evidence, which having been for centuries subjected to the most rigid and scrutinizing investigation, on the part both of friends and foes, may be safely considered as an impregnable basis for faith, and hope, and joy.

We have not, then, in our minds, my brethren, the purpose of originating any proof of "the life which is to come," differing from that which is found upon the sacred page. We wish you to look upon this testimony of God as the ultimate ground of faith.

And yet there is such a thing as commending ascertained truth to the conviction of the human mind. We may, if we are disposed to do so, gather from other sources collateral evidence of the facts of revelation. We may, if we can do so, meet the gainsayer and the unbeliever upon their own ground, and turn the weapons with which they attack revelation against themselves, by driving them, upon their own principles, into the admission of "a life to come." And I am not sure in these days of physiological research and philosophic pride, when the enmity of the human heart against the spiritualities of the Bible is but half concealed under a professed regard for the ascertained truths of science, that it is a waste of time or labour, or an inappropriate work for the advocate of truth, to ransack the analogies of things, to trace the correspondence between the natural and spiritual, if for no other purpose than to show that a skepticism as to "the life which is to come" has no warrant whatever in any of the things which are seen and known as yet; and as an attribute of the human mind is gross and wicked, unnatural and monstrous. Let me, then, for a single moment carry you with me into this field of thought, bespeaking in the mean time your careful and fixed attention to what I have to offer.

It is so well known that I need hardly dwell upon the fact, that the vegetable and animal world around us, when subjected to a careful examination, present constant changes, renovations, and transitions, while the subject of these changes and transitions preserves its identity. The fully formed butterfly, for example, is the same animal it was in its chrysalis, or but partially developed form, and yet the changes through which it has passed seem to us well nigh miraculous. It is worthy of remark in this connection, that the naturalist can very easily distinguish between the kinds of animals which are to undergo changes and transformations, and those which reach their perfection under one form of life. There are indications of incompleteness in the former which are not seen in the latter. There are germs of undeveloped being, there are certain symbols of progression and instinct which point out another mode of existence; and when these indications are observed, and when these animals are seen instinctively preparing for their change, seeking a retreat, and occupied in a way unsuited to their present, but exactly adapted to their future mode of existence, we can predict certainly beforehand, not an end, but a change in life; for here are the leadings of nature, always true in their predictions; it would be, to say the least, unphilosophical to affirm that all these indications meant nothing. They do mean something; they are nature foretelling the changes through which it is to pass.

Now, let us see what light this analogy throws upon the problem of our future existence. It is unquestionably true, that there are mysteries about human nature which nothing in the present life avails to solve. There are powers and instincts, as yet undeveloped, furnishing evidence of their existence, but not reaching their end. We look for the distinctive features of human nature, not in any thing which man possesses in common with the irrational tribes around him, not therefore in any of his animal instincts and susceptibilities, but in those moral and intellectual powers which are his peculiar characteristics as a creature of God. Among these, if any where, we are to find the symbols of another life analogous to those instincts which in the animal creation seem to foreshow a new and higher form of existence.

The materials of the argument for the soul's immortality, which reason has at her command, are neither few nor trifling. The common conduct of mankind, who in all ages and all nations have admitted it, cannot well be otherwise accounted for, than by admitting the substantial truth of the thing believed. The aspirations after something beyond this transitory sphere, longings after the future, always the strongest in those minds whose powers have been most cultivated, the vast compass of the human faculties, the instinctive recoil from the thought of ceasing to be, above all that moral sense, whose power to afflict or gladden the soul is dependent upon future retribution, as it awakens hope or kindles fear, form the grounds, which cannot be removed, of a belief not easily to be shaken. But then, this is the point of my illustration; all these prognostics of futurity, are evidences on the point only as they show the expectation of "a life to come" to be an element of human nature, an original article in the natural constitution of the mind. It is a well known fact, that man generally harbours the thought of living after death. Most men are convinced that they shall live hereafter, and the exceptions to this statement, the skeptics, insignificant in number, who endeavour to evince the groundlessness of this expectation, prove by their ingenious and long continued reasoning, that the belief of immortality is instinctive, or at least too general, and too deeply seated, to be easily removed. With this general view, we can meet the scientific and other doubters of the present generation upon their own grounds, and tell them, that as the forms, and instincts, and habits of certain kinds of animals foreshow a transformation and a new mode of existence, so does the sum of human impressions, opinions, and expectations, constituting, as they do, elements essential parts of our nature, indicate infallibly what awaits the species, and prophecy our certain destiny.

I know we shall be told here, that nothing is more common, than for men to entertain opinions and cherish expectations which are wholly groundless. We are to a great extent creatures of prejudice, adopting sentiments very hastily, upon very little and unsatisfactory evidence, and clinging to them with unyielding pertinacity, simply because we have advanced them; but let it be remembered that we are speaking now not of particular opinions and particular reasonings, but we are speaking of the common reasonings, the common opinions, the common belief, the common instincts of the human family, all of which point in one direction. I may reason falsely in some cases, but it does not prove that the reasoning faculty of the human mind always reaches false conclusions. I may have my prejudices, hastily assumed and unfounded, but all human opinions are not unwarranted. My error on one point does not prove my error on a point which I hold in common with the entire human family—in some articles of my faith I may be chimerical, and yet perfectly rational in my belief of generally admitted truths. So with regard to the point we are now considering. My particular persuasions and prejudices, which may be entirely unwarranted, do not prove the common belief of human nature to be a vanity, but rather the contrary. The particular views which different men entertain concerning a future life may be fanciful and false; but so far from militating against the doctrine itself, they go upon the supposition that there is "a life which is to come." The particular desires, and views, and hopes of the benighted Pagan, the victim of superstition, and even the nominal Christian, concerning this future life, may be all wrong and delusive; their hope of what awaits them after death, may be a dream, but not so the belief that they shall survive death. So the peculiar forms of different religions may be false, but the religious instinct itself in man speaks the truth. The errors on the subject of religion and futurity of which man, individually, or nationally, become the victims, may all be traced to artificial or accidental causes, and vanish the moment those causes cease to operate;

but religion itself, a sense of obligation to a higher power, and the common impressions, expectations and opinions, concerning "a life which is to come," spring from among the elements themselves of human nature. You may warp them; you may exaggerate them; you may deform them; but there they are; you may depress them, or cover them, or secure their temporary denial, as to some extent was done in France at the close of the last century; but they will reappear again every where, with unabated force, and the same essential properties. These are very different in their nature and in their origin from the particular persuasions and prejudices of men, and they must be substantially true, if there is any truth or harmony in the general scheme of God's universe. For a man, therefore, to doubt the truth of the Bible upon this subject, is to cast suspicion, not upon the teachings of revelation merely, but upon the teachings of nature; for it is to say that here is a being, possessed of the most marked and decided indications of a future existence, while yet there may be nothing at all in the future which can meet or correspond with them.

We take our stand then upon the ground of the Bible, "There is a life which is to come." The statement accords with the workings of the human mind, with the analogies of things, as we see them around us, and with the general constitution of nature. The skeptic may put on his incredulous smile, but we can retort upon him as a being who in his unbelief is resisting the clearest and most conclusive evidence, contradicting the analogies of things, and disputing truths which are interwoven in the entire system of God's creation.

II. This point settled, the certainty of "the life which is to come" being established, what are to be its characteristics, what the elements which shall go to compose it? The importance of the question takes away all possibility of evading it. The fact, that I am to be, forced home as a reality upon my mind, shuts me up, irresistibly to the inquiry, "What am I to be?" where am I to be is a comparatively trifling question—one which in view of the other is not worth a thought.

We go then directly to the source of knowledge for light upon this point—and here I need not dwell upon the very obvious and familiar truth with which every reader of his Bible is acquainted, and which he perfectly understands, that "the life which now is," is a scene of probation, and "the life which is to come," is to be a scene of retribution. The present is a world of doing, the future is to be a world of recompenses. It is only for the sake of completeness in my exhibition, that I quote in support of an opinion so fully comprehended, such proof texts as these: "If thou sayest, Behold, we knew it not; doth not he that pondereth the heart consider it? and he that keepeth the soul, doth not he know it? and shall he not render to every man according to his works?" "Say ye to the righteous that it shall be well with him, for they shall eat the fruit of their doings. Wo unto the wicked, it shall be ill with him, for the reward of his hands shall be given him." "And, behold, I come quickly, and my reward is with me, to give to every man according as his work shall be."

Besides these general declarations as to the retributive character of the future economy, there are not wanting intimations clear and decisive upon the sacred page that the future is to be but the full development, in different circumstances, and in a different form of life, of the present. The symbols used in the Scriptures, and the analogies they adopt to illustrate and throw light upon the subject, all show that "the life which is," is to give shape, and form, and impart its elements to "the life which is to come." According as we are we shall be; according as we feel now we shall feel hereafter; and our experience and recompences in the future shall perfectly correspond in nature and degree with our actions in the present; "for whatsoever a man soweth, that shall he also reap; he that soweth to the flesh shall of the flesh reap corruption; but he that soweth to the spirit shall of the spirit reap life everlasting." Precisely as in agriculture, the grain which is harvested answers in kind and quantity to the seed sown, so in spiritual things futurities are to answer to present actions. There are two ideas upon this subject which pervade all the teachings of revelation. One is that hereafter we are to be the same beings we are now. I do not mean the same physically, but the same morally; I mean that we have now, within us, daily and hourly developing itself the germ of our eternal, moral consciousness. Whatever change may take place in us when all that is merely accidental shall have fallen off, when all merely animal sensations shall have disappeared, when our present views of things shall have given place to knowledge derived, more directly from its sources, there will be no change in those emotions, tastes, and moral dispositions which go to make up the very core of our being. The sentiments and affections which have now settled down upon the mind, and which constitute character, will remain, making us feel that we are precisely the same we always were. Thus the future will be the on-going of the present. Whatever passion sways us now will sway us hereafter. The same feeling toward God and his requirements which now determines our character as his friends or his enemies, will be carried out hereafter, and be seen and felt in its bold, and prominent, and unveiled supremacy. If we love God now, we shall love him then; if we hate him now we shall hate him then. Whatever changes may be affected by a transition from one state of being to another, none of them will touch the great elements of our moral nature.

Now, so far as analogy sheds any light upon this point, its teachings are in precise accordance with the revelation of the Bible. We all know that there is a certain illusion attaching itself to everything future and untried. When we look forward to some great change in our outward condition, we are apt to suppose, that though we may personally remain the same, there will be a great and essential alteration in our modes of feeling, habits of thought, tastes, and sentiments. Take, for example, boyhood's anticipations of manhood, or the anticipations of manhood respecting declining years; and yet, as we have reached these different stages of our existence, we have discovered the illusion; our modes of life, our relations, all our outward circumstances have been changed, but our moral consciousness is the same; the passion which prompted us before prompts us still; the appetite which swayed us before sways us still; the characteristics of manhood are the characteristics of our boyish days, brought out more distinctly; and old age, in this respect, is but manhood developed; and analogy and Scripture unite in showing us a great principle of continuity running between the present and the future, in declaring that the law which binds the different stages of human life into one and the same earthly existence, binds "the life which now is" and "the life which is to come" in one continuous, unchanging, uninterrupted being.

But while we are dwelling upon this moral sameness between the present and the future, let it be remembered that we are speaking of a sameness of character, not of degree. We draw from the teaching of the Bible that hereafter there will be a greater fixedness of sentiments, a fuller expansion of the moral powers, and a more intense action and excitement of the passions. We are all aware now, that our principles act themselves out as our sphere enlarges; feeling becomes deeper and stronger as our capabilities of endurance increase. The child, the youth, would be paralyzed and crushed by the intense thought and emotion easily sustained by riper years; while, at the same time, as we advance in life, not only are our powers of endurance stronger, but our range of action is widened.

Now, we are all aware, that in "the life which now is," there is a check put upon all our emotions; love, joy, anger, hatred, fear, cannot pass beyond a certain point of intensity. They are sometimes arrested in their rapid rising by the incidents or interests of common life; or when this is not the case, there is a limitation put upon them by the weakness of our physical powers. When they go beyond a certain point they bring on exhaustion, which warns us of the peril of indulgence. It is with the noblest sentiments as with the most malign passions, we feel that they are thus hampered and kept down; we dare not let them move the soul as they might move it, because they would rend the system and break it into fragments. We know, moreover, that the peril of these excitements grows out of the frailty of this physical organisation. And if here in this world, as man advances from the feebleness of youth to the strength of maturity, sentiment grows and passions become stronger, why may we not suppose that "in the life to come," when all the prudential considerations of this life shall cease to affect us, and the frailties and feebleness of this physical frame shall no longer hamper and fetter us, the soul may take its fill of emotion, and feeling, and passion, rise to a pitch of excitement of which in our present circumstances we cannot form the remotest conception?

It is a thrilling thought to the Christian, whose great moral characteristic is the love of God, that he cannot tell what in his pure and holy emotions he shall be; that in the intensity of them he may rise higher and higher, and be lost in God himself. It is a thought of terror to the slave of carnal desire, that whatever may be the master passion which now sways him, it will completely engross him; and when all its present checks and hindrances shall be removed, it will hurry him away with a fury irresistible, and a rapidity of which the lightning's march is but a feeble symbol. Yes, "the life which is to come" will be but the full development of "the life which is."

III. The foregoing is one of the scriptural ideas respecting our future state, which we find to be sustained by familiar analogies. There is another, viz.:—That while we shall be the same beings, so far as our moral consciousness is concerned, the materials of thought, the objects which shall excite the passions and determine the experience shall be the same. It is a common-sense thought that if there is to be a retributive economy, our feeling now, and our doing now, will determine its nature; and hence there always has been an impression upon the human mind that the feelings we cherish now, and the acts we perform now, are in some way or form to be reproduced hereafter, to tell upon our experience. The joy which springs from a consciousness of right, is as truly, to a certain extent, an anticipated joy, as is the pain of sin the result in a great measure of apprehension. We feel every day that the influence of our every day actions does not terminate with themselves, and with the moment of their performance. We may for the time forget them, but we know that they must rise from the oblivion into which we throw them, and work out their results. The very idea of retribution, the declaration that every man shall eat of the fruit of his doings, and that "God will render to every man according to his work," involves this consideration. Hence these, our daily feelings, our daily actions, are to be the topics of thought, and the motives of feeling hereafter. The present is the great store-house of the future, wherein we are laying up the elements of our future experience. Our emotions in "the life to come," whether present or prospective, shall exist in view of the past. The remembrance of "the life which now is," will be distinct and familiar; and memory, as it calls up each event, each feeling, each action, will, according as those feelings and actions have been agreeable to, or at variance with the will of God, administer to our joy or fill us with remorse. It is so partially in the different stages of our present existence. How do certain actions we have performed, follow us, and follow us continually with their influence, as though God would teach us, in the very nature he has given us, that righteousness must bring its own reward, and sin its own punishment. How do the follies and wickednesses of boyhood rise up and torment us in after years, and make us feel that then we were filling up sources of grief we are now called to exhaust? And why should not the actions of "the life which is" rising up to distinct remembrance, when memory shall be strengthened, as well as all the other powers, for ever the sources of our highest joy, or the instruments of our deepest and most intolerable anguish, in "the life which is to come." Why not? The Bible says that such will be the case; who can furnish an analogy to justify even the slightest doubt? No, my brethren; we never can get rid of the influence of the present upon us, and that because we never can destroy the present. What we have done, and what we are doing, remains, and ever will remain. In the moral world, as in the physical, "no motion impressed by natural causes, or by human agency, is ever obliterated." The sentiment is most clearly and strikingly presented by the author of the "Ninth Bridgewater Treatise," (Babbage), and it bears so directly on the point before us, that you will allow me to call to it your attention. I quote the sentiment from memory, without pledging the correctness of the language. "What a strange thing is this wide atmosphere we breathe. Every atom impressed with good and with ill, retains the motions which have been imparted to it by the will, combined and mixed in ten thousand ways, with much that is worthless and base. The air itself is a vast library, on whose pages are for ever written all that man has ever said, or ever whispered; there, mixed with the earliest, as well as latest sorrows of mortality, stand for ever recorded, vows unredeemed, promises unfulfilled, perpetuating the testimony to human character. If

God stamped upon the brow of the earliest murderer, the visible and indelible mark of his guilt, he has also established laws by which every succeeding criminal is not less irrevocably chained to the testimony of his crime, for every atom of his mortal frame, through whatever changes its several particles may migrate, will still retain, adhering to it through every combination, some movement derived from that very muscular effort by which the crime itself was perpetrated."

And now, my brethren, if this sentiment be correct, and it is in accordance with the teachings of the soundest human philosophy, if our words and actions make such permanent and indelible impressions upon this physical system to which we belong, impressions which will last while the system lasts; must not the same thing be analogously true of the spiritual system, that in whatever part of God's universe we may be, we shall meet perpetually the impressions of our spiritual doings, which as seen in God's light shall awaken within us emotions of intensest joy, or of the keenest and bitterest remorse.

My subject, I find, has so expanded, that its compass cannot be travelled within the time I have allotted to it on the present occasion. I will here, therefore, arrest it, and without anticipating the main results which I have in view, and which hereafter I may bring out, I will simply ask my hearers, in view of what I have advanced, what they think of "the life which is to come," and what kind of a life they have reason to suppose it will be to them? There is not one of us who does not carry about with him the materials of its rational answer in the thoughts he entertains, the desires he cherishes, the passions he indulges; there is not one of us who has not been busy for years, who is not busy now in making and describing his own futurity. Go then into your own bosom, my hearer, and ask yourself what you think of an eternity of the thoughts, the purposes, and aims which now belong to you? What would you think of an eternity of the same passions which now urge you along, only excited to a burning intensity of which you can now form no conception? What will your present course say, what will be the testimony of present influence, when every where eternally it shall be seen in the impressions it has made, and in the character and experience of those upon whom it has acted?

Well, whatever you may think of it, remember that you are standing upon the verge of a life where you will be for ever what you are now. Where you will feel towards God as you now feel towards him; a Christian then if a Christian now; a rebel then if a rebel now. There will be no changes. He that is holy shall be holy still; and he that is filthy shall be filthy still; rising in holiness, or sinking in degradation for ever. Are you prepared for "the life which is to come?"

PREPARATION FOR "THE LIFE WHICH IS TO COME," HEAVEN.

"Say ye to the righteous, that it shall be well with him; for they shall eat the fruit of their doings: Woe unto the wicked, it shall be ill with him; for the reward of his hands shall be given him."—ISAIAH iii. 10, 11.

THERE is, according to the common apprehension of mankind, a mysterious but real and indissoluble link, binding together the present and the future. It is not an intellectual conviction, the result of any process of reasoning, but a feeling, deep-seated in the soul, originating, if we may judge from its depth and power, in a necessity of nature. It is an irrepressible, uncontrollable, governing feeling of the human mind. In fact, my brethren, we are perpetually living in the future. Our places and purposes to-day, derive their meaning from the expected developments of to-morrow; and the joys which gladden, and the sorrows which afflict us, stripped of all reference to the future, would be stripped likewise of their elevating and depressing power. That future, moreover, upon which we dwell so much, is in our apprehension, in a great measure wrapped up in the present. As we are here to-day, we do not feel more certainly that the past has determined, while it has furnished the elements of our present consciousness, than that the present will give character to the experience of to-morrow; in fact, throwing out of our calculation unforeseen contingencies, and supposing that all things will go on in accordance with the regular and established laws of cause and effect, we have no other idea than that to-morrow will be in its views and feelings but the fuller development of to-day. Now, I apprehend, that the common impression of the human mind relative to the certainty of a future state, is but a modification of this same feeling of which we have been speaking. The same law of our nature which binds together the successive stages of our earthly being, binds together "the life which is," and "the life which is to come." The ongoing of the human mind is not arrested by the thought of death. True, that event is seen to separate between us and the scenes which are beyond it, but it does not shut those scenes from the view. There they are, in all their reality, in all their glory, or in all their terror; and though there is a dark valley between, which shows to sense no pathway, and over which we know not how we shall travel, yet there is a feeling which cannot be reasoned down, that in some way we shall cross it, and mingle in the scenes which are beyond.

This feeling, I imagine, goes still farther. It infers not only the reality of the future from the reality of the present, but the experiences of the future from the character and doings of the present. We can no more get rid of the idea of a correspondence between that which is, and that which is to be, than we can get rid of a certain hereafter; here is the commencement, there the consummation; this is the seed time, that is the harvest; here we have the blade, and the ear, there we shall have the full corn in the ear. Every one who carefully analyses the workings of his own mind, will discover that the power of right doing to gladden the soul does not spring more from its own intrinsic nature, than from a connection between it and future results; and crime pains, and tasks, and hardens the spirit, not simply on account of its essentially debasing influences, but also, because it is felt to be connected with a certain coming remorse.

Such are the natural feelings of man as God made him; and every human being will feel thus when he allows nature to have free play; and I need not say how exactly they tally with the disclosures of revelation; and I come this morning to set these forecastings of the human mind in the light of revelation, to give them their proper direction, and point out their appropriate use.

The main thought upon which I design to insist is that suggested by my text; viz., that righteousness and wickedness work out their own appropriate results; that the present is a world of discipline for the future, wherein man is preparing for the scenes in which he is to mingle; that results are to accord with character, as the nature of the harvest agrees with the seed sown, and every one's future experiences will correspond with the moral training to which he here subjects himself.

We have a double picture then to present to you, as the discipline of the Christian and the course of the sinner shall be seen in connection with their respective necessary results.

I. I begin with the Christian, and from the lessons he is taught, and the discipline to which he is subjected in the school of his Master, endeavour to prefigure his destiny. The Christian life has two great characteristics. It is a life of faith; and herein it stands distinguished from the life of unconverted man, which is a life of sense. It is a life of usefulness, and herein it likewise stands distinguished from the life of unconverted man, which in the ends it contemplates is regulated by a principle of selfishness. I need hardly say to my hearers, that the essential element of all spiritual Christianity is confidence in God; for "whatsoever is not of faith is sin." Human apostacy began at this very point, a distrust of the character and word of the living God, and ever since, man has walked in the ways of folly and of transgression, only as he has given himself up to the control and guidance of "an evil heart of unbelief." To bring him back to the exercise of a child-like reliance upon his Heavenly Father is the design of the gospel; and one great object of all God's providential dispensations toward his children is to develope more and more this spirit of confidence in himself. The very first step a man takes in a Christian life is a step of faith, as he renounces all self-dependence, and throws himself upon Jesus Christ in simple reliance upon the word and testimony of God; and as he moves on thereafter, he "walks by faith and not by sight." The circumstances in which he is placed, the trials he is called to meet, the duties he is called to discharge, compel him to look out of himself for direction; force him to fly to the rock which is higher than himself, and to lean upon the promise of Almighty strength. It is not, indeed, without evidence that he is called to believe; not without manifestations of kindness, which alone warrant trust. The first act of faith which belongs to a man, as he casts himself upon the promise of forgiveness in the gospel, is put forth in view of God's unspeakable love in Christ Jesus; and day by day his confidence is strengthened by displays of goodness, seen in the present or called up from among the remembrances of the past. It is the discipline of faith to which the Christian is subjected in this world of trial.

So likewise is he taught by his Master to look out of himself for the objects of life. The scene of the world around us is a scene where every man is describing a circle of which he himself is the centre. Self-aggrandizement is the great end of human ambition. Strip any object of its relation to some selfish desire as the means of its gratification, and to carnal man it ceases to be attractive; but among the first lessons which a man is taught in the school of Christ, is to "look not upon his own things, but also upon the things of others." "If ye love them which love you, what reward have ye;" and "if ye do good to them who do good to you, what reward have ye," is the language of our great Teacher; and "ye are not your own, for ye are bought with a price," are the words of one who had learned, and was exemplifying in his life the great lesson of usefulness which his Master had taught him. And here, while speaking of these great elements of the Christian character, and of the nature of Christian discipline, let me observe that they are no more strongly contrasted with carnality in their nature than in the experience which accompanies them. The condition of a man who, in respect to all his plans and movements, his hopes and joys, is governed by sense, cannot, so far as this world is concerned, be compared in point of happiness with that one who walks by faith. Both must have their trials, in view of those developments of Providence which neither sense nor reason can explain; but the one has resources to which the other is entirely a stranger. The man of sight is not only lost amid the dark intricacies of things, but he has the superadded torment arising from his inability to unravel or enlighten them; while the man of faith can fall back upon the assurances of him who cannot lie, and stay himself upon God, under the conviction that he "doeth all things well." Hence it is, that amid those dark scenes of our earthly history, where the carnal spirit is completely borne down and overwhelmed, there is a wonderful elasticity about the mind under the influence of faith; and when the former is most distressed, the joys of the latter do most abound. In fact, so far as the experience of the mind itself is concerned, there is no true happiness in many cases which does not spring from confidence in God.

So, likewise, a life of passionate gratification is not to be compared with a life of active benevolence. God has so constituted our nature, that a man cannot be happy unless he is, or thinks he is, a means of good. Judging from our own experience, we cannot conceive of a picture of more unutterable wretchedness than is furnished by one who knows that he is wholly useless in the world. Give a man what you please, surround him with all the means of gratification, and yet let the conviction come home to him clear and irresistible that there is not a being in God's universe a whit the better or happier for his existence; let him feel that he is thus a blot upon, because a blank in the universe, and the universe will not furnish a more unhappy being. Herein lies the solution of that to many inexplicable fact, that the schemes of mere selfishness, however wisely laid, however energetically and successfully prosecuted, never add to the joys, but always to the pains of those who originate and are engaged in them. It is not so with a man of opposite characteristics. Take from him what you please, and you do not take from him the elements of his joy, if you leave him the conviction that in any way he is useful. If you contract the circle, and diminish the sphere of his influence, you detract from his joy only as you detract from his means of doing good. And as we cannot conceive of a more wretched being than one who feels himself to be the slave of an uncontrolled selfishness, so we cannot conceive of a happier being than a man of truly benevolent heart, whose wishes describe the circle and bound the sphere of his influence, and whose means are ample to give those wishes a full expression.

The disciple of Christ, then, is one who in this world is disciplined in the school of his master to a life of faith and usefulness. Let us look forward, then, and anticipate the future, and ascertain, if possible, what kind of life is that for which such a discipline will prepare one, or what must be the experiences of one thus trained, amid the circumstances which are to define his deathless being.

It is not assuming too much here to say, that the correctness of many of our views of "the life which is to come," is questionable; and even where our views are correct, generally speaking, they are very vague. If we were now to sit down, I mean those of us who have thought most upon this subject, and analyze our ideas, I think we should be surprised at the indistinctness of our own conceptions, and even suspect the correctness of those which are perfectly clear. That coming world will be a very different world from this. Upon that point we are satisfied; but wherein will the difference consist? is the question which is to test the clearness and correctness of our views. So far as heaven is concerned, it is very easy to say, that there will be no sin there, and of course there will be no pain there, and no death there. Very true; but by these negative assertions we are not advanced one step in our inquiry. We have learned what "the life to come" is not, but we wish to know what it is.

And when we come to this point, the very first distinction we are apt to make between the present and the future is, that while this world is a world of faith, that will be a world of sight; and the second is, while this world is a world of action and toil, that will be a world of rest and repose; and many a one is apt to think, that if we are wrong here, if it is not to be so, that when we enter upon another world, every thing in the shape of mystery shall be gone; if then, and there, we shall not see all things clearly, in the light in which God sees them, with a kind of intuitive perception; if, moreover, heaven is to be a scene of ongoing activity, of ceaseless, restless effort, it would be stripped of its main attractions to beings who like ourselves, groping amid the mysteries of God's dispensations, and wearied by the greatness of their way, are awaiting, in hope, the full revelation of all mysteries, and "the rest which remaineth for the people of God."

Yet, notwithstanding, we are constrained to think, that for our conception here of heaven, as a world of sight, we are more indebted to the Christian poet, who, as he describes the Christian's hope, speaks of it as a world,

"Where faith is sweetly lost in sight,"

than we are to any thing we find upon the sacred page, or any thing we learn even from the analogies of things. In reality, if we look distinctly at this conception, we shall find that it is very hastily assumed, and never can be made good, because it contradicts all the analogies with which we are familiar, and seems to involve an impossibility. If the enjoyments of the coming world are an end, and the dispensations of Providence towards us here are means, if in God's arrangements the wide universe through, there is always a strict correspondence between means and ends, then is this world to us a mystery, if the discipline of faith to which we here are subject, is not designed for its higher exercise, in that other world into which we expect to be introduced. If the training of the present life has, as is undoubtedly the fact, a reference to "the life which is to come," such a reference, that it may be justly looked upon as a course of education for the future, if indeed the two states of being are so alike that the essential elements of the one may be said to be wrapped up in the other, we say that futurity, whatever it may be in other respects, must be a scene where the qualities and habits to which we have been trained here, shall be called into exercise and even set to work more intensely than ever. We cannot believe it any part of God's arrangements to allow the fruits of a long and painful culture to fall to the earth and perish, at the moment of their ripening. Analogy then, if nothing else, teaches us that the future will be a world of faith as well as the present.

But further. We speak of God as the unsearchable God; one, whose movements, because they are constructed on a scale commensurate with his own infinite perfections, must to us be inscrutable; whose steps must be in the dark, and whose name must be "mystery;" hence the necessity of faith to such creatures as we are, grows out of the limited nature of our powers. As our minds cannot take in God's designs in their manifold relations, our reason is incompetent to explain his movements in their varied bearings, the only resource left to us, is implicit, submissive faith; we must lean upon this faith, or be unutterably wretched. And will the disparity between the finite and the infinite ever be any less than it now is? Grant what you please as to the certain advancement of the human mind in knowledge, and goodness, and power, it must always stand at a measureless remove from the infinite, uncreated, and boundless Spirit upon whom it will be eternally dependent. There are other beings, in higher and purer spheres, far more enlarged than ourselves in their views, with nobler powers, and grander capacities; and we may reach their position, we may even far outstrip them, but the interval between the Creator and the creature will not be sensibly lessened by this wondrous, this mighty advancement. God will always be the Unsearchable, because he will always be the Infinite God. Never, never, can the creature measure or grasp his character. Never, never, can he be at peace, reach what point he may, be the subject of any, however great mental enlargement, any otherwise, than as he rests in God with a spirit of simple, childlike confidence.

And if we never can fully comprehend God's attributes, so likewise we never can fully comprehend his doings in which those attributes are embodied. Even now there are things which God has already done, "mysteries of godliness," into which angels "who excel in might" are prying with eager curiosity, as presenting to their minds themes which they must study attentively, because they have not yet divined their meaning; and we believe there will yet be, in the progress of God's great and glorious administration of the universe, developments of his nature in his doings which will open an abyss into which the most exalted mind will scarcely dare to look, but from the edge of which he will shrink back to find his peace in the exercise of simple confidence in the infinite one.

Do not, my brethren, misunderstand me here. I do not mean to convey the idea that we shall never know any thing more of God, or of his doings, with their reasons and ends, than we know now. Far from it. Pitiable, indeed, would be the prospect, if we were never to be extricated from the difficulties which now hamper us, if we were never to understand any more of the dispensations which now try us. God himself has pointed to our hope a very different prospect from this; he has told us that "the vision is but for an appointed time, in the end it will speak and not lie; if it tarry, wait for it;" and the Master has said, "what I do thou knowest not now, but thou shalt know hereafter." There is a day coming of divine manifestation, when God shall make things plain, as he justifies his doings by unfolding their reasons. But you will observe, that this day of divine manifestation is to bring under review only the doings and the trials of the past, and by no means involves the idea that the entire scheme of God's dispensations, for all time to come, shall be spread out as on a map before us. No such sentiment is taught either directly or indirectly upon the sacred page, nor can it be inferred from any of the disclosures which are here made to us. I doubt not, that hereafter, we shall see clearly the way by which God has led us; and every dispensation of his Providence toward us, which at the time tried our spirits, and severely taxed our faith because it was inexplicable, shall be fully explained, and become a source of thankfulness and joy, as its wisdom and goodness become apparent, in view of the end of which it was the necessary means. I doubt not, moreover, that our views of divine truth shall become more enlarged and distinct, and the difficulties which now embarrass us when we attempt to grasp and master many of "the deep things of God," shall entirely vanish when we come to look at them, in the new light which God shall pour upon them; and perhaps we shall be surprised at the simplicity of the points which now disturb and even stagger us. But we are greatly mistaken if we suppose that nothing will remain to exercise our faith in God. As the traveller who in his journey reaches one eminence which commands the road over which he has travelled, sees yet another eminence before him, so we believe it will be with us, when the present trials of our faith are over. We shall be ushered into other scenes, where we shall likewise need a spirit of trustful reliance, and thus the vast hereafter which stretches itself out before us, will be a world which in its successive developments, shall call us to live by faith, and its experience shall be the peace, and joy, and hope of an ever exercised and ever strengthening confidence in the Father of our spirits.

In throwing out these views, while we do not imagine for a moment, that there will be connected with the exercise of our faith hereafter, as is now the case, any apprehension of loss or sorrow of any kind, which now, in fact, gives to the trials of our confidence all their painfulness; we have reason to believe that the evidence of the wisdom and goodness and love of God which now warrants our faith will be unfolded to us in grander and more glorious discoveries, to correspond with the higher exercise of faith to which we shall be called. The light which seen upon one eminence of our journey charms us up its ascent, will seem brighter and more charming as seen upon the eminence beyond. The testimonies to the character of our heavenly Father in view of which now we trust him, will increase in number and power, and inspire us with all the confidence which our joy requires in the new scenes upon which we shall be ushered. In the present life, we find that the difficulties of youth prepare us for the sterner difficulties of manhood, and the labours of manhood for the anxieties of age, and a well spent life grows happier and happier even unto the end. We find too that the Christian who walks by faith as he moves amid the perplexities and trials of time, grows not only in the strength of his confidence but in the spiritual joys which are inseparable from its exercise; so when we reach "the world which is to come," we shall find that the discipline of "the world which is," has prepared us for its scenes, its duties, and its joys, and every successive stage of that coming existence will be one of increasing confidence, and increasing happiness.

Then, moreover, is the other view of the nature of the discipline to which God is subjecting us upon earth to be added to this one. In the school of Christ we are trained to habits of active usefulness, which give expression to that benevolent spirit which religion inspires; and if this is so there must be something hereafter to correspond with this discipline as its necessary and appropriate result. I do not know that any one intelligently entertains the sentiment, but there is a very undefined feeling in many minds that when the human spirit reaches the eternal world there will remain nothing for it to do. To the sanctified it is a world of rest, the happiness of which will consist in pleasing and grateful recollections, in adoring admiration, in songs of praise. It will unquestionably be a world of rest, but not a world of inert repose. The rest of the human spirit is not inaction, but right action. The most restless being in God's universe, is he who has no end appropriate to his powers in view of which to work. The transition from the present to the future, is not to be a destruction, or alteration, but only a full development of the powers of our natures; and if here action and usefulness are essential to happiness, there can be no happiness eternal, separate from eternal usefulness. The government of God is carried on, and his purposes are executed, as we learn from the inspired oracles, and from the teachings of Providence, by intermediate and instrumental agencies. Men are his instruments, "angels are ministering spirits;" and who can doubt, my brethren, that God, in calling us here to be co-workers with himself in carrying out his designs, in giving us our spheres of duty and usefulness, in throwing upon us responsibilities which our own peace of mind requires us to meet and discharge, is preparing us for the higher position we shall be called to occupy, and the nobler, grander parts we shall be called to act in his coming kingdom. It is a hard and rugged path, which man is sometimes called to tread in early life—painful and toilsome are his acquisitions of knowledge, severe the discipline to which he must subject his active and ambitious mind, but the mysteries of God's providence towards him are all explained, when in after life you see him towering high above his fellows, describing a wide circle of influence, and wielding a mighty power. He had never been fitted for his place, never had reached his eminence, but for his previous discipline and toil; and for the most part the men who take the lead in life, who give shape to earthly movements, and direction to the current of human things, are men who have been schooled in scenes of difficulty, and whose upward and onward strugglings, as they have developed the powers of their minds, have prepared them for the relations they sustain, and rightly to use the influence they have gained. And do you not suppose that God has something for us to do hereafter, and that by calling us to duty now, he is training us for usefulness then? Verily do we believe that there will be posts in that upper world to which nothing but a previous life of usefulness will fit one. Verily do we believe that there will be services demanded there, which will utterly baffle the skill, as they will surpass the capacities of those who have never been trained to service here. Every man will there have his place and his sphere, but it will be the place or the sphere for which his previous course has fitted him; and so surely as "every man is to be rewarded according to his works," so surely as "one star differeth from another star in glory," so surely in that future world there will be elevated positions, which are to be reached only by those who have already learned to soar high, and wonderful advantages, which shall belong only to those who have here been taught how to reap them.

There is something, moreover, in the nature of goodness, in its expansive tendency, which seems to demand a sphere for its developement. Some there are, even in this world, who feel that life has its joys only as it has its duties; and they would as soon cease to live as cease to be useful; and this spirit the gospel has implanted in the hearts of all its subjects. Goodness, benevolence, is the essential element of the Christian life. It may be only like the blade springing out of the ground, but it grows by culture, and if God's arrangements are carried out, there will be as certainly "the ear," and "the full corn in the ear;" and oh! what kind of a world would that be, so far as happiness is concerned, where there would be no field of usefulness, which would afford no room for the outgoing and expansion of this benevolent spirit? Just as certainly as that yearning after immortality which God has incorporated among the elements of our nature, demands an immortality to meet it, does that benevolence which the Spirit of God has implanted in every Christian heart, demand that there shall be an immortality of usefulness, in order to an immortality of happiness.

At this point, my brethren, I must again crave your indulgence. I cannot compass my whole design in this discourse. I have yet the other side of the picture to present to you before I have finished my general view of "the life which is to come;" but upon the strength of what I have thus far advanced, I may ask my hearers if the thoughts I have thrown out, do not cast an entirely new and exceeding interesting light upon "the life which now is." There is a very common feeling, I am persuaded, that it would be better that a Christian man should be at once translated to heaven, than that he should be left, if I may so speak, to work his way there through a world of trial and sorrow, of difficulty and toil. It would not, indeed, be better for the world, because it would remove all its light and take away all its salt. Neither would it be better for a man, so far as his earthly interests and relations are concerned. In this respect, the Christian has as strong reasons for life as any other man; but so far as regards his spiritual relations and future rewards, it would be better for himself personally that he should be taken to heaven the moment heaven is sure. But there is a sad misconception here. The Bible tells us that "it is good for a man to wait for the salvation of God." It tells us that the trials which beset us here "work out for us a far more exceeding and eternal weight of glory;" and they do so, by training us to bear it. We wonder that God calls men to such severe trials of their faith. But why is it but to prepare them for the higher and nobler exercises of faith to which they shall be called hereafter, and to which they would be wholly incompetent, but for their previous discipline in a school of affliction. Here you see what trials mean. Each one of them prepares us for a still higher spot and for a richer crown. And every one of us shall find hereafter, that God did not tax us too often or too severely. Every lesson which we learn here, every lesson of confidence and submission, shall come into full play and do its part in fitting us for our work and administering to our joy. We shall then see that not one of them could have been spared without proportionably detracting from our portion. We may depend upon it, if God means to raise us to honor and nobility hereafter, he will prepare us for our reward now; and then " the trial of our faith shall be found unto praise, and honor, and glory."

So too with regard to those scenes of active usefulness in which we are placed, and the duties we are called to discharge. They are none too many; in view of " the life which is to come," I had almost said that God cannot put upon us too many, or too weighty responsibilities. The more we do, the brighter does our reward sparkle with the splendours of eternity. Every duty we faithfully discharge does but put another plume in our angel's wing, another jewel in our seraph's crown. Every effort we make, every responsibility we meet, every act of goodness we perform, does but fix our place the higher in the scale of majesty and triumph. In view of that reward which shall be according to every man's works, we have none too much of labour, none too much of toil; our future recompense requires it all. Oh! let us not, my brethren, shun duties, however painful and self-sacrificing they may be; let us not shut ourselves out from, or seek to avoid spheres of usefulness in the world. If we do we shall find that by our short-sighted calculations we have missed noble and glorious things, and have failed to reach some high point in the kingdom which we might have occupied. We may make the discovery when it is too late. If we are Christians we shall make it, if not before, in our dying hour. When we come to stand on the top of some Pisgah which overlooks the past, as well as the future, then lost opportunities of usefulness will be seen as so much taken from our coming joy; and in that moment, while the firmament is bright with the dawning of heaven, and the music of the spheres is already heard, while the spirit is pluming its wing for its flight, if there shall be a wish to put a check upon it, and rebuke its eagerness to be gone, it will be a wish not concerning earthly things or earthly friends, but it will be a wish to live a little longer, that we might labour a little more for Christ and for good in this world. Let us be instructed by these thoughts: "Walk ye by faith, and not by sight." Be steadfast, immovable, always abounding in the work of the Lord; for as much as ye know that your labour is not in vain in the Lord."

THE DAY OF GRACE.

"And when he was come near, he beheld the city and wept over it, saying, if thou hadst known, even thou, at least in this thy day, the things which belong unto thy peace! but now, they are hid from thine eyes."—St. Luke xix. 41, 42.

The scene, my brethren, which the language of the text pourtrays, is not more touching, than are the principles which it involves, important. We behold the Son of God in tears. The fact derives its peculiar interest from the circumstances in which he was placed, and the influences which seem to have unmanned him. It would not have been at all surprising had the "man of sorrows and acquainted with grief," been thus deeply affected in view of "the hour and power of darkness," the garden and the cross, which were just before him; but however he may have felt at times in reference to his coming and distinctly apprehended trials, they were not now sorrows of a private or personal nature which stirred his strong emotions and compelled his tears. He is, at the present time, in the midst of his greatest earthly triumphs; about to make his public entry into Jerusalem, surrounded by an admiring multitude, and heralded by thousands, who shout "Hosanna to the Son of David." He has reached the brow of Mount Olivet, and beneath him lies spread out in all its extent and magnificence, the city he was approaching; and as his eye rested upon Jerusalem, he thought of it as the scene of his public ministrations and his most splendid miracles, as the city whose inhabitants he had so often taught, so faithfully warned, so marvellously blessed; and yet, Jerusalem, uninstructed, unreclaimed, unmoved, and now abandoned of Him whose hand lingers ere it takes hold on judgment, to the withering curse of slighted mercy and abused long suffering, which was about to descend upon it. Here you have the reason of the Redeemer's tears.

We may not be able to present a correct analysis of our Saviour's state of mind which here finds expression; and yet the language which he uses indicates one thought as serving to give to his feelings of grief peculiar poignancy. The catastrophe which he bewailed might have been averted. They were not unavoidable evils and necessary calamities which awaited that devoted city, but such as were traceable to their source in the folly and guilty infatuation of its inhabitants. Its condition, as now doomed, was the more melancholy, because Jerusalem might have been saved.

Now, I take it that we have in this language of Jesus Christ a general principle of deep interest and importance to ourselves. However widely in some respects our circumstances may differ from those of the ancient Jews, yet so far as our relations to the gospel of Christ are concerned, what was true of them is true of us. As subjects of this gospel, we stand upon the same platform, have the same means of spiritual good, move under the same influences, and must in our character, our position, and the results of our course, illustrate the same general principles. Taking all this for granted, and we do not for a moment suppose that it will be called in question by any of our hearers, we start the question,—what is my position, what is your position, what is the position of every man under the gospel of Jesus Christ in reference to the salvation of the soul? That is the question with which we have to do to-day. A question big with interest, and one which can hardly fail to arrest and rivet the attention of every one who believes that he has a soul which must be lost or saved.

In attempting to answer this question, allow me to advert again to the thought which has been suggested as that which gave pungency to the Saviour's grief while he wept over Jerusalem,—the now certain and dreadful catastrophe might have been prevented. Upon no other ground than this, can the language which Christ uttered be justified to any rational mind; for the sorrow which it expresses regards not simply the event itself, but the event as resulting from human folly and infatuation. Study it carefully, and see if you can find any meaning in the language, or any evidence of sincerity in the feeling to which it gives utterance, but upon the supposition that there had been a time when these inhabitants of Jerusalem might have known the things which belonged to their peace, and when by knowing them they might have averted their coming doom.

Now for my doctrine. Every man brought under the influence of the gospel has a time of probation and hope; a day of grace. This naked proposition which I thus lay down, will not, I presume, be questioned, though some there are who will give to it an interpretation which will strip it of all its power and life. I mean by a day of probation and of grace something more than an arrest of threatened punishment, something more than an hour of respite. I mean a definite season, during which every man who enjoys it has an opportunity for securing everlasting life. We may look upon a day of grace as a means, connected with the salvation of the soul as its end. To preach to a man "Jesus Christ, and him crucified," to set before him the plan of salvation through atoning blood, to throw the light of truth upon his pathway, to press him with the invitations and warnings of the gospel, to send home its varied and powerful appeals to his heart, and yet to intimate that these multiform influences and instrumentalities do not contemplate his spiritual good, and sustain no relation to the object at which they professedly aim, is little else than trifling with human sorrows, and sporting with human helplessness; other and higher and nobler views do I take of the gospel of the grace of God. I could not preach it did I not believe that they who enjoy its light, and are subject to its influences, are prisoners of hope; did I not believe that there is a connection between its privileges and a final redemption from the curse. I could not come and lay the offer of eternal life before you, my brethren, and press it upon your acceptance by the urgency of eternal motives, did I not believe that it was meant for you, and that you might embrace it and be saved. Perish for ever the thought which would thus limit the grace of God, or contract the circle of its wondrous manifestations. The provisions of the gospel are in fullness and extent all that human wants can ask. The message, "whosoever will may come and take of the water of life freely," is the standard by which to guage the dimensions of the love of God; and wherever there is one to whom I may preach the gospel, there is one to whom I may say, "you may be saved."

Such a view of the gospel and of the relations of men as its subjects, throws a new aspect over the world in which we live; if my statement is in accordance with truth, then is this world not a scene of unmixed corruption, hopeless death and irretrievable ruin; then is this day of grace something more than a mere reprieve or arrest of judgment. It is a world of probation and of hope; these hours which we are now spending, and these scenes through which we are now passing, are hours and scenes full of delightful, and elevating, and sanctifying influences; the spot where God has fixed our habitation, is the spot upon which the cross has been erected, whence mercy speaks, and through which God is ready to dispense his blessings "far as the curse is found." Oh, that men did but "know the joyful sound," that they "understood in this their day, the things which belong unto their peace!"

Another remark may be proper at this point, to prevent a misconception of the doctrine which I have laid down. When, then, in delivering the message of the gospel, I say to a man, that he may be saved, I do not intend to convey the idea that there are no difficulties in the way of his conversion, no hindrances to his salvation. I mean simply, that all outward hindrances, growing out of his past sinfulness, and out of the claims of God's violated commandments, over which, from the very nature of the case, he could have no control, because he cannot live over, or redeem, or atone for the past, are entirely removed. Nothing of this kind intervenes between him and the attainment of everlasting life. The glory of God, as a reconciling God; the secret of his mighty power, as revealed in the gospel, over the human conscience and the human heart, is found in this, that he has taken it upon himself, and succeeded at an amazing cost, in his plan to remove every obstacle on the part of God's government, leaving nothing to intervene between a man and his salvation, but what derives its preventive influence from the state of his own heart. Therefore do we say to a man that he may be saved, because every obstacle of an outward character insuperable by man has been removed, and because the influences connected with the gospel, which are brought to bear upon him, are in their own nature recovering influences. If this is so, then, two positions are reached; the one is, that before man, under the gospel, a door of hope is opened; the other is, that no one can close that door but himself. He may be saved; if he should be lost, it will be because he did not know, in his day of grace, "the things which belonged to his peace."

Guided by this, the main thought, as I apprehend, of my text, when I come to my hearers with the messages of eternal truth, I say to them generally, "this is your day of grace." It is so, because you are the subjects of that gospel which with its privileges and offers has appeared unto all men. The means of grace which God has appointed seem in their enjoyment necessarily to involve the opportunity for securing eternal life. The Sabbath sun which shines upon us, and lights our way to the house of God, by means of its interesting associations with the cross, points our thoughts to the wondrous work of redeeming love as the ground of our hope and the source of sanctifying influence. The messages of mercy which are addressed to us, bringing our minds as they do into contact with questions of privilege and duty, seem to open to us the door of life, as they demonstrate God's readiness to save. Providence, too, subordinating all its movements to the cross as the instrumentalities of its designs, arranges a man's circumstances and fixes his changes and allotments with a view of giving efficacy to the truth. From the moment when we first listened to the tale of a

Saviour's love, to the present hour, have we been moving amid such associations, and under such influences. There is not one of us without a hope in Christ, whose career, whether it has been long or short, must not be essentially varied from that of the vast majority of his fellows, if, as he looks back from his present position over the scenes through which he has passed, he cannot discover many opportunities of which he might have availed himself, and which might have been turned to account in effecting a great change in his circumstances and relations; seasons during which, had he rightly estimated and improved them, he might have become a subject of the kingdom of Christ.

Thus, when speaking in general terms, we say that "life is man's day of grace and hope;" because while life lasts he is cheered by the Sabbath sun, instructed by the teachings of the gospel, and plied by the varied means of conversion. "Life is the day of grace," because now the calls of mercy fall upon the ear, and the life-giving and sanctifying Spirit moves over the human soul; and God is near to each one of us, and may be found of those who "search for him with all their heart." Need I add that this is man's only day; once past, and the shades of evening gathered over him, it never more returns; once past, the gates of that everlasting kingdom are for ever closed, and the invitations of truth and the whispers of the Spirit are hushed in the silence of an eternal night. What human mind can calculate the amazing change which a month, a day, an hour may make in all a man's spiritual circumstances and relations? Now we look at him—he is in a world of light; he is a prisoner of hope; the message of a reconciling God falls upon his ear, the power of a recovering spirit moves over his heart; there is the mercy-seat to which he may lift up his prayer, and there the advocate within the vail. We look again, and he is not; the curtain has fallen, the scene to him is changed, and where he dwells,

> "In that lone land of deep despair,
> No Sabbath's heavenly light shall rise;
> No God regard his bitter prayer,
> Nor Saviour call him to the skies."

This general position admitted, and a believer in this written testimony of God will not dispute it, what a withering reflection it casts upon a career of worldliness and spiritual unconcern. I need not say any thing about the uncertainty which attaches to this probationary scene; at the longest it is short, in circumstances of the greatest security it is doubtful. The thousands who are falling around us, the seeds of disease, the workings of death, of which we are conscious, what are these but the daily, hourly remembrances of the certainty and rapidity of our flight away from this land of promise and of hope; which, as they force themselves upon our minds, compel our sympathy with the spirit which sung,

> "Great God! on what a slender thread
> Hang everlasting things;
> The eternal states of all the dead,
> Upon life's feeble strings!"

And if upon these few days, fleeting as the morning cloud, and evanescent as the early dew, hang the interests of these deathless spirits, what is the man, thoughtless and unconcerned about his spiritual welfare, doing, but burning out the lamp of life, and spending his only day of mercy, and of hope, upon the pleasures and follies of a world fleeting as himself? What is spiritual indifference but a downright robbery of the soul? nay more, but draining the very life-blood of the human spirit, to gratify the desires of the flesh and of the mind? I would ask the man buried in the present, and forgetful of, and wholly unprepared for the future, to pause a moment, and ponder the path of his feet, and tell me whether he honestly thinks that his course is in keeping with his circumstances? Admitting the uncertainty of probation, is he not rapidly pushing on to a spiritual bankruptcy; and while he cannot but acknowledge that this Sabbath's sun is lighting his pathway to the grave, what is he doing but spending what may be the last cent of his spiritual property, and intelligently wasting upon the vanities of earth, the hour which may push him amid the untried and unprovided for realities of another world. Surely he knows not, in this his day, the things which belong unto his peace.

The appeal which my subject makes to the conscience, the hopes, and the fears of man, is regulated as to its power very much by circumstances. True, it is invested with interest to any man, wherever he may be, and in whatever circumstances he may be placed. Confessedly, is the folly amazing of any man, who, without a hope in Christ, treads his pathway carelessly to the grave. Yet there are circumstances in which the appeal is peculiarly strong, because the light in which its grounds are presented, is peculiarly vivid. There are seasons in every man's history strictly characterized by a suitableness to a religious change, and when Providence seems in an especial manner to force upon his attention the things which belong to his peace. There are crises in men's lives, when God is very near unto them, and hope and eternal life are very near them. If we could point to a human being whom in a particular and pointed manner, God seemed to be addressing, whom he had selected from those around him, as a subject of his special solicitude, upon whose mind the unfriendly influences of the world had less than their wonted power, to whom the invitations and warnings of the gospel were particularly directed, one, in short, who by reason of his outward circumstances, his mental susceptibility, and his real feelings, was occupying an attitude exceedingly favorable to his conversion to God, we should look upon him with wondrous interest, as one who, in an emphatic sense, was enjoying a day of grace. How wonderful to him would be the associations amid which he moved. How much of peace or sorrow, hope or despair, life or death, would be dependent upon his movements, in the circumstances which Providence had so kindly arranged for him. If in any man it is folly, in him it would be madness not to know the things which belong to his peace.

We are very apt, my brethren, to look abroad and endeavour to define the character of others, and determine the relative advantages and disadvantages of the positions which other men occupy. I would that we might come home to day, and ask ourselves if there are none here, who, in their feelings and circumstances, meet the supposition which we have just been making? I acknowledge, that in these remarks my mind turns with a very deep and affectionate interest to those of my hearers who are in the spring-time of life. To them would I for a moment address myself, and to their hearts would I minister the appeal which my subject furnishes. You, my youthful hearers, are now spending the best and brightest part of your day of grace. I do not intend, in any of the remarks which I am about to utter, to limit the operations of the grace of God, or intimate that the day of grace terminates with any particular year of human life. God forbid that we should, as the Bible has not, shut out the aged unbeliever from hope. It is never out of place; it is never too late, while the eye, though dim, yet sees, and the pulse, though feeble, yet beats, not though the winter of life be at its depth, and the sun be touching the horizon, to say, "now is the accepted time"—but it does seem to be implied in the whole strain of inspired teaching, that repentance deferred, if not impossible, is doubtful.

There is a peculiarity about the messages of

truth, which give them a special emphasis to the youthful mind, in that while they are addressed indiscriminately to all men, they apply them particularly to the young. The man of middle life, and the man of riper years, is never selected in the word of God as the subject to whom it presents a specific invitation, or to whom it holds out a specific promise. There is a meaning and a point which cannot well be overlooked, in the exhortation, "Remember now thy Creator in the days of thy youth," and a richness unspeakably precious in the promise, "They that seek me early shall find me." This much, certainly, we may infer from the statements of the inspired oracles, that God looks upon the young with peculiar interest, and his Spirit strives with them in a peculiar manner. In the spring time of life is man the special object of divine instruction, divine expostulation, and divine solicitude. You cannot doubt it in view of the inquiry, addressed with so much tenderness to every youthful conscience, "Wilt thou not from this time cry unto me, my Father, thou art the guide of my youth." You cannot doubt it, in view of that delight which God takes in those who consecrate unto him the dew of their youth. That quick susceptibility, that tenderness of heart, that wakeful conscience, those prompt responses of the mind to the truth of God, those frequent movements in accordance with the appeals of heavenly mercy, those deep and strong emotions, which are stirred within you by the power of the cross, as the Saviour from amid the scenes of his humiliation, appeals to you, and asks your hearts as a cheerful tribute to his benevolence, all show that God is striving with you, and that you are very near the entrance into his kingdom. How precious to you is this your day of grace! Would you rightly estimate its value, and fully appreciate its importance, let the testimony of inspired truth be strengthened by your own observation, as you see how men depart from God as they move onward in life. He who has entered upon those scenes of active engagements to which manhood calls him, unconverted to God, may have indeed his hours of deep reflection and solemn thought, and agitated feeling, but he knows nothing of that tenderness of soul, of that susceptibility of impression, of those strivings of the Holy Spirit, which formed characteristics of his early years. Believe me, there is no day of grace, there is no season like that of youth, in which to make one's peace with God. Skeptical upon this point you may be, but against that skepticism is arrayed the testimony of the Bible, and of all, without a single exception, of those who have gone before you. Nay, more than this, your honest convictions are against it; for there is not one in early life, who hears me to-day, who, however willing he might be in respect to some worldly associations or circumstances, to exchange places with another more advanced in life, would be willing to exchange with him, if he is out of the kingdom of God, his hope in reference to eternal life. Give me then your mind, my youthful hearer, and suffer my appeal. This is your day of promise and of hope. Oh!

let it not slip by unheeded and unimproved; scatter not, in this spring-time of life, the seeds which can produce no other harvest than one of anguish and despair. Youth is the season of action in spiritual as well as temporal things, because the season of quick apprehension, buoyant spirits, and elastic energies. There is a season coming when there will be ice in the blood and snow on the brow, and all the emblems of winter will be thickly strewed over the man; and if there has beeen no action before, it will be a hard thing, a scarcely possible thing, when the limb has grown rigid, and the blood has become congealed, to put forth the energies which a successful action demands. In spiritual things, the man who has been successful in drowning anxiety, and stifling conscience, as every man must have been, who has passed onward in life unconverted, must have closed up all the avenues through which the gospel message might find an entrance to his mind—never in after life, will he be a willing, certainly not an intelligent auditor of the message, that judgment is coming to all, and that eternity is big with terror to all who have not been born again. The state of his mind will not be adapted to grapple with so stern a communication—his apprehension will not grasp the tidings in their length and breadth—or if we should endeavour to stir him with the touching spectacle of a Redeemer's crucifixion, his sensibilities are too benumbed to appreciate our appeal, his heart too indurated to feel its force. You might as well try to melt a

16

substance with the same fire which hardened it, as move a man by those appliances of truth which have served but to fasten him where he is. Thus hope becomes weaker, as time rolls on—and he who in youth might have been converted, is unimpressible in age—precisely as the oak, which an infant might have crushed in the acorn, when rooted in the ground, defies the might of a giant's strength.

Every thing, then, my youthful hearer, depends, in all human probability, upon your prompt action in this your day. Your own honest convictions accord with what I utter. The man of middle life, cumbered with the cares, and harassed with the perplexities of active business, which no more agitate his mind than indispose it for spiritual things—the aged sinner, as he trembles on the verge of the grave, shattered in body, and enfeebled in mind, unable to bring home to his conscience and heart the truths of the gospel, and essaying in vain, after some clear discovery of the way of life,—look back to you and say, in tones of emphatic and solemn warning,—"Act now." Nay more, there is a voice coming from yonder dark prison house to-day. Listen to it—it is full of meaning. It is the voice of those who passed on earth through scenes of privilege, of promise, and of hope; and they say, "If you would not be united to us at last, in our tears and sorrows of unavailing regret, and bitter self-reflection, as we look back over the scenes of early life—now in this your day attend to the things which belong to your peace." We meet you, then, to-day, my youthful hearers—some of you are just crossing the limit of this day of grace—with our kind, yet powerful appeal. I cannot tell its issue, but if I could, I would write it on the conscience and burn it into the heart. And if it fail of its end, it will yet not be lost. You will meet it again, and dread it again, and feel it again; and when your day has gone, and your sun has sunk beneath the horizon, and a darkness which may be felt, gathers over your spirits, putting out the last ray of hope, this Sabbath day will rise up in freshness and vividness to your mind, and its remembered argument, and its recollected appeal, oh! how they will tell upon the stricken, mourning spirit, and what an oppressive load will they throw upon an already overtasked and sinking soul! Oh! "that you did but know, at least in this your day, the things which belong unto your peace."

But if the appeal of our Saviour's lamentation has a peculiar pertinency in reference to the young, it is not without its force as addressed to others. I doubt not, my brethren, that there are some thoughtful, troubled spirits here to-day. I doubt not that in some minds, among those out of the kingdom of God, there is a conscious interest, more or less deep, upon the subject of religion. There are those who have their hours of thoughtfulness, their sincere and honest convictions, their half-formed, secretly cherished, sometimes almost expressed purposes of a change. There is this peculiarity about such a state of mind that the things of religion have an aspect of vividness and reality. Its subjects are not satisfied with what they are; they cannot reconcile their position in a religious point of view with their intelligent convictions of duty or safety. Such facts, and others kindred to them, can no otherwise be explained than upon the supposition that God, in the instructive and recovering influences of his grace, is very near. I doubt not that he often thus acts upon and tests men when others know nothing about it, and they themselves hardly suspect the true nature and tendency of their mental movements. Now, I meet a man in such a state, and interpret his experiences. God is trying him—it is his day of grace and hope. I know not what he will do under the spiritual pressure which rests upon his mind. But I would have him feel how much hangs upon his action. He will do something; he will pass through some processes of thought, through some mental changes. He is now doing so; and these processes of thought, and these mental changes, will tell; tell certainly, tell effectively; tell, perhaps, decisively upon the question of his final, permanent spiritual condition. He is shaping his course at this very moment for a world of sorrow, or a world of joy. Such a man, in such a state, hardly needs to be taught; he is taught already. He does not need to be moved; he is moved already. He is in his consciousness a living witness to himself, and in his words and actions a demonstration to others of the reality and power of spiritual influences. It is a day of grace with him; a day of hope; and yet a day of peril; many a one has passed through it unchanged; and in doing so has put away from him the words of everlasting life; and, thereafter, a deep insensibility has fallen upon his spirit, and a thick darkness has settled upon his prospects. The Bible to him, in its promises and warnings, has been a sealed book, an unmeaning book, a powerless book. Every message of mercy has fallen upon a stupified conscience, and an indurated heart. Every step which he has taken has been onward to a certain, dreadful catastrophe; and at last he stands, the hero of many victories achieved by "the lust of the flesh, the lust of the eye, and the pride of life," over the influences of the truth and the manifestations of the Spirit, unshaken and unaffected; until he is awakened, at last, to find that "the harvest is past, and the summer ended, and he is not saved."

I do not know, my brethren, of a more painful spectacle than that of a man, who, having advanced far in his earthly career, confessedly without confidence and hope in God, is yet a subject of spiritual indifference. You will find him wrapped up in a garment of self-satisfaction, perfectly impenetrable—he does not need to be taught—he will not be taught in spiritual things—he may be very much obliged by the well-meant but mistaken interference of others who would endeavor to enlighten him, but he does not wish to be troubled. His path is beset by danger, but he does not see it—there are pitfalls before him, but his prejudice covers them—it is darkness all around him, deep, moral, midnight; but his vain arguments and false confidences are like meteors, which, filling the horizon and colouring the sky, make his midnight seem like the blushing of the morning—and there he is, passive and unconcerned, waiting till the grave opens to receive him, and destruction to engulph him. Some men wonder how any one can reach such a state. It is a painful state, but there is nothing mysterious about it. This is the secret of it—the man has sinned away his day of grace, and God has left him.

And if there be a man here to-day, of thoughtful mind and awakened conscience—if there be one to whom religious truth is invested with interest —who feels dissatisfied with his present spiritual position, and is convinced of the necessity of a change, I would remind him, that this blinded, and infatuated, and morally speaking, sepulchred man, whose picture we have just drawn, once had his day of grace—once passed through the very processes of thought and feeling which now belong to himself—he was once just like you. Oh, see to it that you do not, by postponing the subject of religion, become just like him.

My thoughtful, my convinced hearer, bear with my appeal. You have your day of grace; and now I press upon your attention, the mighty theme of an interest in Jesus Christ. Oh! "that you knew, at least, in this thy day, the things which belong unto your peace"! There is an hour coming, when, sympathising with your speaker in the views he has taken, you will no more wonder at his earnestness and importunity. There is an hour coming, when the door of hope will be shut, and the conviction will be clear and irresistible, that it never again can be opened. Then will the views of men concerning their day of grace be vastly changed. Then the scenes through which they have passed will rise up to the view unobstructed by any of the delusions of sense, and unperverted in their features by any of the sophistries of a deceitful heart. The time when God was near, and waited to bless, will be seen to have had a meaning and a preciousness which do not now belong to it; and as memory runs back along the line of one's history, every day of promise will be seen. The season of youth, with all its susceptibility and tenderness, and quickness of feeling, the hour when in the sanctuary God drew near unto the soul, and the wakefulness and reproofs of conscience demonstrated the presence and power of his spirit; the dealings of Providence, which brought eternal realities home to his mind, all seen as gone, gone unimproved, will all be to him, not more proofs of his certain ruin, than evidences of the doctrine that he might have been saved, had he but known in his day of grace the things which belonged to his peace. My brethren, that hour is coming; this day of grace is rapidly passing away. This Sabbath, this argument, this message takes so much away from the opportunities which God has afforded, while he still waits to be gracious, and his message is one of invitation. While his Spirit yet moves in his quickening influences over those hearts, while the door of life is yet open, while conscience approves the claims of the truth, and the mind is accessible to the persuasive arguments of the cross; ere the sensibilities become callous, and a sinful world has obtained the mastery, oh! heed the appeal, which the lamentation of the Saviour ministers with so much power. He wept over Jerusalem because her inhabitants knew not the time of their visitation; and if after having poured out his soul unto death, and brought to you an offer of mercy, and plied you with so many and such tender and forceful entreaties, he should be compelled to weep over your infatuated resistance, those tears, believe me, will be scalding drops, the torture of which the human spirit can never bear. Oh! "that you knew, in this your day, the things which belong unto your peace."

THE NATURE OF THE ATONEMENT.

"Christ hath redeemed us from the curse of the law, being made a curse for us."—GALATIANS iii. 13.

THE necessity of some wonderful expedient to restore friendship between God and his alienated creatures; of some ground or reason of forgiveness out of, and independent of man himself, has not been more clearly taught by all just views of the character and government of our Maker, than fully demonstrated by the irrepressible convictions of every human bosom. "Wherewithal shall I come before my Maker?" and "how shall man be just with God?" are questions, which have tried, and agitated, and palsied the mind in every age of the world. The human intellect has felt its own littleness when it has attempted to grapple with them, and no human sagacity or invention has availed to furnish of them any thing like a competent solution. The light manner in which some men treat these questions, and the unseemly and really flippant air with which they speak of the ease of forgiveness, and consequently of the scruples and anxieties of others, are due to a want of moral sensibility, which makes sin a very trifling matter in their estimation, and to an ignorance of God, which blinds them to the unsullied and necessary holiness of his character. If the wisest and purest of heathen sages, one who from many of his disclosures, seems to have caught a glimpse of light from other sources than nature's revelations, yet could never perfectly satisfy himself as to the possibility of forgiveness, if notwithstanding all his reasonings, doubt preponderated over faith, and fear over hope, surely it cannot be a trifling question, nor one to be disposed of so easily and summarily as some men suppose. An awakened conscience will start difficulties, of which spiritual insensibility never dreams; and an intelligent conviction of sin will render ineffective all the efforts of human wisdom to remove them. The human mind never yet has found a rational and satisfactory peace, save in the light which the revelation of God has thrown upon the problem of forgiveness. Conscience has served only to start the question, but not to furnish the answer. It lifts an accusing voice, and heralds a coming storm, and there it leaves its subject without furnishing him with a justifying plea, or directing him to a covert from the tempest whose approach it announces. Reason ransacks the analogies of nature, but finds nothing which furnishes any help for the mastery of this wondrous problem. The works of God are full of evidences of order, magnificence and bounty, but among them all not a trace of pardon can be found.

The only light which has ever broken in upon

this darkness, and banished those forms of horror which walk around us in the gloom, comes from this book of God. "The word made flesh," is the revealed solution of the difficulty. "Christ and Christ crucified," is the only source of peace and hope to the distracted and despairing spirit. With the simple narrative of the gospel we are all familiar. It is the story of the Son of God, clothed in our nature, tabernacling in the world. It is the tale of his life of suffering and his death of agony. It is human nature, illustrating by a course of unswerving obedience, and spotless innocence, the excellence, and so magnifying the righteousness of the broken law. It is the picture of "a man of sorrows and acquainted with grief." It carries us with him every step of a painful pilgrimage. It shews him to us as he struggles in the garden with his anticipations of coming woe, as he agonizes on the cross, carrying on there a mysterious conflict, and enduring an incomprehensible anguish, and expiring amid throes of convulsive pain with which all nature sympathized. We feel, while we read the tale, that we are communing with a singular being; singular in the constitution of his person as harmonizing and embracing the divine and the human; singular in all his experience, singular in his conflicts, and singular in his death; and while we study the exhibition, we are told that in view of it God can be just, and yet forgive; that on the ground of the doing and the suffering of Jesus Christ, pardon, full and free, may be extended to sin, to any sin, to all sin. This is the simple narrative, the answer which the Bible gives to the question, "Can a man be just with God?"

If we have thus before us the fact, we may well summon to it our most interested attention. How many inquiries at once start up in the mind in view of it. He can hardly be said to think, who has never asked himself, how do the sufferings of Christ constitute a ground of pardon, or what is the great principle of atonement? Does the sacrifice of Christ meet the sinner's case, honoring God, and satisfying the human mind? Is the scheme throughout consistent with itself, and so completely free from difficulties as not only, to warrant, but to demand a rational faith? To the substance of these questions, involving, as they do, the nature, reality, and reasonableness of atonement, our thoughts shall be for a few moments directed.

And here, I am well aware, my brethren, that we are treading upon what, to some minds, seems to be very uncertain ground. It has been distinctly avowed, and that upon high authority, that the nature of the atonement, or how the sufferings of Jesus Christ can be a ground of pardon, is absolutely incomprehensible. We know it is said, merely, that God, for Christ's sake, does forgive sin—but why or how he can consistently do so, are questions about which we can merely speculate, without the possibility of arriving at certain truth. If this is so, then the very thing which it is the purpose of Christ's propitiation to declare, is as much a mystery now as ever—then, though we may be assured that the atonement meets all the difficulties growing out of the government of God, we cannot tell whether it meets all the difficulties originating in the mind of man. It cannot, therefore, be the subject of a rational faith, nor the source of a settled, unwavering peace. I grant you that there are some things connected with the atonement, which, to us, in our present state, are incomprehensible. We cannot unravel the mysteries of our Saviour's person, nor fathom the depths of his anguish, nor analyze perfectly the character of his experience; but the relation of his sufferings to our forgiveness, as its procuring cause, the manner in which they become available to such a result, seems to me to involve some of the first principles of the doctrines of Christ—principles radical in the system of revealed truth, without an apprehension of which the Bible is a sealed book, and the whole plan of redemption is an inexplicable and unprofitable, and even an embarrassing mystery. If we are at a loss here, we are at a loss every where. If we do not understand these first principles, we do not understand the spirit, the essence, the very life of the gospel.

The necessity of atonement (as we have already seen) grows out of the nature of God, and the nature of man—out of the nature of God, whose righteousness seems to demand the punishment of sin—out of the nature of man, whose feelings seem to demand a reparation of the past, and a preventive to the future evil of his sinfulness, in order that he may have perfect peace. Now, it strikes me as assuming the very point in dispute to say, that justice or righteousness necessarily demands the literal infliction of the threatened penalty, the strict and unfailing punishment of the transgressor. If it is so, in reality, that every man must receive the punishment he has merited, in order that justice may be kept unsullied, then there can be no forgiveness ; and every man who admits that there is forgiveness, admits that justice does not necessarily require a literal punishment, and that it is perfectly consistent with treating men differently from their deserts.

I doubt not, my brethren, that not a little of the indistinctness which marks men's views upon this subject, arises from a want of discrimination—discrimination, I mean, between the ends of justice and the modes by which those ends are to be secured. The grand end is one thing, and the primary and essential thing, the method of securing that end, is another thing, and comparatively speaking, unessential and unimportant. Now, surely, I need not say to my hearers that the punishment of crime is not the end of justice—it is but means to an end itself, in the maintenance of the authority of the law-giver—the manifestation of the majesty of the law—the preserving unweakened the securities of righteousness. Wherever, and by whatever means, rights are preserved untouched and interests unimpaired, the great ends of justice are secured. The penalty attached to the law, and the infliction of it, in case of transgression, are the means through which justice is to attain its ends. But can we undertake to say that they are the only supposable means? If, indeed, these results can be reached in no other way than the literal punishment of sin, then, indeed, is the infliction of penalty essential to justice—but if we take this ground, then we again beg the question, and pronounce beforehand forgiveness on the part of God, to be impossible, because inconsistent with his character, as a just God, and an upright, moral governor.

It is, however, by no means an extravagant supposition, that cases may occur under any administration, where the infliction of punishment upon a criminal may not be necessary to answer the ends of justice. A wise parent, for example, may see in the case of a disobedient child, that the great object of parental oversight, the welfare and order of his family, may be perfectly attained, without inflicting the punishment which had been threatened to the disobedience in question. In such a case the inquiry arises, do the claims of justice imperatively demand a strict and literal adherence to the threatened penalty? Has wisdom nothing to say in this matter? Does benevolence put in here no claims which must be heard? It is but an artful evasion to say, that there can be no goodness, no wisdom, contrary to justice; whatever is right, must be wise and good. True, but if there can be wisdom and goodness without any conflict with justice, who will stand in the way of their manifestation? The great end of government is order, and suffering in case of crime, only where it is essential to order. It never seeks or inflicts suffering for its own sake, but in view of some good results which are to flow from it; and if those results can be secured, while at the same time the amount of suffering necessary may be diminished, where is the injury? Goodness accomplishes its purpose, and justice is satisfied because its ends are attained. The case is a much stronger one, where the ends of justice can be better secured without, than with the literal infliction of the penalty. If I, as a parent, can discover any way in which I can better secure the welfare of my family, and exhibit the uprightness of my character, than by the literal punishment of disobedience, surely in the adoption of that method, while I exhibit my wisdom and my benevolence, I do at the same time show myself more regardful even of justice, than I should do were I to decline the adoption of such an expedient. Nay, in the latter case I could not, I imagine, escape the charge of vindictiveness, a disposition to inflict punishment for punishment's sake, irrespective of the ends to be secured by it, when I refuse to adopt a method by which the suffering might be spared, while at the same time the object of that suffering could be much more certainly and easily attained.

These principles, it strikes me, are unquestionable, and they commend themselves to the common sense of every thoughtful mind; and these, I imagine, are the principles upon which the doctrine of atonement proceeds, and which serve most clearly to illustrate its nature. We do not indeed suppose that any transaction has ever taken place among men which in every respect is a parallel to the sacrificial offering of Jesus Christ; and there are no analogies in any of God's procedures with which we can compare it; it is a procedure perfectly unique in its nature, without parallels and without analogies; and yet there are many things which, when closely examined, furnish us with a key by which to unlock its mysteries, and introduce us to an acquaintance with their meaning.

Now, when we look at the revelations of the Bible upon this subject, we find a being, called the Son of God, presenting exhibitions which shew him to be more than human, and yet clad in the vestments, and wearing all the sinless attributes of humanity; we find him going through an experience of shame, suffering, and death. The untold agony which convulsed his frame, and the deep anguish which preyed upon his spirit, invest the scene with an air of mystery. We feel that this suffering must have some connection with sin. No man can read the record of the garden scene, or the scene upon the cross; can trace the evidences of mental anguish which there present themselves, anguish over and above, and entirely different in its nature from that which was connected with the external circumstances of the sufferer, without being compelled to bring, in some shape or form, sin as the only exponent of the scene. The Bible tells us that for "others' guilt the man of sorrows wept in blood." It gives the detail of his experience, and as we read it, it adds, he "was made a curse for us;" he "bore our sins in his own body on the tree." "God hath set him forth as a propitiation to declare his righteousness in the forgiveness of sin." The doctrine of atonement, as I gather it from the inspired testimony, is this: that God has substituted the sufferings of his Son in place of the punishment of the guilty; and that those sufferings answering the great ends of justice which the threatened penalty contemplated, constitute a good valid reason for the remission of the penalty itself. This is the way in which the atonement becomes available as a ground of forgiveness. We are forgiven, if we know any thing of forgiveness, only because the sufferings of Christ have come in the place of the punishment due to our sins, as answering the end of our punishment equally well and much better.

He who underwent that great travail of his soul, clothed himself with our nature, and became one with us, not simply that he might become capable of suffering, but that he might identify himself with the nature of sinful man; that the same nature which had sinned might suffer; and that the relation between his sufferings, and our forgiveness, might be at once and clearly perceived. And as we look at the whole subject, can we doubt for a moment, that his sufferings answered the great ends of justice, and preserved unsullied in its glory, and unimpaired in its sanctions, the law which had been broken, and which they were designed to sustain? The infinite dignity of his person, gave an infinite value to his work. The higher and nobler the subject upon whom, in case of transgression, the law takes its course, the more impressive the lesson taught of its majesty, and the mightier the enforcement given to its sanctions. And if the Son of God, notwithstanding the excellence and dignity of his person and station, was not spared that bitter cup of suffering, when he consented to assume the legal responsibilities of the transgressor, what an effective lesson is taught us of that sternness which belongs to the righteousness of the eternal throne, and of the certainty that sin shall receive its just award? Take any view of penalty you please, and see if its ends are not better answered upon the cross. What lesson does it teach, which is not better taught—what warning does it utter which is not more distinctly heard—what security for order and righteousness is gathered from it which is not better gathered from the cross? Every thing which punishment, in its own nature, as a mere sanction of law, involves, is involved in the great sacrificial offering of Jesus Christ—and more—for punishment, strictly speaking, has no remedial influence about it. Penalty contemplates not so much the good of the offender, as the good of the community or state whose rights he has outraged and whose interests he has sacrificed. The atonement of Jesus Christ contemplates both. By one and the same means, it upholds and illustrates the righteousness of God, and reforms and renews the guilty. It constitutes the mightiest, nay the only power which can be brought to bear upon the alienated heart, and recover it to the love and service of its rightful Sovereign; and thus it gives to justice all its claims, and affords goodness free scope for its exercise; makes kindness to the sinner consistent with righteousness—blends mercy and truth, good will and justice together, shewing to every intelligent being, how God can be just and yet justify the sinner. And if this is so, what difficulty can there be in clearly comprehending the doctrine of atonement, when it amounts simply to this: the sufferings of Christ are substituted in the place of my punishment, and thus secure my forgiveness, while they answer a much better end, and teach far more impressively all the lessons of penalty, than my punishment could in any circumstance possibly have done.

To sustain this view of atonement, I know we must consider the sufferings of Christ as strictly vicarious—to be available to me as a sinner, those sufferings must come in the place of my punishment. I can, upon no other principle, understand the doctrine of atonement; and if I greatly mistake not the spirit of the Bible, this idea pervades and gives meaning to all its teachings. The very terms which it uses to describe the Redeemer's work, are borrowed from sacrificial offerings, every one of which in its own nature implies a transfer of some kind from the person sacrificing to the victim sacrificed. The whole Jewish ritual, which derived its meaning and importance and value from a Redeemer's atonement, which was, in fact, but a shadow of good things to come, is full of the same idea—and when you see, under that ritual, the offender bringing his victim to the altar—when you see the high priest, on the great day of expiation, confessing the sins of the whole congregation over the head of the scape goat, it would be marvellously strange, if, when we come to the sufferings of Christ, which they were intended to typify, we should find nothing at all to correspond with the essential idea of the type. We confess to our fixed, settled conviction on this point, that if you take away from the sacrifice of Christ the idea of a strict substitution, and convert it into a mere instructive or declarative lesson, you take away that which constitutes the very nature of atonement, and render the whole story of our Redeemer's passion a tale of inexplicable mystery. Without this idea, the Bible, to my mind, is a sealed book. I may open its pages and read, but upon every leaf there rest "shadows, clouds, and darkness," which conceal the meaning of every one of its passages from my view.

And yet, while I stand so strongly by the vicariousness of Christ's sacrifice, as an essential truth of revelation, I am not to be considered as intimating that there is any thing like a transfer of personal character or desert from the guilty to their surety. We do not require to be told that sin and righteousness are moral and personal qualities and acts, and therefore cannot be transferred —we know it. The beings for whom Christ suffered, are none the less sinners because Christ suffered for them, nor was Christ the less innocent because he "bare their sins in his own body on the tree;" and yet, while we agree to the moral impossibility of transferring moral qualities or acts, we see no such impossibility in transferring their legal connections. Such a principle is common in the administration of God—to a certain extent, it is common in the transactions of human governments; and, while we see children suffering every day for the sins of their forefathers, in which they had no agency; while men suffer for the mistakes, the faults, the sins of their rulers and representatives, which they themselves abhor and disavow, it is idle for any one to say that it is absurd to suppose that Christ could assume the liabilities of the guilty, and so "suffer the just for the unjust."

Nor do we mean that the vicariousness of Christ's sacrifice implies that the threatened penalty of the law was literally inflicted upon him, and that he suffered in kind and amount precisely what all men would have suffered had he not offered his atonement. Such a notion, constituting as it does the only idea which some men have of atonement, is, to say the least of it, exceedingly crude; and when examined is seen to be wholly untenable. In the very nature of things penalty inflicted upon the personally guilty must be different from the suffering for sin endured by one who is personally innocent. If I choose to step in between an offender and a violated statute to screen him from punishment by suffering in his place that which will honour and sustain the law, it is perfectly absurd to say that my experience must be precisely the same with the experience of the offender, as it would have been had he endured the threatened penalty; the absence, in the one case, and the presence in the other case of all sense of personal sinfulness and desert of punishment, must essentially alter the experience. The sufferings of the Redeemer, therefore, could not possibly have been what the penalty of the law would have been had it been literally inflicted on the personal offenders.

The idea, moreover, that the atonement of Christ consisted in his suffering what those for whom he atoned deserved to suffer, is, in my apprehension, a contradiction of the very nature of atonement. Its source is goodness, as its design is to diminish the amount of suffering resulting from sin; and its wisdom is apparent from the fact, that it secures the great ends of the divine government at a less expense than the literal infliction of the penalty upon all offenders. But if Christ suffered in kind and amount precisely what all the redeemed would have suffered, what is gained? where is the goodness, where is the wisdom of God's wondrous plan of mercy? There is just as much suffering with the atonement as there would have been without it; and nothing, absolutely nothing is gained by this wondrous expedient, which fills all heaven with astonishment, which is to give its greatest glory and brightness to a world of light, and pour its richness and sweetness into its eternal song, but a simple transfer of punishment from the guilty to the innocent. We have no such idea of atonement. The sufferings of the Redeemer were indeed vicarious, strictly so, inasmuch as he stood in the place of man when he suffered—putting his endurances in the place of human punishment, endurances which deriving their value from the dignity of the sufferer, were a full equivalent for the punishment remitted, and served amply to compensate for the absence of its infliction.

I am perfectly aware, my brethren, that notwithstanding all these explanations, we may be told that we do not meet the real difficulty of the case, which grows out of the fact, that the doctrine of atonement still supposes, after all, a substitution of the innocent for the guilty, an exaction from one who never sinned of that which justice could claim from the transgressor alone; and there are not a few who think that such a substitution is wholly inconsistent with the principles of an upright administration; it supposes, we are told, God doing that which is unjust, in order to maintain justice.

And yet I cannot possibly see the difficulty, because I find the principle of the atonement, that of substitution, interwoven in the very texture of the human mind, and in all the operations of human society. Yes, this doctrine of men's being benefitted or injured by the acts of others, in which they took no part, is the very soul of the social system, the life-spring of intercourse among men, and the affairs of the world could not move on one step without it. We find the same principle pervading the administration of God; and while children suffer for the wickedness, or are blessed for the righteousness of their forefathers; while God pours out the vials of his wrath upon the posterity of those who betrayed his truth, and shed the blood of his people; while we read that "in Adam all die," and see thousands of Adam's children, before they can distinguish between their right hand and their left, writhing in agony, and sinking into death, in consequence of his transgression, in which they took no part, we have facts to prove that substitution is not inconsistent with God's administration, and that upon the very same principle upon which men die in Adam, they may be made alive in Christ.

Now, to apply this principle to the case in hand. If there is any injustice in the substitution of Christ, it must be injustice to the person who is forgiven, or injustice to Christ who suffered, or injustice to the interests of God's kingdom, which demanded the punishment of the offender. If the sinner is not injured, and Christ is not injured, and the kingdom of God is not injured, where is the injustice? In all earthly administration, a magistrate may do wrong in allowing a substitute to take the place of a murderer; that substitute may have no right to lay down his life, and the community might justly complain that a valuable member of society had been withdrawn in place of a worthless one, and that thus the securities of its interests were diminished rather than increased. But in the case of the atonement, Christ had a right over his own life, and voluntarily gave it for the life of men. Had it been otherwise, then the substitution would have been inadmissible. We admit, moreover, that any substitution, which would have told out in less impressive and overcoming tones, than the punishment of the transgressors would have done, thenature and consequences of sin, would have been inconsistent with God's character, and unjust, because injurious to the well-being of God's kingdom. But who can make such a supposition concerning the arrangement by virtue of which Christ "bare our sins in his own body on the tree"? Who will say that the majesty of law was less rigorously asserted, when he who was "in the beginning with God," sunk under his woes, than it would have been, had the whole population of the globe been ground to powder under the weight of divine indignation? Who will venture on the bold statement, that as piercing a voice would have gone out through the peopled immensity from the wailing cry of the lost children of our race, given up hopelessly to the penalties of their transgression, as now issues from the cross on which Christ was bruised by the Father, that he might reconcile man unto himself? So far from there being any room for such a supposition, if there is any thing which can make a man fear to sin, it is the atonement, in its mysterious awfulness. There is a power in the scenes of Gethsemane and Calvary, which could not be surpassed or equalled, if we had present before us all the torments of all the lost. The overwhelming thing about the atonement is that "God spared not his own Son." A substituted angel would have made sin appear "exceeding sinful;" but when we go beyond the angel, and have before us the substitute, incomprehensible indeed, yet confessedly "the brightness of his Father's glory, and the express image of his person;" when we find that his dignity is no shield against suffering, but that he is reckoned with rigidly and unflinchingly, so that the poison of death for a time overcomes him, oh! then there is set in array before us, such an exhibition of God's thoughts of sin, and determination to punish it, as leaves far behind the highest picture which the imagination can sketch, of the whole earth visited with the extreme of divine indignation. If thus there is no injury done to the securities of righteousness, which indeed are strengthened; if there is no injury done to Christ, who voluntarily became our surety; if no injury is done to us, who receive redemption through his blood, where is the injustice of that atonement which was wrought out by Christ's redeeming us from the curse of the law, as he became a curse for us?

This, my brethren, is the view of the nature of Christ's sacrificial offering, and its vindication, which I would desire to commend to your rational faith. And I am the more earnest in insisting upon clear views here, because I apprehend many have little or no distinct notion of atonement, and therefore are so easily carried about by every wind of doctrine. If we could but incorporate these views among men's elements of thought, we should be satisfied; we should fear neither the inroads of heresy on the one hand, nor the baneful influences of mere formalism on the other. Study the atonement, gain clear and discriminating views of the work of the Redeemer, and we know you will stand firmly by every essential principle of evangelical truth. Be loose, or wrong in your notions here, and in reference to no one point of religious truth can you have clear or correct apprehensions.

I insist upon clear views here, because without them, we cannot feel the power of the gospel. It is not the simple proffer of forgiveness, which gives to the gospel message such a penetrating and affecting character, but it is the awful, fearful, wonderful fact, upon which that offer is based. When we listen to the proclamations of the gospel, if we would feel their power, we must listen to them as utterances from the cross. It is not enough that there be laid before us a picture of man, brought out from that condition in which sin had placed him, and again brightening in the smile of his Maker. It is not enough, though it may waken in you emotions of gladness and wonder, that you should be addressed with the tidings of mercy, and that the ambassadors of God should make proclamation that pardon now requires only penitence. In that picture, radiant though it be with the glorious and the beautiful, there would be one spot hung with thick clouds and darkness, but from this spot would issue all the light which falls so beautifully and transportingly on every other part. We need not tell you, that this spot is Calvary—a spot on which, indeed, the sun dared not shine, but which, nevertheless, is the centre of illumination, whence the beams go forth to irradiate and give life to a world in the darkness and horror of spiritual death. With the gladdening proclamation of life, there should always be made mention of the dreadful death which secured it—the death, I need hardly tell you, of that mysterious being, that "word made flesh," who indeed yielded to the curse, but who by yielding, abolished it, yea, converted it into a blessing.

If we would feel the power of the reconciliation, we must understand the process by which it is brought about. It can hardly fail to make us listen with deeper interest to the offer of pardon, and shun with greater fear the idea of neglecting or resisting it. Christ, Christ in his deep, unknown, mysterious agony in the garden; Christ bearing our sins in his own body on the tree. Oh! remember, when in the Master's name we offer you forgiveness, it is the result of this untold anguish, this immeasurable sacrifice. And if you do, what a lesson does it teach you, not only of your own sinfulness, which demanded such an offering, but of the love of God which provided it. You cannot comprehend this thought without feeling that "herein is love." You may trace love in the arrangements of Providence, in the furniture of the universe, in the operations of nature; yet you must fall back upon the cross as that which transcends every other manifestation, and say, "herein is love." If it had not cost God much to redeem us, if man might have been saved as man had been created, by an act of will, by a word of mouth, then, perhaps, we should not have been staggered by the wonderfulness of the love. But when you remember the obstacles to be surmounted ere the purpose could be reached, when you remember that, unlike creation, redemption required an effort on the part of God, (and, oh! what an effort) you cannot fail to be confounded by the love, and to confess that of all mysterious, overpowering, subduing truths, this is the most mysterious, overpowering, subduing, and, at the same time, most encouraging. God gave his Son "to be the propitiation for our sins;" and when you go hence, take the gospel, read the account of the sufferings of Christ. Read it with true prayer to God that he would take away the "heart of stone," and give you "a heart of flesh;" and we cannot but think that you will know the gushings of a penitent and thankful spirit, and feel a thrill of joy and hope at the announcement. "Christ has redeemed us from the curse of the law, being made a curse for us."

EXTENT OF THE ATONEMENT.

"And he is the propitiation for our sins, and not for ours only, but also for the sins of the whole world."—FIRST EPISTLE OF ST. JOHN, ii. 2.

THE amplitude and all-sufficiency of God's provision for the lost, is a no less important article of the Christian faith, than the fact itself, that such a provision has been made. Every one must feel, the moment the subject is laid before him clearly, that the value of the atonement, to any one, is inseparable from its sufficiency for all. To tell me in my sorrows, under a sin-oppressed conscience, that provision is made for forgiveness, and yet to cast suspicion upon its fulness, is but to awaken a hope, the warrant of which is uncertain, because it leaves me entirely in the dark upon the question, whether that provision is within my reach. There is nothing here to relieve my straitened spirit, nothing to authorize my confidence; so far as all practical effects are concerned, I am in very much the same condition as before the announcement of pardon, through the atonement, was made. Better not say any thing of forgiveness of sin, if in the same breath you must suggest a doubt as to the possibility of my forgiveness. You do but make my case the more wretched, as you awaken a hope only for the purpose of destroying it.

The great question which throws its overwhelming burden upon the mind, in view of its spiritual relations, is, after all, a personal question—it relates to my own individual circumstances and hopes. The value of the gospel, therefore, to me as a sinner, grows out of the answer which it furnishes to this question. The mere fact that God can forgive sin, is nothing, except as it is brought home to my own personal interests. The pages upon which that fact is announced, may beam with the bright and the beautiful, but if they do not bring home to me, as an individual, this truth as a certainty, that God can be just and forgive my sin, they have no brightness and beauty for me; they do but put me in the condition of the famishing wretch, who is told of abundance, but not that he may touch it, or the victim of some dreadful disease, who is told of a certain remedy, but not how he may reach it.

The question, then, as to the extent of the atonement, is not a question, as some men would have us believe, of mere speculative theology, but one of vast practical interest. Every man can understand its importance, if he will but observe how the whole aspect of the gospel will vary; how its power over his own spirit will be increased or diminished, according to the views which he may take of this single question; and I cannot, therefore, think that I am giving myself up to a useless task, or one without its interest to all my hearers, when I undertake to agitate, for the purpose of reaching a satisfactory conclusion, the inquiry as to the extent of the atonement of Jesus Christ.

I need not say to my hearers, that in taking up this subject, we are entering upon disputed ground. The Christian world here presents to us opposite extremes of opinion, as well as diversities. If we except, on the one hand, those who put a limitation upon the intrinsic value of the Redeemer's sacrifice, who by a kind of arithmetical process, estimate the worth of atonement by the number of those whom it actually saves; and on the other hand, those who infer universal salvation as a necessary consequence from the atonement of Jesus Christ—extremes of opinion held by comparatively few in the Christian church, and with neither of which we can sympathize—the remaining discrepancies are, I apprehend, for the most part, the result rather of misapprehension, than of any opposition of view. It is perfectly obvious, that the same object will strike persons differently, as they look upon it from different points, and consider it in different relations; while if they look upon it in the same light, they are perfectly harmonious in their views. So the man who looks at the sacrifice of Christ, in view of some secret purpose of God, and of the actual results which shall flow from it, becomes the stern and unflinching advocate of limited atonement, and seems to be directly at war with another, who, looking at the intrinsic nature of the sacrifice of Christ, and its adaptation to other and larger, and more general results, becomes the no less stern and

18

unflinching advocate of unlimited atonement, while in reality the difference of opinion between them is not what at first sight it might appear to be.

In defining my own position, and stating what I consider to be the scriptural truth upon the subject, I must be permitted to exhibit what I consider to be the true state of the question, so as to prevent all possibility of misconception.

There is, I apprehend, a distinction to be always carefully maintained, between the work of atonement and the work of redemption. The one does not necessarily imply the other; redemption includes atonement, but it includes more; it includes its actual results; it is the application of the atonement issuing in final and complete salvation. The one, therefore, in its nature may be more extensive than the other. An unredeemed sinner has even now a deep interest in the atoning sacrifice of Jesus Christ, and whether eventually lost or saved, will feel that interest through the ages of his deathless being. With this understanding, redemption certainly is not general; and to affirm that it is limited is but stating the plainly revealed fact, that all men will not be saved.

In the view which we take of the subject, moreover, we separate the nature of the atonement from any secret unrevealed purpose of the infinite mind respecting its application. We do not deny the existence of such a purpose; so far from it that we cannot conceive of an intelligent, all-wise being acting in any thing without design, and we cannot, without detracting from the honour and glory of him who is no less wise than holy in all his works, suppose otherwise than that in this great plan, and I may add effort of forgiving mercy, he had in view some certain, specific results. We do not believe that the issue of the atonement is in the infinite mind an open question. The results of a Redeemer's work are not contingent results. They are absolutely certain. It is fixed, unalterably fixed, that the Saviour is to be rewarded for his life of toil and ignominy, and his death of shame and agony. He is to "see of the travail of his soul and to be satisfied;" and a multitude greater than any man can number, of those who "have washed their robes, and made them white in the blood of the Lamb," shall give grace and glory to his triumph. But the ultimate design of the atonement as it exists in the mind of God, is a very different thing from the nature of the atonement itself, as it is spread out before our view upon the pages of revealed truth. The question before us is not, what God intends to accomplish by virtue of the sacrifice of Christ; not how far the efficacy of that sacrifice will in point of fact reach; for upon these questions God has thrown a veil of impenetrable darkness; but what is the great moral, revealed purpose of the atonement; what is its intrinsic value and sufficiency; how far is it available in its own nature to the salvation of men? Did God mean to spread it over only a part, or the whole of the race? Are men, all men, as lost sinners, so interested in the atoning death of Jesus Christ, that they may, if they will, be saved by it? This is the question, and we unhesitatingly take the affirmative. Our position is, that through the sacrifice of Christ, God can be just, and yet forgive. Such is the character of the atonement, that "it would comport with the glory of the divine character, the sustentation of God's government, the obligation and honour of his law, and the good of the rational and moral system, to save all men, provided they accepted of Christ." "Every legal bar and obstruction in the way of the salvation of all men is removed."* Such is the nature and efficacy of the atonement of the Son of God, that the relations not merely of some men, but of the entire race, are totally different from what they would have been, had the Saviour never suffered and died; different, I mean, in this sense, that since this great atoning sacrifice has been offered, God can upon the ground of it consistently pardon the sins of all, and nothing now shuts a man out from forgiveness and hope, but his own unwillingness to accept of the offers of mercy made to him in the gospel. Such is the view of the fulness of the atonement which we desire to advocate, and which we would fain commend to the intelligent faith of our hearers.

And in proceeding to the illustration of this general view, I cannot but think that we have, at least, strong presumptive proof of its correctness in that characteristic of universality which marks other of God's dispensations. All the laws by which he governs the different systems are general in their character, all his arrangements for our world

* Associate Reformed Synod's Report, p. 53.

are made upon general principles. He has placed his sun in the heavens to give light unto every man who cometh into the world. He sendeth his rain upon the entire surface of the earth. "He causeth his sun to rise upon the evil and the good, and his rains to descend upon the just and the unjust." The same thing would be true though the population of the world were increased a thousand fold, and the earth's surface vastly enlarged. In this case, we should need no other sun to lighten the world, no other laws to regulate the earth's productiveness under the refreshing showers of heaven; and though half the population of the world should be smitten with blindness, still the sun would shine as brightly as ever, and still it would be true that it would enlighten the world, and the rains fall upon the sterile earth and the impervious rock as well as upon the thirsty fields and the fertile soil. It is changing the question entirely, and carrying the mind away to another subject altogether, to say that God did not surely mean, when he put his sun in the heavens, to give light unto him who refused to open his eyes; or when he sent his rain upon the earth, to fructify the barren rock. We would consider him a very silly reasoner who should argue against the general character of God's arrangements for the natural system, from the fact that some men could not or would not open their eyes; and the fact that the earth presented a surface as well of rock as of soil. All we need to establish the general nature of his provision, is, that the sun is designed to give light to all who will open their eyes to behold it, and the rain is designed to refresh and fructify the earth wherever there is a capacity of production. That man certainly does not understand God's works, who imagines that if one now blind should recover his sight, a new sun must be created, or the light of the present sun must be increased; or if a single pebble upon the earth's surface should be converted into soil, a new arrangement must be made to meet the increased demand for moisture. The light of the sun is enough for all; the rains of heaven are enough for all. And if a man does not see the light, the reason is in himself and not in the sun, or in any purpose of God respecting its nature when he set the sun in the firmament; and if the surface of the earth is not fertile, the reason must be in itself, not in the rain which descends upon it, nor in any purpose of God which respects its falling.

This illustration, which we have borrowed from analogy, is perfectly simple and level to the comprehension of every one; and so far as the argument from analogy goes, it demonstrates the general character of Christ's atonement, and meets and removes all the objections which are usually urged against it. If, when we pass over the line which separates the spiritual from the natural world, we are arrested in our progress, and told that the two are entirely distinct from each other, and therefore the principles of the one do not and cannot furnish us with any key to the interpretation of the principles of the other, we cannot be considered unreasonable, if we are not satisfied with a mere assumption, and ask for some proof of the doctrine which is thus unceremoniously thrown in our pathway. For ourselves, we believe that in the respects already mentioned, the provisions of God in the natural and spiritual worlds run perfectly parallel with each other. The same characteristic of universality belongs to both, and the same difficulties (if any) are found in both. And we question whether a single objection to a general atonement can be brought forward, which may not be urged with equal force against plain and palpable facts.

Having cast our eye abroad over the arrangements of nature, and observed the principles by which they are all manifestly pervaded, we turn now to the word of revelation, which unfolds God's gracious arrangements for the spiritual world, that we may see how far they sustain us in our supposition of the parallel between the dispensations of nature and of grace.

And here you cannot fail to be struck, my brethren, with the character of universality which marks the terms in which the Bible speaks of the sacrificial work of Jesus Christ. "God so loved the world, that he gave his only begotten Son, that whosoever believeth in him might not perish, but might have everlasting life." "Christ gave himself a ransom for all." He is "the Lamb of God, who taketh away the sin of the world." "He was made a little lower than the angels, that he by the grace of God should taste death for every man;" and "he is the propitiation for our sins, and not for ours only, but also for the sins of the whole world." Language like this cannot well be mistaken. I may add, it can have no meaning, if it does not convey distinctly the idea, that every member of our apostate race has a positive interest in the atonement of Jesus Christ.

To a certain extent, this general thought is admitted, even by those who question the universality of the atonement as a spiritual provision. It is not denied that the arrangements of God, so far as man's interests for time are concerned, are very essentially modified by the mediation of Jesus Christ. There is not a human being in our world, believer or unbeliever, whose circumstances are not, at the present moment, vastly different from what they would have been, had the Redeemer never suffered and died. This much, at least, has been effected by his intervention, that the execution of the curse has been staid, and men, though sinners, live in a world of light and peace. The comforts of men's earthly lot, the joys of their social condition, and all the circumstances which make this a pleasant world, are the result of the grace which is in Christ Jesus. The sinner farthest from God, may learn his interest in the atonement, from the arrangements of his earthly circumstances; and the veriest outcast of wickedness might be taught a lesson of his obligation to redeeming love, by the very forbearance of his insulted Maker, which that love alone has secured. In this sense, then, and to this extent certainly, all men have, without exception, an interest in the sacrifice of Christ, as there is no man who does not enjoy some good as the result of that sacrifice.

And why should it be otherwise, when we come to look at the atonement as a spiritual provision? Why should not its nature be as extensive with regard to man's eternal as to man's temporal interests? If its primary reference is to the former, why should its main be more restricted than its incidental design? But we come again to "the word and the testimony," and there we read that the gospel is "glad tidings of great joy which shall be to all people;" we are commanded to "preach the gospel," as a system of forgiving mercy, "to every creature." Our commission recognizes no distinctions among those to whom we are sent; our message is a message for the world, for the whole world, for every individual of this whole world's population; its language is, "Ho every one that thirsteth, come unto the waters; let him that heareth say, come, and let him that is athirst come, and whosoever will let him come, and take of the water of life freely."

"Rivers of love and mercy here,
In a rich ocean join;
Salvation in abundance flows
Like floods of milk and wine."

I confess, my brethren, I do not understand the gospel, if this is not one of its cardinal doctrines; if the indiscriminate offer of Jesus Christ, and of pardon and eternal life through him, is not made to the race, and as truly and honestly and sincerely made to one individual as another of the race. This, I apprehend, is its great central point of light and power, which gives meaning and beauty and consistency to the system, without a clear apprehension of which the whole seems but a formless mass. If the entire population of the globe were before me, and there should be one in the mighty assembly for whom there was no provision, I could not preach the gospel; for how could I say in sincerity and honesty to all and to each, come and take of the waters of life freely?

Such are the views I take of the offer of the gospel; and though for the ultimate authority of these views we must and do fall back upon "the word and the testimony of God," as the only reason of faith, yet it may give strength in many minds to our position, if we can sustain it by the authority, likewise, of human opinions, as put forth by those who have been considered standards in the interpretation of the sacred oracles; while, at the same, it may serve to wipe off the obloquy which ignorance has thrown upon them as men of narrow and contracted views. I do but quote the language of one whose name I bear, and whom I honour not less as a spiritual progenitor than as a father after the flesh, when I say, that in the gospel "God hath made a grant of his Son Jesus Christ, as an all-sufficient Saviour to a lost and perishing world; he hath not merely revealed a general knowledge of him, but has distinctly and solemnly given him to sinners *as such, that they may be saved.* The gift is indiscriminately to all the hearers of the gospel, and to every one of them in particular."*

There is, however, something more than this. The gospel is not simply an offer of mercy, it is a law. It has its own duties, and prescribes its own penalties. It does not simply make it the privilege, but the duty of all men, without exception, to embrace Jesus Christ, and to accept the offer of forgiveness which is made to them. It makes the question of eternal life or eternal death to every hearer of the gospel to hinge upon his acceptance of proffered mercy, coming to him on the ground and through the provisions of the atonement of Christ. "This is the commandment of God, that we should believe on the name of his Son Jesus Christ." He is set before us, before every one of us, in all his fulness and freeness, and it is at our peril if we reject or neglect him. With these views of the gospel offer, I cannot advocate a limited atonement; I cannot put a restriction of the provision which I do not find in the offer; I cannot believe that God would make to a sinner in his wants and his woes the tender of a relief which did not exist, or which he did not wish him to embrace; I cannot believe that God would command his creatures to embrace a provision which had never been made for them, or sanction by the peril of one's everlasting interests a commandment which he never meant should be obeyed, and which itself precluded the possibility of obedience.

* Act concerning Justification. Mason's Works.—Vol. iii. pp. 321, 322.

It does not at all meet the difficulty of the case to say, at this point, that we are required thus indiscriminately to offer the gospel, and thus to enforce its acceptance upon all, because we do not know the persons for whom the provision is made, and whom God designs shall accept it. The offer is not ours; we are but the channel through which it comes. God himself makes the offer; we but take up God's words, and announce them as he has given them to us. We are ambassadors of Christ, not speaking in our own name, but according to our instructions, which bind us to say to each and every one of our hearers, "Come, for all things are now ready.." In this matter we have no responsibility beyond the simple utterance of the message, "This is the will of God, that ye believe on him whom he hath sent;" and the question returns upon us, how can we reconcile a universal offer with a limited provision? How can we acquit God of the charge of insincerity in making to men a tender, and enforcing upon them by the high sanctions of eternity the acceptance of that which not only was never designed for them in any sense, but which, in fact, has never been provided?

And yet it is said, at this point, "the Lord knoweth them that are his; it is not a matter of doubtfulness to him, who sees the end from the beginning, who shall and who shall not be saved through the atonement; he has his all-wise purposes in reference to this subject, and the final result will not vary one hair's breadth from his purpose;" and while the truth of this principle is claimed from us, and cheerfully admitted by us, the difficulty of the subject is supposed to be thrown over upon ourselves, as the question is retorted upon us, how can we reconcile a universal offer with God's secret purpose; an unrestricted provision with a well-known definite and limited result? Why should God make a provision to an extent he knew would be unnecessary, and be guilty of an expenditure beyond what the well-known circumstances of the case required? If he knew that in many cases the atonement would be rejected, why for such cases provide an atonement? If he saw distinctly that there would be some, and knew who they were, who would treat the blood of the covenant as an unholy thing, where the honesty of pressing it upon their acceptance, and bringing such mighty sanctions to bear upon them to enforce obedience?

I do not know, my brethren, a better example than the foregoing questions furnish, of that rule of logic which forbids us to allow a weak argument to stand isolated and unprotected, and requires us to combine such arguments and present them in one view, so that they may help each other, and have the appearance, at least, of overwhelming force. When you take all the questions together, they seem to have no little weight; but when taken singly they are wholly pointless and irrelevant.

For we may ask in return, what has any secret purpose to do with our rule of judgment and action? "Secret things," we are told, "belong unto the Lord our God; but things which are revealed, unto us and to our children." The question taken from the hidden purposes of the divine mind, can have no force whatever, because it is an appeal to our ignorance. We know, and can know nothing about them. One thing, however, we do know. God must be always and every where consistent with himself; and whether we can understand it or not, it is certain that there can be no inconsistency between revealed and unrevealed truths; and if God has made an offer of eternal life through the atonement unto all men, and commanded all men to embrace it, there cannot be in any purpose of God concerning its nature, any thing which will clash with, and so contradict this universal offer.

This argument, however, from God's purposes, which is so often brought forward to limit the nature and availableness of Christ's atonement, like many other arguments, destroys itself by proving too much. With equal pertinacity, it might be brought forward to put restrictions upon the law of God, and prove it not to be a law for the race. No fact is more palpable to human observation than that the requirements of God do not bind all men. This is a sinful world; the race is corrupt; men have thrown off their obligations to their Creator, and have turned rebels against his rightful authority. And God knew beforehand that it would be so. Every thing has eventuated in precise accordance with God's expectations. And now we turn the question, and ask, is not the law of God a law for the race? Was it not designed for and adapted to secure the obedience and happiness of the race? Did not God mean that it should be obeyed? And where is the consistency of his publishing such a law, and enforcing it with the tremendous sanctions of his eternal throne, when he knew beforehand that it would not be obeyed? Look at these questions for a moment, and as you see the absurdity involved in them, you can judge whether they are not quite as pertinent, and do not contain an argument quite as forcible as those by which some men would attempt to put restrictions upon the atonement of Jesus Christ, when they ask where is the wisdom, where the consistency of preaching an unlimited provision, and the sincerity of enforcing it universally, when it was well known beforehand that it would not be universally accepted.

And now, if you still press the question, why should God make provision for forgiveness, to an extent he knew would be unnecessary, and be guilty of an expenditure of means beyond what the well known circumstances of the case required? We answer, by referring you to the characteristic of universality, to which we have already adverted, as marking his dispensations in the natural world, and ask you why his sun shines and wastes its beams upon sightless eye-balls, or upon those who will not open their eyes to behold his goodly rays? Why does he send his rains upon the barren rock, or waste his showers upon the sandy and sterile soil, in which the seed can never vegetate? If I propose this question, you tell me in reply, that I mistake altogether the nature of God's creations, and the general principles of the system which he has established. You tell me that the necessity for the sun being what it is, does not depend upon the number of the persons who are to be enlightened by his rays, but grows out of the fact that it must be what it is to give light to any one—that atmospheric laws are general, and cannot in their nature be so arranged as to secure the descent of rain only where it will render the earth productive. You cannot consider that there is any waste of light or moisture, because there are some who do not see, or because in some places the surface of the earth presents the impervious rock to the rains of heaven.

We admit the explanation, and falling back upon the authority we have already quoted, we use it in reference to our present subject. The spiritual system, as well as the natural system, is governed by general laws—and the atonement of Christ must be general. "Its necessity does not arise from the number of sinners, but from the nature of sin. The very nature of sin requires an infinite atonement in order to its honorable remission. Such an atonement as Christ offered, was indispensably necessary to the pardon of one act of sin"—and as the sun must be what it is, whether it lightens one man, or every man who cometh into the world, so it makes no difference as to the nature or availableness of the sufferings of Christ, whether one sinner, or a race of sinners, is to be saved by them. There is no more waste or unnecessary expenditure in the one case than in the other.

And yet, my brethren, I feel that I would be doing injustice to you and my subject, did I here arrest my remarks. In advocating the doctrine of unlimited atonement, I am not advocating the doctrine of universal salvation. There is a limitation to the application of the atonement. It reaches not to all men. It reaches only to those who embrace it. God pardons not the sin of unbelief, because that is a rejection of his only method of pardon. Upon the ground of Christ's propitiation, he can be just, while he justifies him who believeth. He can save any man who accepts of Christ, he can save none who refuse him. And this is the limitation we are required to preach to you, and the only limitation we dare put upon the suffering of an Infinite Saviour. And in behalf of the correctness of these general views, we summon the evidence of every enlightened conscience, and the experience of the lost. Those self-reprovings which often trouble the spirit of the worldly-minded, when he turns away from the offer of a free salvation, have their origin in the distinct conviction that he is shutting himself out from hope and forgiveness. It would hush many a clamour of an injured conscience, it would obliterate in many a mind that deep sense of guilt which disquiets and harasses it, could man but satisfy himself that forgiveness is beyond his reach, and that the atonement of the Son of God was never meant for him. But he cannot do it. No arts of sophistry, no special pleading, can convince any one that he is innocent in "neglecting the great salvation." Every man feels that he might be saved if he would be, and that very feeling tallies exactly with the teachings of the Bible, which shew us unbelief, and nothing else, as the barrier to eternal life. The same feeling will be deeper and more distinct hereafter, and go to form one of the most effective elements in that poison cup from which the spirit lost will for ever drink. The man who fails of the great salvation, will stand speechless before his Judge; the vain apologies of earthly impenitence, will not bear looking at in the light of eternity. And when the wretched victim of abused mercy and a neglected gospel, shall self-convicted go to his final allotment, as he begins to sink in his deep perdition, remorse, undying remorse, will prey upon his spirit; and as he sees in the mighty, and still increasing distance, the brightening glories which cluster around those who have washed their robes, and made them white in the blood of the Lamb, oh! this will be of all the most overwhelming thought, I might have been there, but I chose death.

My brethren, I am commanded to preach to you, to-day, a full and perfected atonement. I preach Jesus Christ as an all-sufficient Saviour for each and every one of you. God says to you, "come, for all things are now ready." Whosoever will, may take of the waters of life, freely. I wish you to take home this subject as a personal matter—I speak to you in the name of my Master, as individuals. If you never have been placed in such close contact with your Saviour before, I would place you, my hearer, as an individual, in this close contact with him, this morning ; I would testify to you, to-day, in behalf of the gospel. I would testify to you that you are a sinner, under condemnation ; that God offers to save you from your ruin by the mediation of his Son. I testify to you, that if you would no more make sure to yourself an eternity of anguish and remorse, you must rise at once and accept of this offer of forgiveness and eternal life ; I testify to you, to-day, my hearer, by the majesty of God, by a deluged world, by the sufferings of Calvary, by the death-beds of saints, by the wailings of the reprobate, by the anthems of the ransomed, that everlasting life is placed within your reach. But if you refuse to lay hold upon this hope set before you, there remaineth no more sacrifice for sin ; there can be no propitiation for him who rejects the propitiation, and you must go down to the grave and enter upon an eternal scene unforgiven, unsaved, lost for ever. You may be indifferent, you may go away from the house of God careless about Christ as you entered it, but here is the point—I wish you to ponder it—believe me, there is meaning and truth and power in it. Though you should never hear my voice again, as a messenger of the truth, I have fastened myself to you, and time cannot wear away the links, and the earthquakes of the last day cannot dissolve them. I could not keep back the testimony I have already given you, in the words you have heard, words which express nothing but the simple, well-known truths of the Bible. They have sprung forward, and they cannot be recalled ; you have heard them, they have written themselves in God's book, and oceans cannot expunge them; and, when we shall meet again, hereafter, and memory, to which God shall have given such a resuscitating power that the events of every day and every hour shall come back in their order and freshness, and shall present this our assembly, and recall this my testimony, it is not being too bold in imagining the stirrings and heavings of the thoughts, when "the great white throne" is erected, to suppose that there will arise in your bosoms, and in my bosom, the feeling that the ministry so imperfectly discharged, is nevertheless fulfilling itself with terrible accuracy.

My brethren, there are great ends to be answered by the infinite atonement of the Son of God, and by this testimony to its fulness and all-sufficiency, which I give you to-day—ends to be answered in the experience of those who reject it as well as in the experience of those who receive it. I would not attempt to be wise above what is written. But yet I know that the testimony which I give to you, in behalf of Christ, though it may seem not to prevail with you, is not fruitless. There is no more waste in preaching, than there has been in making an atonement which is not received. The precious seed which, Sabbath after Sabbath, is thrown out upon the moral desert, which resists and sets at naught all the diligence of the husbandman, is not lost. It will bring forth fruit—the broad field upon which at last shall be gathered the sublime, and awful, and mysterious, and stirring magnificence of the end, is white unto the harvest. Every grain is there giving produce —every particle of gospel truth springs up and waves on that awful field. I preach for a testimony—oh! it is in feebleness I speak. I cannot throw might into my language. I cannot breathe words which shall take a lasting form and substance, and fall upon my worldly-minded hearers —but yet they die not. I seem already to hear their reverberation from a thousand echoes, louder and louder, and deeper and deeper, responding to the anthems of the saved, or the bitter and deep-toned knell which shall be rung over lost spirits. God prepare us, my brethren, for the end.

MAN UNWILLING TO BE SAVED.

"Whosoever will, let him take the water of life freely."—REVELATION xxii. 17.

THE statement which thus closes the book of God's inspiration, is no more remarkable than interesting. "The Spirit and the bride say, come. And let him that heareth say, come. And let him that is athirst, come. And whosoever will, let him take the water of life freely." No salvation but one absolutely free, could justify such language; none but an all-sufficient atonement for sin could warrant an offer so unlimited. It seems to be the spirit of the testimony of Jesus, concentrated in a last appeal to those for whom he died. As we dare not add to, or detract from either the fulness or freeness of the offer, but at the peril of the heaviest plagues which are written in the book of God, we can say nothing less of the gospel, than that it is a message for the lost, for all the lost; for men of all climes, all classes, all conditions; men of every shade and variety of character, men in all the supposable circumstances in which any of the race can be found. Thus it sets before each and all, an open door of life, which no man can shut. All the blessings purchased through a Redeemer's death, symbolized by "the water of life," are brought within their reach. There is light for those who are in darkness, pardon for those who are guilty, purity for the vile, strength for the weak, joy for the sorrowing, hope for the desponding, life for the dead. "Whosoever will," and here is the only limitation which the Bible puts upon either the efficacy of the atonement, or the offer which it publishes, "Whosoever will may take of the water of life freely." Beyond all question, then, the position in which the gospel places the man to whom it comes, is one where every external obstacle to his salvation is removed, and where, if he will, he may have eternal life. Looking at this truth from one direction, it is the most precious and delightful truth which can be commended to the human mind; looking at it from another direction it is the most solemn truth which can engage human thought. That there is forgiveness for the guilty, and hope for the lost,—who does not hail the announcement, that has ever felt himself to be a sinner, and has apprehended the retributions of eternity? and what voice can be more cheering to the man who is no more aware of his indebtedness than of his inability to meet it, than one which assures him that salvation is "without money and without price?"

But then, is it not so, in view of the fulness and freeness of God's provisions and arrangements, that the responsibility of the result rests with man himself? Is the gospel of Jesus Christ, as thus we look at it, any more the measure of the rich grace of God, than it is of our obligation? Had the provision been less full, or its offer been less free and untrammelled, our responsibility had been proportionably less. Every restriction you put upon the fulness of the gospel is a limitation put upon human duty; and in proportion as you impair its freeness, you take off from the weight it throws upon the human conscience. If you insist upon a full and free salvation, you must take it in all its necessary connections and results—and there is no truth which its fulness and freeness more conclusively demonstrates than this, that every man to whom the message of Christ comes, is responsible for his failure to secure eternal life. To all his reasonings to the contrary, to all his suggestions of difficulty in the way of pardon and acceptance with God, we oppose the simple language of the text, which, if it means any thing, teaches us beyond all controversy, that since Christ has died and the offer of salvation in his name has gone forth to the world, nothing can shut a man out from eternal life, but an unwillingness to embrace the offer.

It is this simple truth (as a fitting and legitimate inference from previous discourses) that we wish to commend to the minds of our hearers, in the hope (God grant that it may not be a vain one) of leading them to a clear perception and a just appreciation of their circumstances as subjects of the gospel of Jesus Christ.

The point then which we design to illustrate

this morning seems to grow necessarily out of a clear and consistent view of the Saviour's atonement. The glory of the gospel as a revelation of that atonement is found in the fact that it represents every external obstacle over which man had no control removed out of the way of eternal life. As a sinner, man has put himself in a position of utter helplessness; do what he may, he never can amend the past so as to correct his errors, or recover what he has forfeited by transgression. If eternal life is brought within his reach, it must be by virtue of some provision which shall relieve him from this difficulty, and place him in circumstances where the responsibility of past transgression may be removed from his conscience. To meet this exigency is the design of the sacrificial offering of Jesus Christ, which demonstrates its value in the assurance which it gives, that God can be just and yet forgive. Now it must be perfectly obvious to the most superficial thinker, that if any outward obstacle of this kind remained, the atonement of the Son of God is a failure, because it does not meet all the difficulties it was designed to remove. If God could not be just and forgive all a man's sins, it is, so far as the result is concerned, the same as though he could not forgive any of his sins; upon such a supposition the offer of eternal life could not be laid before any man. No less manifest is it that if there is a single human being, all of whose outward difficulties the atonement does not meet, there is one to whom the offer of eternal life cannot honestly be made; and upon either supposition the language, "whosoever will may take of the waters of life freely," involves a palpable contradiction of the truth. The free and unlimited offer of the gospel, therefore, necessarily involves a provision for all human wants, a removal of all external obstacles, a provision of unlimited value and unrestricted sufficiency, a provision within the reach of every one to whom it is presented, and who is charged with its acceptance upon the peril of eternal death. For ourselves we cannot see how you can separate such an offer from man's responsibility as to the result. The two doctrines must stand or fall together. If it is true, that whosoever will may take of the waters of life freely, it must be true that if man partakes not, it is because he will not.

Of the position which we here assume, every man carries within him the most clear and convincing evidence. No testimony, upon any point, is more conclusive than that which is furnished by human consciousness. If I do not know that I exist, I do not know any thing; and yet consciousness is the grand evidence of my existence. If I do not know that I am free in my actions, I do not know any thing, for consciousness is the evidence of my freedom. It is the glory of my nature, as an intelligent and moral being, that I choose my own course, and fix my own position; I may not be able to answer all the metaphysical questions you may propound to me upon this subject, nor to meet and overthrow all the subtle arguments which would convert me into a machine, or a victim of uncontrollable fate, and perhaps I might suggest some puzzling inquiries as to the reality of your existence; but you consider all my inquiries as I do all your subtleties, wholly forceless, because they are every one of them met and refuted by the testimony of consciousness. And does human consciousness, my brethren, bear no testimony as to the position which every man occupies in reference to the gospel? Go catechize the man who has found peace at the foot of the cross, and who rejoices in the hope which that cross has brought nigh unto him, and he will testify that in no act which he ever performed was he more conscious of his perfect freedom, than when he embraced the offer of eternal life, made to him by Jesus Christ. The impenitent and unbelieving hearer of the gospel gives a no less forceful testimony—the consciousness of his own spirit is the best answer to all the arguments by which he would throw off from himself the responsibility of his unbelief. Talk as he may of his peculiar circumstances, as interfering with his submission to Jesus Christ, when he comes closely to scrutinize them, he finds, for the most part, that they are circumstances of his own arrangement, and even when they are not, they are no farther hindrances in the way of life, than as his own heart has invested them with preventive power. Talk as he may of the obscurity which rests upon the pages of the gospel, preventing a clear perception of the principles they unfold, he perceives them with sufficient distinctness to know that they involve truths which are dis tasteful to his mind, and enforce claims to which he is unwilling to submit. The difficulties of religion are not found in its obscurities—the insuperable obstacles to obedience are not found in any outward circumstances—a child has understood the gospel so as to embrace it, and men have walked with God, in the midst of abounding sensuality and crime. But those difficulties are found in the spiritualities of the gospel, in the holiness of its principles, and the self-denying nature of its duties; the child of sense will not govern himself by faith, the being of earthliness will not submit to spiritual influences, and the slave of appetite will not put a curb upon his passions. Did men but love the truth as they love error, love holiness as they love sin, regard the glory of God as they do their selfish gratifications, the obstacles to religion would vanish, and the path of life would be as plain and as easy to travel as is now the path into which their desires lead them.

There are moments in every man's history, when the truth of these remarks and of the position they are designed to illustrate, comes home to him with irresistible power; they are moments when conscience breaks loose from the trammels which sin had thrown around it, and emerges from the darkness in which sin had enwrapped it, and acts in the light of the gospel; they are moments of self-reflection, sometimes deep and overwhelming, in view of a neglect of the great salvation. Not one who hears me, and is not in reality a Christian disciple, but feels, and often deeply, that in reference to the claims of the gospel, he ought to be vastly different from what he is. And yet, my brethren, we never reflect upon ourselves, in view of events which are wholly beyond our control. We may mourn over their occurrence, and bitterly lament their influence, as it defeats our plans and desolates our joys, but they inflict no wound like that of conscious guilt. The self-condemnation of the unbeliever, is the testimony which his own spirit yields to the truth, that he might be different from what he is; that the responsibility of his present position, and of all its apprehended necessary consequences, rests entirely upon himself; and so in the workings of his own mind he is illustrating at one and the same time the fulness and freeness of the provisions of the gospel, and the doctrine which our Saviour advanced as the exponent of man's unblessed condition, when he said, "Ye will not come unto me that ye might have life. And in view of this testimony of con sciousness, harmonizing as it does so perfectly with the plain statements of the word of God, will any man who is out of Christ presume to throw off from himself the responsibility of his hopeless condition? Will he undertake to say that the question of his eventual safety is one the decision of which is so wholly independent of himself, that feel and choose as he may, the final result can in no way be affected by the operations of his own mind, and the state of his own heart? Is there one of my unconverted hearers who can look at the plain statements of the word of God, and at his own experience, so fully accordant as it is with all the principles which those statements involve, and then define his circumstances as those of one against whom the straight gate is closed by a power over which he has no control, and in whose pathway to eternal life there are insuperable obstacles, whose existence and magnitude are wholly independent of his own feelings. In taking such a position, man must array himself not only against God, whose truth he disputes, but against his own spirit—whose evidence he rejects. He has here nothing upon which he can fall back for support in this unequal and painful controversy. So far from it, that when God throws upon him the fearful responsibility of the issue of his course, and he examines the testimony of his own consciousness upon the subject, it tells him that in a moral point of view he is precisely what he chooses to be; that the path upon which he is travelling, leading him, as he sees it does, away from the forgiveness, and peace, and hope of the gospel, is the one which, upon the whole, is preferable to his mind; and thus, out of deference to the desires of his own heart, which cling to the vanities, and pleasures, and honours of this perishable world,—in the face of motives, infinite as God can make them, forceful as the retributions of a coming scene, bright as the fascinations, and dark as the forbidding gloom of an eternal world, he turns away from an offered salvation, and with his own hand, closes against himself the gate of heaven, and puts the seal upon his everlasting destiny. For this controversy between

God and man, God has the human spirit on his own side, and no one can wring from it a testimony in contradiction of the statement of the Saviour, "Ye will not come unto me, that ye might have life."

The doctrine of man's responsibility for his own salvation which we have thus deduced from the free offer of the gospel, and which we have seen to be so fully sustained by the testimony of human consciousness, so far as human consciousness can give its testimony upon such a point, I may here add is not only uncontradicted by, but is in perfect keeping with the entire strain of the inspired record. The whole Bible is throughout perfectly consistent with itself. There is a beautiful harmony subsisting between its different truths, which, like the different parts of an edifice, all in keeping with each other, indicate one design and one designer. Any alleged discrepancy between one and another statement of the sacred oracles is apparent only, resulting from the medium through which we look at them; correct the medium and the discrepancy vanishes. I advert to this fact, because of the contrariety which has been supposed to exist between the position I have assumed and some of the acknowledged doctrines of the inspired volume. It is not without an air of apparent triumph that we are sometimes called upon to reconcile our statement of human responsibility with such doctrines, for example, as that of human dependence, which refers the conversion of the soul to the grace of God as its only efficient, adequate cause, and the sovereign agency of the Almighty, which we are told respects results in the spiritual as well as the natural world, and without which no event of any kind, much less such an event as that of the salvation of the soul, can possibly occur. An appeal like this demands the attention of the expositor of truth, not more with the view of relieving an honest mind of its difficulty, than of removing the obstacle which false apprehensions interpose between the conscience and the full force of revealed truth.

We admit then the scriptural doctrine of human dependence. We admit that men are "born not of blood, nor of the will of the flesh, nor of the will of man, but of God." The Spirit of grace and truth must breathe upon the dry bones, ere they live. It is the mighty power of God, by which a man is brought from the error of his ways, to embrace an offered salvation. We admit, moreover, that there is something, at first sight, exceedingly plausible in the assertion, that an effect which demands superhuman agency for its production must be beyond the reach of human effort, however disposed the heart may be towards it. The special agency of the Holy Spirit, is the standing argument of a deceitful heart against the doctrine which I now inculcate. It is sufficient, however, to strip this objection of all its speciousness, to direct our attention, for a moment, to the reasons out of which grows the necessity for this wondrous agency. If any man supposes—I know the Bible does not teach him—that the special influence of the Spirit of God is designed to remodel him as a rational being. It does not involve, by even the remotest implication, the idea that either the elements or laws of our mental organization must undergo a change, in order that we may become new creatures in Christ Jesus. We repudiate such fatalism as unworthy of a thinking man, and hurl back upon its authors, as dishonouring to God, the imputation which it casts upon his revealed truth. The spiritual change upon which the Bible insists, is a change of feelings and passions, hopes and joys, rules and ends of action. The Spirit of the living God, in translating a man from the kingdom of darkness into that of his dear Son, does not give him a heart, but a new disposition of heart—does not give a man affections, but new objects of affections. He is "alienated from the life of God, through the ignorance that is in him, because of the blindness of his heart." The difficulty of his case is, not that he cannot embrace Christ, if he will, but that he will not embrace him. The Spirit acts upon the heart, and man becomes "willing in the day of God's power"—and the difference between what he is and what he was, the secret of his wondrous change lies in this, that he loves what formerly he hated, and hates what formerly he loved.

Do not suppose for a moment, my brethren, that I have lost sight of human depravity, or that I am disposed to fritter it away, or make any less of it than does the word of God. Human depravity, who doubts it? Who that calmly studies human nature, or analyses his own experience, will question either its reality or extent? I do not need an argument to prove it. I will not insult the understanding of my hearers, by constructing an argument to demonstrate it to their minds. We do not need it, when we can see for ourselves, how men treat the things of God. We do not need it, when we can see men treading day by day upon the very verge of an eternal world, and though they behold one and another dropping hourly into its retributions, living as secure and careless about futurity, as though God has stamped immortality upon their present mode of existence. We do not need the argument while this sanctuary stands; and the messages of mercy tell no more of the kindness of heaven, than does their fruitlessness tell of man's deafness to the voice which utters them, and his insensibility to the thrilling motives which enforce them. And yet I find I have given you the argument! I need not—no man needs any more conclusive proof of the totality of human sinfulness, than the position of this discourse has furnished. But then let us remember that it is the wilfulness of man's depravity which throws around him so dark a shade, and brings down upon him so heavy a curse. Man's wickedness is not mechanical action; it is inseparable from the feelings, and desires, and choices of his heart. It consists essentially not in the absence of a mind to think of God, a conscience to approve of his requirements, affections to give to his Maker, but in such a cherished blindness to spiritual realities, such a fixed aversion of heart from all that is pure and excellent in the character and government of God, that without the influence of heavenly grace he never will love holy things, nor give his heart to his Saviour.

The doctrines of the gospel vary their aspect according as they are looked at in or out of their scriptural connexions. Take them as isolated doctrines, totally separatéd from their relations to other truths which serve to explain them, and in view of them, man, as a sinner, may seem to be a subject deserving of pity rather than of blame. But look at them in the light which they mutually shed upon each other, and they serve to place men precisely where we have put them, with the free and untrammelled offer of the gospel set before them for their acceptance, and with the words of Jesus Christ written over them, as the only true exponent of their unsaved and unsanctified condition, "Ye will not come unto me that ye might have life."

If we have disposed of this difficulty, we turn your attention to another, and apparently a more formidable one, growing out of the Sovereignty of God, and his inscrutable purposes concerning man. And here, my brethren, allow me to say, if God is a sovereign, he is not an arbitrary despot; if he has his purposes in respect to all things, and unquestionably he has, they are formed in view of all-sufficient reasons every way worthy of himself, as a God infinite in his wisdom and his love. I do not undertake to explain them; far from me be the unhallowed temerity which shall attempt to unravel the mystery which enshrouds the unsearchable God. What is beyond my power of comprehension, I receive upon the testimony of Him who cannot lie, and refer its solution to that august day, when the great white throne shall be set, and God shall make plain all that was intricate, and shed light upon all that was dark in his administration of the affairs of this lost and ruined world.

But, I would ask a man who talks of God's secret will, and God's electing purposes, what he can find in them by means of which he can throw off from his conscience his responsibility in reference to the great salvation which has been offered to him? True, he may answer me, (and this is the interpretation which thousands put upon the doctrine of election,) "That God, according to his eternal purpose, saves some and casts off others, whether they reject or embrace Christ; and if I am to be saved, I shall be saved, do what I may, and if I am to be lost, I shall be lost, do what I can." My hearer, if you ever thus have reasoned, let me ask you if you are honest with yourself, or honest with the word of God, the authority of which you pretend to quote? I take your argument and set it before you in another form. "If I am to live to-morrow, I shall live, though I should die; and if I am to die to-morrow, I shall die, though I should live." God's purpose has settled it. Will you as a thinking man, claim the paternity of such a senseless and contradictory argument? If not, never say again, never even let your heart whisper to your conscience, "If I am to be saved, I shall be saved, do what I may; and if I am to be lost, I shall be lost, do what I can." The plea has no meaning; it is absurd; it contradicts itself.

God is indeed a Sovereign God. We do not question it; but then sovereignty, as I understand it, has to do with the dispensation of blessings, not at all with the arbitrary infliction of punishment. I can easily understand how God can shed down his mercies upon a human being, for reasons which are wholly irrespective of the character, and independent of the doings of their subject. But I cannot understand how he can send down his curse upon any other ground than the guilt of its subject. He may bless a man who does not deserve his blessing; but he cannot punish a man who does not deserve punishment. The sovereign infliction of evil would be an anomaly under any government, a contradiction of all the principles of equity, and all the laws of righteousness, and never can blot the administration of him whose throne rests upon justice and judgment. The sovereign grace of God! What being in the universe does it injure, or what obstacles can it interpose between any man and eternal life? It surely injures not the being whom it saves, by making him willing in the day of its power; not surely the being whom it does not constrain, but whom it permits to rest in his own chosen objects, and walk in his own chosen path. If there were two worlds of sinful beings,—our own and another—and if to us God made an offer of eternal life, full and free, the responsibility of the result would rest entirely with ourselves, and the character of his dispensations toward that other world, whatever it might be, could not in any degree or in any way affect our position.

To make our point still plainer, we will suppose for a moment, that the doctrine of the Divine Sovereignty had never been revealed in the Bible; that not one word had ever been written upon its pages concerning the purposes of God, and then, as we read, "Whosoever will may come and take of the water of life freely," nobody would doubt man's perfect liberty of choice, nor hesitate a moment as to the question where rested the responsibility, if any being who heard the offer should be lost—and if upon the supposition, that man knew nothing of any of God's purposes, he would be under God perfectly free, the author of his own character and the framer of his own destiny, I see not how the revelation of the doctrine can alter a man's position in the least, when in case of a failure of the great salvation, it leaves a man precisely where and what it found him.

But, my brethren, let me remind you that the purposes of God, as he has revealed them, are universal. They extend as truly to the sparrow, which falleth to the ground, as to the seraph who burns before his throne. They embrace the hairs of your head, which are all numbered, as well as the greatest events of your life, all of which are controlled by an overruling Providence. If they respect man's future allotments, they must respect with equal certainty man's present movements. I have, however, yet to learn that any one feels their constraining power in any of his earthly plannings and actions. I have yet to learn that any man considers himself a mere passive instrument in the doings of his daily life, or looks upon the results of his undertakings as in no way connected with his own sagacity, his own energy, and his own perseverance. To convince me of a sinner's honesty, when he refers the spiritual results of his course to the purposes of God, I must find him in perfect carelessness, giving the same reference to the actions of his daily life, to the plans and movements of the morrow. I must see him refusing the nourishment which nature demands for its sustenance, or quaffing the poison cup which contains the elements of death, upon the plea that the question of his life or death is regulated and to be determined by the purposes of God, irrespective wholly of his own doings. When I see this, then, but not before, will I believe a man sincere when he says, "If I am to be saved, I shall be saved, do what I may; and if I am to be lost, I shall be lost, do what I can." Who can doubt, my brethren, that men take refuge in God's election, only that they may garnish and persevere in their own election—and every man ought to know better, and does know better than to say, "If I am not elected, I cannot be saved." This is making a false issue altogether. The great question for me, as a sinner for whom Christ died, and to whom the offer of eternal life has been made, a sinner responsible to God and to my own soul for every step I take, and every decision I form, and every choice I make in reference to my everlasting interests, is, am I willing to embrace the offer of eternal life which is placed before me? If I am not, it is not God's purpose, but my own election in opposition to the will and commandment of God, which destroys me, body and soul for ever. This is the thought I would have distinctly apprehended, and which I would throw with all its fearful and crushing weight upon the conscience of every man who has not accepted of Jesus Christ.

Divest the thought for a moment from its relation to ourselves. Go back to the scene where the voice of "peace on earth and good will to men," was heard breaking from the heavens when the sun of righteousness rose in spotless and unshadowed splendour upon the plains and mountains of Judea, and lest the light should dazzle, and the heat destroy, gentleness and condescension tempered his rays; and the languishing revived, and the dying lived. And surely the favoured people hailed his rising; and the voice, "Come unto me, and I will give you rest," awakened strains of gratitude and joy as they exclaimed, "Lo! this is our God, we have waited for him, and he will save us; lo! this is the Lord, we will rejoice and be glad in his salvation." But, no! they saw no beauty in him that they should desire him; they did but glance at his glories, and then firmly closed their eyes against his penetrating beams, and retired into the deep recesses of their ignorance and unbelief, lest the light of life should shine into them. And since they loved darkness rather than light, because their deeds were evil, *this was their condemnation*, they found the night they sought, a night without morning, the blackness of darkness for ever.

We do not, for a moment, question the equity of God's judicial administration in their case. Dreadful as it was, it was no more than their flagrant and inexcusable unbelief deserved. "But thinkest thou, O man, who judgest them which do such things, and doest the same, that thou shalt escape the judgment of God?" To what in yourself will you ascribe that which in others you ascribe to criminality? Compare yourself with others upon whom you have been sitting in judgment, and wherein are you dissimilar? Be not deceived, God is not mocked. What are you doing, as estranged from him who came to save you, but fulfilling the desires of the flesh and the mind, and walking in your own chosen way? You may talk of your weakness, your inability to embrace the offer of eternal life; but if you felt it, it might give rise not to apologies but to sorrow, and lead you to humble yourself before God, and exclaim, "O! wretched man that I am, who shall deliver me from the body of this death?" But when or where, my hearer, have been your desires for the salvation of the gospel which you have been unable to gratify? In what hour of your history,—be candid with yourself—did you ever put forth an effort corresponding in any just degree with the importance of religion and eternity? When did you strive against sin, resist the devil, and agonize to enter in at the straight gate? Rather has not your heart leaped to meet the follies of the world, and has not the prince of darkness been invited to hold dominion over its desires? Have you not exerted yourself rather to repress than to strengthen religious influence in the soul? Have you not laboured to resist the conviction which truth has sometimes forced home upon the mind, and fled to the vanities of earth to free your thoughts from the intrusion of eternal things? Let conscience do its duty; let it speak unchecked by the influence of a false philosophy, or a crude and partial theology; let conscience freely speak, and yield its first unbiassed testimony, and you will own your unbelief to be your guilt, your separation from Christ to be the result of your own choice.

Talk not, my beloved hearer, of the power of surrounding temptations, which constrain your movements contrary to your better feelings. What gives these temptations their power, but their harmony with your own desires? But the world cannot constrain, it can only allure. And what are the allurements of the world compared with the attractions of the cross? Look to that blessed, though accursed tree on which Christ your Saviour loved and died; look to the peerless glory which now encircles him; and remember that all which his sinless blood and unknown agony could merit; that all the grace which his Spirit can afford, that all the bliss which his presence can impart, and all the honour, inestimable and undying which he can bestow, are yours, unalterably, for ever yours, if you will embrace his offer. Compared with such treasures worldly affluence, worldly joys, diadems and thrones are but "trifles light as air;" and if you can withstand the powerful attractions of the cross, oh! surely, you can, if you will, withstand the pitiful allurements of this poor and fleeting world.

My beloved hearers, I would have you to understand your true position to-day, and to apprehend the truth I have been striving to commend to your mind. I appear before you, a messenger from a Redeemer's cross, empowered to publish to you a full and free salvation. This is the message which I am instructed to lay before you, "Whosoever will, may take the water of life freely." If you drink not it is because you will not. You are not straitened in God, you are straitened in yourself. And here, in the name of the Master, in whose words, and by whose authority I have spoken, I would this day, in view of the judgment-seat of the Son of Man, throw over the responsibility of the result upon you conscience. God has put it there, and there it must remain. You never, no! never, while "life, or thought, or being lasts, or immortality endures," can shake off that dreadful responsibility from your spirit. At times you feel it now, and it seems a crushing weight, as you know you are not what you should be; but in a little while, after a few more Sabbath suns shall rise and set, you will perceive it more distinctly and feel it more deeply. And if it sometimes torments, and harasses, and almost crushes you now, under the feeble and partial light which is thrown upon it, what will it be in the light, brilliant and unclouded, of the judgment throne? "If thou hast run with the footmen and they have wearied thee, then how canst thou contend with horses? And if in the land of peace wherein thou trustedst, they wearied thee, then how wilt thou do in the swelling of Jordan?" We can shut the subject from our thoughts now, but then we shall not be able to do so. We may invent a thousand apologies, and they may satisfy conscience now, but then every mouth will be stopped. And tell me, my unconverted hearers—bear, I pray you, with the pressure, which the solicitudes of a pastor's heart put upon you—tell me what you wiil answer, when he whose salvation was proffered to you, and urged upon you, and rejected by you, shall say, as at the last, he turns away from you and leaves you to sink in the darkness of that night which knows no morning—"How often would I have gathered you together, as a hen gathereth her chickens under her wings, but ye would not!"

"Stop, O! stop and think, before you further go."

A STIFLED CONSCIENCE.

" And as he reasoned of righteousness, temperance, and judgment to come, Felix trembled."—ACTS xxiv. 25.

IT has been often and justly remarked concerning Felix, the Governor of Judea, that the convenient season of which he spake, when he should give attention to the truths which now agitated his spirit, never arrived. His succeeding history presents the same characteristics, though more fully developed, which when set before him in the light of truth, made him tremble. We see no change in him but for the worse; and so far as we have any evi dence concerning his end, it tells us that he utterly perished in his own corruption. As we look at him, under the preaching of Paul, we find that he had a conscience, a conscience which reproved him of sin and filled him with dire apprehensions. As we look at him afterward, we find him the subject of a stifled conscience, going on from bad to worse. We doubt not that the moment when Paul reasoned with him of righteousness, and temperance, and a judgment to come, was a crisis in his moral history, upon his action in which, the whole character of his future life turned. He might, at the bidding of conscience, and under the teachings of the truth, have changed his whole course and become a new man, but he stifled those monitions, and resisted those teachings, and went on more confirmed, and hopelessly confirmed in his old unrighteousness.

In this brief exhibition of the text, and its connections, we have presented to us a subject of painful, but intensely interesting study. It is the human mind, in two distinct states, or stages of its spiritual history—first, as agitated in view of the appeals which truth addresses to the conscience, the subject of strong moral influences, and of clear and decided convictions of truth and duty; the other is that state, in which after having resisted these influences and suppressed these convictions, it remains inaccessible to the power of truth, and goes on in a career of determined and growing sinfulness, uninfluenced by any of the counteracting agencies which may be brought to bear upon it. The two states are intimately connected with each other, the movements of the mind in the one state determining the character of the other. And thus we have before us the thought upon which we design to dwell this morning. *A stifled human conscience*, or in other words, the nature and consequences of resisting one's own convictions of truth and duty. Without any further introduction, then, we proceed to the illustration of our general thought.

The careful observer of human things cannot have failed to notice the fact that every man's peculiar history dates its commencement, and takes its cast from his conduct in some particular combination of circumstances. It is true, as a general principle, that one period of life regulates to a very great extent those which succeed it, and certain trains of conduct give shape and colouring and character to those which follow them; thus youth receives its cast from childhood, and in its turn gives a cast to mature years. In early life elements not unfrequently disclose themselves which promise future dignity and usefulness, or threaten future inefficiency, degradation, and crime. The analogy in this respect is very striking between the physical, intellectual, and moral world. A deformity resulting from accident or carelessness in early life regulates all subsequent bodily developments. The mental powers, when fully disclosed, shew the character of the early training to which they were subject, and in the absence of powerful counteracting causes the moral temper of maturer years will be but the clearer and fuller development of the spirit of childhood.

Without giving countenance to any of those forms of fatalism now so current in the community which make man the sport of casualties, and give to events an irresistible power to control his character and destiny, in perfect consistency with his entire freedom of action, we may say that there is generally, in every man's history, some particular combination of circumstances, his conduct in which determines the whole course of his after life. The idea which I make the basis of my illustration this morning will be perceived in view of facts with which, doubtless, many of my hearers are familiar. There have been men in our world who at a critical juncture of their temporal affairs have taken some immoral step; as you have looked at their subsequent course, you have found them unable to recover themselves from the influence of that step; it has followed them continually, marring their every project, defeating their every plan, and they have passed onward in their course exhibiting a character constantly deteriorating in a moral point of view until death has closed their earthly career.

Now, it strikes me, that a principle which thus runs through the physical, intellectual, and moral world, must find some analogies in the spiritual world likewise, and the exhibition of those analogies is our object on the present occasion. If it is true that man's conduct in early life has an important bearing upon his temporal relations, it may be true that it has an important bearing upon his eternal relations likewise. For ourselves, we believe that in the majority of cases, if the truth upon this point could be reached, it would appear that the question of man's destiny is settled before his habits of thought and feeling are confirmed, and he is found busied amid the cares and perplexities and struggles of life; his conduct anterior to that time has shaped his course and determined its results. There have been in his spiritual history circumstances, his conduct in which has placed him beyond the reach of change; in which his spiritual relations have been altered; a crisis in his history when he was introduced to an acquaintance with the hopes and joys, and sanctifying influence of the gospel, or when a seal was put upon him which, humanly speaking, determined his condition as hopeless. Whether this be so to the full extent of our supposition or not, this much is certain, there is in every man's history a combination of circumstances, a crisis, his conduct in which determines whether his character in a spiritual point of view shall deteriorate, and his prospects of future good become more equivocal, or his character improve in moral excellence, and his hope grow brighter.

To some of these circumstances, and to man's conduct in them leading to such issues, we shall turn our attention, and we ask our hearers to follow us step by step, and closely examine the positions we assume.

The salvation of the soul, my brethren, is always to be viewed in connection with, and as dependent upon the influence of the gospel. We do not mean to say that the gospel has in itself any direct efficiency, but that such is the constitution of the human mind, and such the corresponding arrangements of God, that men are not ordinarily converted, separate from the means which God has wisely appointed. I bring in this thought here, to neutralize the influence of a sentiment entertained by some, that circumstances, or a man's conduct in them, can have no vital bearing upon the result of his conversion, which is brought about by a power above all circumstances, and which in fact controls them. True it is, that man becomes the subject of a spiritual change by the agency of the Holy Ghost, but that agency is put forward in connection with means; and if the sentiment adverted to is good for the purpose for which it is used, it is equally good to prove that the means of God's appointment have no manner of connection with conversion as an end; that the end is quite as probable without them as with them, and that God's ability to work a miracle is a good ground for their belief that he will do so. And yet, in opposition to this, men feel universally that there is a very great difference, so far as their prospects for eternity is concerned, between those who are, and those who are not favored with the means of grace. Not one of us would exchange his circumstances in this respect for those of an opposite character, shewing that however we may reason from the efficiency of the Holy Spirit, circumstances have, in our own estimation, a very important bearing upon the question of our destiny. In short, it is a common-sense opinion, which no reasoning can change, a deep-seated feeling which no philosophy can eradicate, that when a man has placed himself beyond the reach of means, he has placed himself beyond the reach of hope. It is immaterial to the point, what agency secures the conversion of the soul, if that agency is put forth only in circumstances in which I never can be placed; and so far as a man's conduct has an influence in defining his position, so far has his conduct a happy or a disastrous bearing upon the question of his eventual safety.

We will then take a man and place him under the preaching of the gospel, and the means of grace.

It is not to be denied that there is much which is stirring and exciting in revealed truth. There is a remarkable adaptation on the part of the gospel both to the conscience and the heart. Under its developments feeling is often enkindled which concedes the righteousness of its claims, and does honour to the power of its motives. Facts in every day's history show how the human mind may be reached by the simple verities of the gospel, and thrown into a mood of thoughtfulness upon spiritual subjects. Whatever may be a man's controlling spirit, there are seasons when subjected to the power of heavenly truth, it is for the moment, at least, suspended in its influence. It often is so in the house of God, when he who ministers the sacred oracles arms himself with the strength of his master, and brings the mighty force of truth to bear upon the conscience. Though there may in such circumstances be no outward display of tremulousness, there are beating hearts, and throbbing and agitated spirits. If the attention is once gained, and rivetted to the declarations of the inspired testimony, very little effort is required to awaken feeling. There is not an announcement of God's word which, when its nature is distinctly perceived, does not commend itself as reasonable to the mind, and which, when its claims are presented in the light of their own appropriate enforcements, does not kindle conviction of duty, and a feeling of self reflection on account of its neglect. I am not surely speaking mysteries to any who hear me, for within the walls of this sanctuary has the gospel been honoured in its truth, and felt in itspower, as here under its simple ministration has many a wakeful conscience, and many a beating soul testified to the righteousness of its claims, and the forcefulness of their sanctions.

Similar states of mind are sometimes produced under the influence of divine providence, when God so arranges or disorders men's private circumstances as to compel thought; yet here you will perceive, that as in the other cases, thought has been kindled in view of truth, and the only difference is, that in one case truth has been ministered by the living voice, and in the other by the providence of God.

We direct your attention then, for a moment, to the human mind in these circumstances, and ask you to analyze its experiences. Thought is awakened in view of truth and duty, set out in the broad, clear light of the gospel. There is a conviction of error, of guilt, of danger; there is self-dissatisfaction; and the man retires perhaps from the scenes amid which his mind has been so stirred within him, feeling the necessity of subduing the spirit which has carried him away from the path of truth and duty, and purposing to wrestle against it, and if possible to obtain the mastery. The movements of the conscience of Felix under the demonstrations of Paul, were not unaccompanied by purposes and resolutions.

And, my brethren, is this the whole of it? Are there no results pending? Are there no consequences of mighty magnitude hanging upon the conduct of a man in these peculiar circumstances? Or is it not so, must it not be so, that there is here something like a crisis in his moral and spiritual history, which is to throw its influence over his whole future course, if not to give shape and character to his future destiny? Let us look at this question for a moment.

We suppose then, for the sake of example, that in these circumstances, the subject of such exercises yields to his own convictions, and at once carries out his purpose into execution, in an intelligent and cheerful submission to the terms and requirements of the gospel. And do you not perceive that all his spiritual relations are at once changed, and that a new light is thrown upon his future experience? If he has truly given himself up to the service of Jesus Christ, he never will be the same man he was before. In every respect, of character, condition, prospects, he is an altered man. He has commenced a process of improvement, and his path will be "as the shining light, which shineth more and more unto the perfect day." What has been the spiritual history of every true Christian, but the history of a process of ongoing sanctification, commencing with such a movement of his mind in circumstances like those we have detailed?

We make an opposite supposition, and we think you will find the converse of the foregoing statement to be true. We set before you now, a man who in these circumstances turns away from the commandment delivered unto him. It is immaterial how this movement of his mind is explained, so long as the fact is certain. The impressions of truth wear away, his convictions are hushed, his purposes are forgotten, and he appears to be the same he was before. It may have been the result of resistance offered, either directly or indirectly, to the responses of his own mind to the truth and Spirit of the living God. It may have been the result either of an intelligent throwing away from him of the truth which has affected him, or of an effort to relieve himself from its present pressure, by a simple postponement of its claims to a more convenient season, as it was in the case of Felix; but in either case, according as the convictions of truth and duty have been more or less clear and deep, there has been a conflict more or less painful and severe between them and the desires of their heart. His energies must have been taxed for strength to oppose the influences which acted upon him, or his ingenuity for cunning to evade their force. In whatever way he may accomplish his purpose, he at all events succeeds in mastering his conscience, and in schooling his moral sensibilities to submission to the dictates of a sinful and deceitful heart, and he appears to be what he was before—but when this process is ended, and he who but just now trembled under the truth is unmoved and unaffected, is he really the same, has no change whatever come over the spirit of that man, over his relations and his prospects? Or is it not so, that he has gathered about him the shades of a deeper depravity, wrapped himself in a garb of more impenetrable adamant, and stirred still more bitter ingredients into the cup from which hereafter he must hereafter drink? Was it not so with Felix? And must it not be so with every one, who in the same circumstances acts the same part, as the movements of the human mind are uniform, regulated by the same general laws? This is the plain, but at the same time startling and thrilling doctrine, which I wish to commend to the minds of my hearers. Here you have the picture of a stifled conscience, in the results which it certainly developes.

I. In commending this doctrine, there are three views of these results which I wish to set before you; the first respects the moral and spiritual character of their subjects. I need not surely say to any of you, my brethren, who believe in these sacred oracles, or who have been at all attentive students of human history, that by nature the tendency of the human mind is sinful. We do not enter upon a philosophical inquiry here which would carry us too far away from the object at present before us. We assume the fact as granted by those to whom we address our argument. It is certain, moreover, that the outward developments of moral feeling are regulated, checked or fostered by circumstances and influences of God's arrangement. Among these influences, conscience as the most powerful, holds, probably, the most important place. In fact, it is by means of conscience mainly that God controls his sinful subjects. So long as it remains unperverted, no one can advance any great length in outbreaking sin; and sinfulness is progressive only as man obtains by degrees the ascendancy of his moral judgment. Hence the plain inference, that every new triumph over conscience is connected with a new impulse in the career of unholiness, and the more unequivocal the dictates of conscience which have been silenced, the clearer and brighter the light of it which has been put out, the deeper the succeeding darkness, and the fewer and feebler the restraints to lawless desire, and the more rapid and fearful the development of the innate depravity of the human heart. The man whose case we have been considering is one who has succeeded in stifling his conscience when it acted under the clear and decided light of God's truth. Its convictions, which he could not disprove, and its remonstrances in all their palpable propriety, have been overborne in the conflict with the heart. Worldly ambition, carnal passion, sinful desire have triumphed over it when it acted in circumstances most favourable to its success. And do you think that the subject of these experiences will, in the same circumstances, ever be similarly affected by the truth of God? Will he tremble as he formerly did in view of sin, and shrink back from the thought of trifling with sacred things? Or, having broken through the restraints which controlled him, will he not feel a freedom in sin, and be prepared to perpetrate without much scruple actions at which, antecedent to these struggles with his conscience, his soul would have shuddered? In this simple thought, we have the whole philosophy of progressive iniquity. We have explained to us, what to many wears an aspect of mystery—how a man can go on step by step in a downward course, becoming less accessible to the influences of good, and more and more open to the suggestions of evil. His onward movement has its stages distinctly marked by contests within, a mysterious something within him to which he has risen superior, and at each of these stages he has received a new impulse in his downward course, until, at last, his character becomes that of one who, neither fearing God nor regarding man, drinks in iniquity like water, and sins without compunction and without remorse.

I am not dealing in fancies, believe me, my brethren, as I give utterance to these solemn thoughts. Alas! alas! the world is too full of their painful illustrations, to leave room for any skepticism here. You will find them in the contrasts which men, no more matured in age than in every form of ungodliness, whose consciences seem to be buried in the darkness of an eternal death, present to the quick susceptibility of impression, and tender moral sensibilities of their early years. You will find them in the children of prayers, and tears, and parental instruction, who for a while, it may be, moved on full of promise and of hope, till they were brought by the Providence of God into decisive circumstances, where the light of truth shone with more than ordinary brilliancy in upon their minds, and they felt in deeper and more awful sincerity than ever the impressive simplicities of the gospel, as conscience spake with unusual power, and with unwonted emphasis. That was a crisis in their history. There was a severe struggle between a sense of duty, and the love of sin—doubtfully for a time may the conflict have been waged—but eventually the love of sin triumphed, and they who before would have paused in their course, in view of the simplest prohibition of the word of God, who would have melted down under the influences of heavenly entreaty, are heedless to the one, and insensible to the other ; yea, are often heard boasting their deliverance from the prejudices of early education, and as an evidence of their emancipation, sporting on the lip of profanity the solemn realities, in view of which once they trembled, and laughing with an almost maniac's sneer at the influences which formerly controlled them. And when the convictions of which men have been the subjects have been peculiarly deep, and the struggles through which they have passed have been severe, you will often find their subjects coming forth unsubdued by all of them, and entering upon a course, in which in respect to principle, they seldom stop short of the most unblushing infidelity, and in respect to practice, they give themselves up to an open abandonment to every vice. Such are the effects of a stifled conscience upon the character, more or less strikingly manifested, as the convictions stifled have been more or less deep, and the efforts to overcome them consequently more or less severe.

II. I turn to another view of my subject, viz., the results of the course I have described, upon the moral and spiritual *condition* of its subject. We use the term condition here, to designate the state of a man in relation to any particular experience, or event, as that state is defined by the circumstances in which he is placed. A man's worldly condition is determined from his temporal circumstances, as they administer to his present happiness or discomfort, or may be ominous of his coming prosperity or adversity. And a man's spiritual condition is determined by his circumstances, as they bear upon the question of his future destiny.

The salvation of any man out of the kingdom of God, is, as yet, an unsolved problem, because there are difficulties to be overcome, which we cannot say that he will ever master, and sacrifices to be made to which we do not know that he ever will submit—and yet the circumstances of some men are more favorable to a happy issue than those of others, simply because some men are more accessible to the influence of the truth than are others; and a man's circumstances are promising or otherwise, according as they prepare the mind for and give enforcement to these influences, or tend to close the mind against them, or neutralize their power. A man's relation to the means of grace may be determined by feeling as well as by locality—that is, a man living under the light, and blessed with the privileges of the gospel, may be, on account of his moral feelings, as wholly unaffected by them as though he were living in a land of pagan darkness. Upon a man who closes his eyes, an object set before him will produce no more effect than if it had no existence. The thought then, I would here have you ponder is, that a stifled conscience puts a man in a position where the truth of God has no effect upon him. The conversion of the soul is difficult, because it is difficult to make upon the minds of men deep and effective impressions of spiritual things. They may be brought under the action of the gospel, and summoned to think upon themes of an import so high and solemn, that one would suppose they never could forget them; and yet they carry away with them an impression, at best, but transient, of the truths with which they have been communing, and that because the conscience, to which these truths appeal, is laid in so deep a slumber; hence, the man who by stifling his conscience has obtained the completest mastery over it, and has laid it in the deepest slumber, is most inaccessible to the influences of the truth, and consequently in the most hopeless spiritual condition. Never is man brought into that state in which he becomes the subject of a spiritual change, except as his conscience is roused to action under the influence of heavenly truth. While it slumbers, all our demonstrations, however clear, and all our appeals, however forceful, are but "like a lovely song of one who hath a pleasant voice and can play well on an instrument"—as pleasing it may be to the ear, but as evanescent in their impression upon the mind; and when we know that stifling conscience is but throwing it into a stupor, we can easily understand that he who has been able to keep it down, and to smother its remonstrances, under the clearest light of the gospel, has, in so doing, triumphed over his better self, and over all that is powerful in the means of grace, and all that was hopeful in his condition—and when you look at him, after having thus mastered his conscience, sitting unmoved when the messenger of truth takes his stand for God, and clearly illustrates and enforces with mighty urgency the claims of his Saviour, it seems as though all that was impressible about him, had been turned to ice and iron and adamant; and we do not hesitate to say that as he has rendered himself more inaccessible to recovering influences, he has to the same degree, rendered his spiritual condition hopeless. You have then the premises and conclusion of my argument before you. The most hopeless of God's creatures in this world, is not, necessarily, the man of the greatest outward deformities of character, not necessarily the man of the fewest spiritual advantages, but the man of the most; the man who has been the subject of the deepest and most pungent convictions of truth and duty, which he has mastered; the man who has been brought nearest to the kingdom of heaven, yet has never entered it.

III. I have one more view of my subject. What kind of an experience, hereafter, think you, must a stifled conscience describe? It is unquestionably true, that the scenes through which we are passing now, and our action in them, have something to do with our coming destiny; and if I mistake not, the workings of our minds now will show with some distinctness what will be the workings of our minds hereafter. It is perfectly immaterial whether you look at the coming scenes in the light of inflicted punishment, or as the results of the natural operations of the human mind. In either view the subject of a stifled conscience must prepare for a bitter experience. The teaching of the Bible upon the subject of retribution, is very simple. "Unto whomsoever much is given, of him shall much be required." Responsibility, and of course guilt, are measured by the light and privileges enjoyed, and there will be degrees in punishment, as there are gradations in wickedness. And upon whom can we fix, as in circumstances of greater responsibility, than upon the man upon whom not merely the truth of God has been brought to act, but upon whom that action has been effective, into whose mind the Spirit of God has been pouring light, and upon whose heart the most solemn and impressive motives have been urged? The man who in these circumstances does not bow to the authoritative announcement of heaven, robs himself forever of the plea of ignorance in extenuation of his guilt, or in abatement of the fearfulness of his coming catastrophe. And if his doom, in its sorrows, is to be determined from the intelligence which has marked his spiritual resistances, oh! there must be many stripes for him, because he knew his Master's will. Better for him that his conscience never should have been roused to action, than that it should have awakened only to drink the anodyne which he himself had mingled for it.

Or, look at the coming scenes of another world, simply as the natural results of our feelings and movements here; and is not he who is smothering the reproofs of his spirit, and hushing the remonstrances of this faithful monitor within him, laying up the stings and the goads which shall madden him for ever? Will not the spirit which is so ingenious now, in inventing excuses for sin, and methods for getting rid of convictions of truth and duty, be equally ingenious hereafter, in teaching the undying worm new modes of torture. He cannot then but see that the cup of sorrow from which he drinks, has been mingled by himself, as he finds that the repressed movements of conscience, its smothered convictions, its hushed remonstrances, constitute its bitterest ingredients; and the reason why he cannot escape from, or alleviate his miseries, will be that he cannot escape from or blot out the remembrance of himself.

Believe me, my brethren, there is an intimate connection between the scenes through which we are passing now, and the scenes amid which we are to mingle hereafter. You and I, and all men everywhere, are now defining the future, and giving birth to the elements of its experience. And he who now moves upon the confines of the kingdom of God, without entering it, will move at the greatest distance from it forever. We had better not think upon spiritual things, if thought amounts to nothing. We had better not feel under the influence of spiritual realities, if feeling does not lead to obedience to the truth. Better that we should never have known any thing of the way of righteousness, if we do not walk in it. Better had it been for Felix if Paul had never reasoned with him on "righteousness, temperance, and judgment to come," or had he never trembled under the truth.

Of the general subject, which I have thus set before you, it is hardly necessary for me to make a particular application, for I see not how any one uninterested in Jesus Christ, can fail to take it home to himself. We are here, my brethren, in the providence of God, under the preaching of the gospel. It cannot be that the ministrations of the truth have been powerless upon the conscience, or that the appeals of the gospel have been without effect upon the mind. It cannot be that the providence of God has in vain seconded these ministrations, or to no purpose added its enforcements to the truth. Experience has proved that uniformly, in these circumstances, thought is awakened, and feeling more or less deep is kindled, and that men have evidence within them, of the reality of that mighty agency which works upon the mind and heart in connection with a preached gospel. You will let me speak to you, my brethren, not in unkindness, but from the fulness of a heart which seeks as the source of its highest joy the salvation of your souls. You will let me speak to you in view of the truth which I have been illustrating. Under this gospel you have thought, under this gospel you have felt, under this gospel you have purposed—but, these convictions have been hushed—perhaps by direct resistance, perhaps by evasion, perhaps by promises—I know not how—but conscience has been stifled. Thought, feeling, conviction have not led to obedience. And are these, my brethren, circumstances which justify apathy and spiritual unconcern? If I am right in the position I have assumed to-day, I know of no circumstances of greater moral peril in which a man can be placed. My beloved hearers, whose history tells of frequent seasons of the strivings of the Spirit of God, and as frequent resistances to them, is it not so that you are called to an agony of effort? The scenes through which you have passed, and the position you now occupy, give emphasis to the voice, and power to the exhortation which calls upon you to "agonize to enter in at the straight gate." It will be a mighty conflict with a heart so long triumphant, which shall issue in a spiritual deliverance; but that conflict must be joined, and won, or all is lost. "Agonize while yet there is hope; while yet "the Spirit of God worketh in you." You may not think it, but, believe me, there is a hand upon you which will palsy and crush you if its grasp be not loosened; there is a withering influence thrown over you which will overcome you, and sink you far beyond the reach of hope, if you struggle not with superhuman strength, like the agony of man for life. Oh! "agonize to enter in at the straight gate;" for, if ye are saved, there is an eternal crown; if ye fail, there are scorpion stings, and flames fanned by the breath of the Almighty; a heart of joy or an undying worm, a garland of glory or a wreath of fire; these are the issues pending; "agonize to enter in at the straight gate."

It is quite possible that there may be some who at this very moment may be going through the experience upon the result of which hang such mighty issues. I confess I should be surprised if there were not, especially among my more youthful hearers, some active, troubled, and reproving consciences; if there were not some to whom a "still, small voice," was whispering, "Behold now is the accepted time, now is the day of salvation." If there is one such in my hearing, I beseech him to give me his mind one moment. You know not, my dear friend, you cannot conceive the issues which may, at this very moment, be hanging on the movements of your mind. There may be more of glory or more of shame, more of life or more of death, more of heaven or more of hell than you imagine; and of one or the other, according as you act in this crisis through which you are now passing. Oh! beware of a stifled conscience, beware of smothered, overpowered convictions. They are so death-like in their influence, so dirge-like in their sound, that they seem to indicate the fatal grasp of the great destroyer. You will be tempted, and I fear successfully, to stifle that conscience, and hush its convictions now, by the hope that God may awaken it to more powerful action hereafter. Oh! be not deceived; do not build a hope of God's gracious influence hereafter upon your provoking him to withdraw it altogether. You would not be tempted to take a viper to your bosom by the hope that

God would extract the sting. You would not be tempted to fill and mix and quaff the poison cup, by the hope that God might neutralize its hemlock; give up such a vain hope, it is one of the deceits of a sinful heart. You may hush that conscience, but in doing so you may sink it into a sleep from which nothing but the trumpet of judgment will awaken it. You may drink of that poison cup which a deceitful heart is mingling, but you may drain the very dregs of the second death. You may stifle that conscience—Felix did it, and trembled no more—you may do it, and cut the last tie which fastens you to God, and sever the only cord which binds you to a world of hope. Beware! beware of stifled convictions, and of seared and hardened consciences. You will act in your circumstances; you must act; but, remember, oh! remember the amazing issues. "To-day, if ye will hear his voice, harden not your heart."

RESISTING THE SPIRIT.

"My Spirit shall not always strive with man."—GENESIS vi. 3.

THE agency of God in all his works, in all places of his dominion, is a first principle of truth, which on the present occasion, I may consider as unquestioned. How that agency is exerted, through what channels that influence, which upholds, and directs, and controls all things, and evolves all results, is put forth, no man may be able positively to determine. Here we may have our theories, varying from, or if you please, opposed to each other, and they are all perfectly harmless, so long as they do not shut out from the view of men the fact itself of the divine agency and control. This much is clear and certain: God's hand is in every thing. This physical system is upheld by his power, and moves at his bidding, and each individual part of it, demands for itself, in order to its existence and motion, the power of God, as truly as does the wondrous whole. The moment it is withdrawn, each and all sink and revert to their original nothingness.

This characteristic of dependence is not, however,

peculiar to the physical or inanimate creation; it as truly pervades and marks with equal distinctness the intellectual and moral world. God's influence runs through every department of being, upholding each, and controlling and regulating the movement of each according to the laws which he himself has given to each respectively. I am as truly dependent upon God for thought, as I am for muscular action; and in the exercise of my mental powers, and in the play of my varied feelings, according to the laws of my own mind, God is as really engaged as in the motions of the planets, the revolutions of the earth, or the changes of the seasons.

The moral or spiritual world has precisely the same attribute of dependence. The nature of the divine influence here, and the mode of its exercise, may be somewhat different, growing out of a difference in the constitution of the subjects upon which it acts; but the dependence here is as real as in the other case. I can no more do without God, as a spiritual being, than I can do without him as an intellectual or merely animal being; and I will not stop to quarrel with a man respecting his philosophical theory of dependence, so long as he does not on the one hand deny its existence and absoluteness, nor on the other reduce dependence to fatalism.

For every proper thought then, for every holy emotion, for every right purpose and action, we need the power of God. We need it as creatures, but oh! we need it especially as sinful creatures.

Man wakes to righteousness only at the bidding, and under the influence of him who gives life in the spiritual world; and holiness is sustained only as the same power which originated, nourishes and preserves it. If this be so, and if every Christian knows, however far he may have advanced in the experimental knowledge of Jesus Christ, that,

> "When God withdraws, his comforts die,
> And all his graces droop;"

surely if he ceases to act, if his peculiar influence as a renewing God be withheld from a lost and ruined world, not a single ray of light will break in upon the darkness in which it is shrouded, nor a single element of life break the deep repose of spiritual death to which it has been hushed.

The peculiarity of the gospel, therefore, as a recovering system, is, that it is a dispensation of the spirit of God, and as such it is the only source of hope to apostate man; and it cannot surely be an uninteresting or an unprofitable occupation for ourselves, to study for a few moments our position and our circumstances, as subjects of this dispensation; and keeping distinctly in view the fact of an absolute dependence, to ponder some truths which the gospel has revealed respecting the agency of the Spirit; truths of deep moment to us, and which should have a very effective and decided influence upon the movements of our minds and the feelings of our hearts in our spiritual relations.

My object, then, upon the present occasion, is to lay before you three distinct trains of thought, all leading to one and the same general result. The first, relating to the fact itself, will direct your attention to some indications of the reality and power of the Spirit's influence upon the human mind. The second, relating to the suspension of that influence, will furnish the evidence of the position, that the Spirit of God does not always strive with man; and the third, relating to the condition of one thus abandoned, will furnish an argument for carefulness as to the movements of our minds under the gospel of Jesus Christ.

I. There are certain states of mind, belonging, I think I may with safety say, to all who are placed under the clear and faithful exhibition of "the truth as it is in Jesus," which shew them to be the subjects of an influence greatly different from that of their own hearts, or that of the world around them, and even superior to both. We do not now say how marked these states are, nor how decided their manifestations. We merely state the fact, that every man is at times conscious of peculiar conditions of thought and feeling, which he may not be able fully to explain to himself, which are not in accordance with his prevailing desires, and are not originated by any of those objects, in view of which he naturally loves to act. Sometimes his state is that of uneasiness—he is dissatisfied with himself. Not that there is any source of disquiet in his outward relations and circumstances, these may all be peaceful. As a mere creature of sense, he may be in possession of all the elements of enjoyment, and yet, surrounded by the means of gratification, he is disturbed and restless.

These experiences, it must be remembered, are inseparable from the influence of the truth of God upon the mind. They exist, as their subject is brought to think upon the statements of the word of God. If he can banish the truth from his thoughts, his painful emotions often cease; but under its light and power he is unhappy, and his uneasiness, in its degree, is generally proportioned to the clearness of the truths' manifestations, and the power of the appeals which they make to his conscience. There are circumstances, moreover, in which the light of the gospel shines very strongly in upon the mind. "The power of the world to come" takes hold upon the spirit, and while he is conscious of contrariety to the being who controls him, he cannot but be fearful of the retributions which await him. Spiritual things have an air of reality, and as he feels that he is not what he should be, he dreads to think of what he may be; in short, he is now awakened to a perception of his condition, and to a sense of his danger as a sinner.

Connected with this state of mind, as either accompanying or succeeding, though essentially distinct in its character, is another, often belonging to man in the same, or very similar circumstances. It is a state marked not simply by a perception of danger, but also by a conviction of guilt. In ordinary circumstances, when the moral judgment is but partially enlightened, man can without much compunction, take an attitude of opposition to every thing like spiritual religion. He can either very ingeniously evade all the requirements of the gospel, or he can work out a very elaborate justification of himself in his neglect of them; and it is truly admirable to observe what sagacity the human mind can display in reasoning against the commandments of heaven, and in what a close web of skilful sophistry it can entangle itself, in its endeavour to get rid of the righteousness of heavenly claims. But now, he can do so no longer; the conviction of his guilt is too clear to be resisted, and under the combined influence of his apprehension of danger and sense of sinfulness, he feels the necessity of doing something which shall change at once his character and his state.

These are mental experiences, by no means uncommon under the faithful preaching of the gospel. How are we to explain them? To what cause, or causes, shall we attribute them? You will not surely account for them by supposing them to be the results of any independent movement of the human spirit! "Dead in trespasses and sins," man does not of himself awaken to a sense of his spiritual danger. The human heart does not spontaneously come to the light, that its mysteries may be revealed. Left entirely to the workings of his own mind, under the influence of the purely sensible objects by which he is surrounded, there is no reason to suppose that man will ever think of any other than his merely sensible relations, or ever dream of his sin and danger as a subject of the spiritual government of God. There is such a thing, we admit, as natural conscience, and it has indeed a wondrous power to overwhelm with its rebukes and distract with its terrors—but then it must be roused by an influence independent of itself—for sin stupefies the conscience as well as blinds the vision. The human mind acts, as it is acted upon, and experience, as it illustrates this great characteristic of our mental nature, testifies that all mental, and of course all moral changes, are secured by outward influences. When the Son of God was about to leave this world, having finished the work which the Father had given him to do, he left behind him this promise, "I will send the Comforter, who shall convince the world of sin, and righteousness, and judgment;" and in this promise we have the explanation of these mental phenomena, which are themselves the evidences that the promise has been fulfilled.

Have we not, then, the proofs of the power and reality of the Spirit's influences among ourselves? If the word of God is the sword of the Spirit, is not that Spirit present in his sanctuary, where that word is illustrated in its principles and enforced in its claims? What means that almost breathless stillness which sometimes pervades the house of God, when the simplicities of the gospel are exhibited? What does the mind made thoughtful indicate, but the presence and agency of him who with "a still small voice," does "stop the sinner's way;" of what are all our awakened anxieties the fruits, if not of his influence, whose province it is "to convince the world of sin." And what mean those oft-formed resolutions, to which kindled fears give birth, and what those oft-repeated vows, originating in intelligent conviction, if they are not the evidence of some mighty though mysterious agency at work upon the mind? Lo! we carry within us the proofs of the position that the Spirit of God strives with man. Truth, a thousand times heard before without awakening emotion, now rousing us to thought; claims a thousand times before presented, and at best but listlessly received, now securing a prompt and intelligent response from conscience; feeling, quick, deep, permanent, perhaps excited under the demonstrations of the gospel; these as facts defining our own circumstances, and testified to by our own consciousness, are the evidences of our subjection to the influences of the Holy Ghost.

II. Now, we cannot tell beforehand, in reference to any given case, what are to be the results of these spiritual movements upon the human mind. We know what their tendency is in themselves considered. The gospel is a recovering system. Christ came "to seek and to save the lost," and the Holy Spirit is the agent for carrying out the great moral purposes of the Gospel; though his influences do not always lead to such an issue. Viewed in this light, the operations of the Spirit of God are to the mind of man invested with amazing interest. They stand connected with the best welfare, and the highest hopes of his immortal spirit; they furnish the only ground for the expectation that he may be born again; they are the only security he has against perdition. Let them but cease, and the question of his spiritual destiny is decided. Let it be certain that over that mind the Holy Ghost will never again move, that he will never again touch that conscience, or influence that heart, and the eternal enslavement of that soul is sure, as it is placed forever beyond the reach of any power which can break its chains, and it must sink under their weight into the darkness of an everlasting night.

And are we not taught by the very words of our text the possibility of such a condition? Do we need any plainer indication than is here given us of the reality of spiritual abandonment? Has not the history of our world furnished its comments and its proofs? What have become of the convictions which belonged to those who have shewn themselves strangers to the hopes of the gospel? How many have apprehended the terrors of the world to come, trembled in the retrospect of the past, and the prospect of the future? Under the influence of an awakened conscience and solemn premonitions, have thought, have resolved and promised, and yet have either entered upon the experience they so much dreaded, or else live only to manifest an entire unconcern about spiritual things, and to present to the realities and claims of the truth an indurated heart and a callous conscience. We have read of an Esau, who shed the tears of a bitter but unavailing repentance; of an Ahab, who humbled himself in view of threatened judgments; of a Saul, from whom God departed; of a Judas, who rushed upon the very ruin which gave to his conscience its tormenting and appalling power; of a Felix, who trembled on his judgment seat; and an Agrippa, who was "almost persuaded to be a Christian." These are gleanings from amid the memorials of the past, in perfect keeping with the demonstrations of the present. We point you to the man who has been laid upon a bed of sickness, and whose mental exercises, in his hour of solemn thoughtfulness, told of the workings of the Spirit of God. We point to the man once alarmed by some startling dispensation of Providence, or awakened by the faithful preaching of the word in the sanctuary, whose emotions, and the language which expressed them, revealed the agency of some mysterious power; and then I turn over another page of their history, and there stands that once troubled sinner, brought back from the gates of the grave, and there is a smile of skepticism, or indifference upon his countenance as he is spoken to of "the powers of the world to come;" and yonder moves that once thoughtful and inquiring one, and he receives with an air of the greatest unconcern every appeal upon the importance of spiritual and eternal things; and here is the subject of providential discipline, from whose spirit the impressions once made upon it are entirely gone, shewing not a trace of the influence of the trials under which his heart once bled profusely. And these are the proofs which every day and every hour are heaving into being, of the truth that the Spirit of God does not always strive with man. I can appeal then, for my arguments upon this point, my careless hearer, to you. Subject of stifled convictions! Child of tears and prayers, and entreaties and warnings, you whose conscience has ere now been wakened to action, and whose feelings have been excited in view of truth, over whom a mother's heart has yearned while she wrestled with her covenant God, and to whom a father's tenderest anxieties have been given as he has laid hold on your behalf of the heavenly promise—you who have wept at the bedside of sickness, or formed the purpose of repentance at the grave of a departed friend; while your past experience is my proof of the reality of the Spirit's influence, your present apathy shall be my demonstration of its suspension.

Considering this point as established, allow me to turn your attention to some of its connections, that my doctrine may be made to subserve the great practical purpose it contemplates.

The position, then, which I here assume, is that such a dispensation upon the part of God, as the withdrawal from a man of his Holy Spirit, is never the result of a dark and mysterious sovereignty. Most men are very prone to resolve every thing into sovereignty, and they mean by it only caprice, arbitrary action, without any reason. There is, however, no such sovereignty taught in the Bible, and it is incompatible with a wise, and intelligent, and upright administration. God is a sovereign, but he has the very best possible reason for every thing he does, though he has not made known to us the reasons of all his doings, and probably our minds are not large enough to comprehend them, should they all be revealed. But then sovereignty is an attribute of grace. God may bestow favours upon a being in the exercise of sovereignty, that is, for reasons wholly irrespective of the character of the being himself. Thus the salvation of every sinner is an act of sovereignty; but the infliction of evil falls within the province of justice, and its reasons are always taken from the character and doings of its subject. Hence, when you read in the Bible of the suspension or withdrawal of divine influences from a man, you always find it represented in connection with some previous wrong conduct on his part, and as a punishment of that conduct. Spiritual abandonment is the judicial result of spiritual resistance. The Spirit of God ceases to strive because he is driven from the human bosom.

We have already adverted to certain states of feeling, certain conditions of thought, of which man is the subject under the preaching of the gospel, and we have traced them to their source in spiritual influences, and exhibited their general moral tendency to draw us away from sin to holiness, from the world to God. These influences are, in the results they contemplate, opposite to the natural bias of the heart. Hence, when a man becomes their subject, there is a counter movement often times of the human mind; there is a sudden and distinct recoil from the impressive power which comes upon the soul. There is generally an effort to throw in something between the mind and the realities which affect it, and in all this there is resistance to the Holy Ghost. The forms in which this resistance is seen, are varied by the manner in which truth approaches a man, by the character and force of its appeal, by his own natural temperament, and by the outward circumstances and associations in which he may be thrown. Sometimes it is shown in an effort as determined as it is direct, to get rid of his convictions. He will preoccupy his mind with other subjects, or with views of the truth different from those which impress him. Sometimes he will break up entirely his associations, in which he comes under these troublous influences, or he will put himself in a position where he thinks the arrows of the truth can never reach him, by vacating his seat in the house of God, or forming his Sabbath associations where he thinks the truth will be less clear in its light, less pointed in its application, or less urgent in its enforcements. His design is apparent. It is to give the mind an opportunity to recover itself from the shock it has received from the demonstration of the gospel, or to secure a counteracting movement which shall neutralize its power. There is a wonderful sympathy between our outward aspect and our inward feelings. We all know how very easily and quickly we can secure any particular emotion, simply by assuming its corresponding outward expression. A forced smile will not infrequently wake up a momentary gladness in the heart, and a tear started, we know not how, and dropped, we know not why, will sadden the spirit, and a scornful look will at once excite something like contempt for the person to whom it is directed. Hence, it is by no means an uncommon thing for a man, whose conscience has been affected in the house of God, to assume an air of entire indifference, not simply for the purpose of screening from others the workings of his bosom, but also of securing in himself that very feeling of unconcern of which he has assumed the outward expression. And I surely need not tell you, that here is a clear evidence of a strife between the mind and the Holy Ghost. There is a direct and intelligent resistance to his influences, the result of which is to banish him from the soul.

Such a method, however, may not be successful. There are circumstances in which it must prove itself a failure; circumstances where no direct opposition will be of any avail. The gospel in its influence over the mind, is at times not unlike some other attractions, powerful in proportion as they are painful, when a man cannot pass beyond the bounds of that charmed circle which the truth has drawn around him. If he cannot by any direct effort rid himself of the impressions which the gospel has made upon him, if its claims so disturbing to his conscience follow him wherever he goes, and present themselves to his mind in whatever direction he turns, then he will endeavour to gain by evasion what he cannot effect by any direct resistance. He will not meet manfully the claims of repentance, and throw them entirely away from him. He will not say intelligently and determinedly of the Son of God, "I will not have this man to reign over me," but he will do it indirectly. Conscience cannot be forced into quietness, but it may be hushed into stillness by stratagem. Hence originate those false trains of reasoning so common in the world, those sophistries by which the human mind is carried, to its own undoing. It is a remarkable fact, my brethren, that men never reason so much upon the subject of religion, and popular errors, and false and delusive pleas never spring up with such mushroom growth, as when the Spirit of grace accompanies to the mind the clear and powerful enforcements of gospel claims. Men do not argue from their peculiar circumstances against holy devotedness, except as they feel the pressure of its obligations. They do not fly to the doctrine of sovereignty, or take shelter behind that of divine decrees, except as they are driven there by some influences which they cannot directly resist, and to which they are unwilling to yield. And whenever you find a man endeavouring to reason down the claims of God—whenever you hear him using such arguments as these: "I would be a Christian if I could"—"I must wait God's time for my conversion"—"If I am to be saved I shall be saved, do what I may; and if I am to be lost I shall be lost, do what I can"—you may set it down as a settled point that the Spirit of God is striving with him. And in these false movements and ingenious pleas, he is only retreating to, or falling back upon what he deems a secure position, where he may successfully resist the mighty demonstrations of the Holy Ghost.

There is yet another form in which opposition to spiritual influences manifests itself, more common I imagine, and more effective, than either of those which have been mentioned. There are circumstances in which the light of conscience is too strong to be in this manner extinguished. Whatever the human heart, or a sinful world may say, many a man has reached this conviction, clear and decided, "I must repent or perish, there is no other alternative; I must be interested in Jesus Christ, or be lost;" but then he feels that the question before him is not one which demands an immediate answer. A dying hour is not so close at hand, a judgment bar is not so near, the realities of eternity are not so pressing as to force me to a prompt decision. "To-morrow shall be as this day"—"I will hear thee again on this matter"—"When I have a convenient season I will send for thee." Thus runs that siren song, which has hushed more souls to the sleep of death than all other influences combined, soothed more troubled consciences, driven the Spirit of God from more souls, and added the largest number to the frightful catalogue of the lost. For when the Holy Ghost saith, "To-day if ye will hear his voice," while he lends enforcement to the message, "Now is the accepted time," can there be a more certain, though covert resistance to his influences, than to promise for the future what he urges as a present duty? A man had much better intelligently and openly throw from him the claims of Jesus Christ, than thus tamper with and gain the mastery of conscience, because in doing so, he is but yielding to the arguments and throwing himself under the power of what has not inaptly been called "the thief of time" and "the murderer of souls."

It is impossible to follow these illustrations farther, and I must content myself, therefore, with a statement of the general principle. The Spirit of God is the agent of conviction and conversion. Any movement of the mind, therefore, which does not accord with his design, any restlessness under or dissatisfaction with the truth and providences of God, which are the instruments of his agency; any reasoning which tends to weaken a sense of personal obligation; any apology for sin, any promise for the future, no matter how sincere, honest, and well meant it may be at the time of its utterance, puts a man in a position in which he resists the influences of the Holy Ghost, and drives him from the soul.

The question has often been asked, how long may such a process be carried on in the mind without reaching the catastrophe of a final abandonment? In other words, what are the limits of a man's day of grace? To this question the answer must be, we cannot tell. You might as well propose the analogous question, how long may a man live in this world? We cannot tell. It does not belong to us to fix, or to point out the limits of human life. Who but the Sovereign disposer of all things can say with certainty when death shall meet a man? But yet, we know what God has said, "Bloody and deceitful men shall not live out half their days." We know, moreover, from the laws of our animal economy, and from experience and observation, that there are some habits and courses of life which lead to its termination more rapidly than habits and courses of an opposite character. And, therefore, analogy may, perhaps, throw some light upon this question. We cannot tell how long the Spirit of God will strive with a man; we cannot, we dare not set the limits of God's forbearance, but then if we throw aside speculation and take a practical view of the subject, we know that there are some states of mind which induce far more rapidly than others a condition of confirmed impenitence and undisturbed spiritual death. If the Spirit of God always departs from a man in judgment because of resistance to his influences; then it would seem that his strivings would be regulated in their duration not so much by the time as by the degree of their resistance; and this must be determined from the amount of influence exerted upon him. Such a principle draws deep, and tells with mighty effect wherever it applies. The more hopeful a man's circumstances are in view of his opportunities, and the spiritual influences of which he is the subject, the more perilous is his resistance. The man of few privileges, whose mind has seldom been called into action by the truth of God, occupies a very different moral position from the child of prayers and tears and counsels—a very different position from the man who has lived long under the full blaze of gospel truth, whose spiritual experience has been that of alternate anxieties and insensibility, of painful convictions and successful strifes with conscience. Tell me what a man's past spiritual history has been; paint me the scenes amid which he has moved, describe the influences to which he has been subject, and shew me what has been his action under them, and I will shew you how you may rationally calculate his hopes for the future, and determine how near he is to the crisis of his spiritual being. If we may draw an inference from God's recorded dispensations towards men of old; then, when we read, "they vexed and rebelled against his Holy Spirit, therefore, he turned to be their enemy and fought against them," surely, we are right in saying, that often stifled convictions, and long continued resistances to the truth, if they are not the attributes of the reprobate, are fearfully ominous of a fatal and speedy catastrophe.

III. And now, my brethren, we do not pretend —language would fail us in the effort—to pourtray the condition of a man who has reached this melancholy crisis, and has been abandoned of God. The scriptures have given us upon this subject but a few hints, yet those are hints of unutterable painfulness. They talk of being left to the desires of one's own mind, and the devices of one's own heart. They speak of there being "no more sacrifice for sin, but a fearful looking for of judgment;" of being given up to "delusion, so as to believe a lie." The sinner forsaken of God, has his doom forever sealed; for him hope has been blotted out; and he has inscribed his own name upon the catalogue of the lost. He may live in the world, but only to harden himself the more; and under the withering influence of heaven's judgments, to develop a character, which, in view of the whole universe, will fully justify the dread chastisement which shall certainly be measured out to him. He may hear the gospel, and at times there may be something like a momentary start from his deep slumbers; but it is only the spasmodic action of conscience after the death blow has been inflicted, or the fearful looking for of judgment. Thus he moves through the world, becoming daily more callous to the impression of spiritual good, till in an hour when his security is most profound, with his heart more than ever wedded to the world, he bursts with all his unpreparedness upon an eternal scene, and his doomed spirit falls into the hands of the living God. The bare thought is one of agony. It is almost enough to break one's heart, and make him shed tears of blood, to think of a human being gone so far that a God of forbearance must forsake him, beyond the reach of heavenly compassion, standing upon the verge of the world before him, his heart-strings about to snap under the sorrows which are coming, and his voice nearly strung and pitched to his eternal death-wail. Oh! that there never had been the original of such a picture! Oh! that there was no danger of any one reaching such a painful catastrophe.

But I read, "My Spirit shall not always strive with man;" and when I read, I turn with peculiar emotions to those who are out of Christ. I speak to the subjects of the Spirit's influence. Are there none within my hearing? Has the Spirit of God moved over none of these minds? Have there not been under the demonstrations of the gospel feelings which none but the Spirit of God could excite, anxieties which none but the Spirit of God could kindle, and purposes which none but the Spirit of God could lead you to form? Ah! when you were forced to think upon your ways, there was the Spirit of God. When you were checked by some startling providence, there was the Spirit of God. When under the convincing arguments and forceful appeals of the truth, you were "almost persuaded" to be a Christian, the Spirit of God was there. When you left the sanctuary, and turned your back upon the emblems of a Saviour's body and blood which invited you to peace, the Spirit of God was there. Am I mistaken, or have none ever resisted the Holy Ghost? Am I mistaken, or have there been no inward struggles to drive away from the mind religious impressions? Have there been no apologies and excuses in answer to the claims of spiritual religion? No promises and purposes numerous as the Sabbath's arguments, and frequent as the Sabbath's appeal? No, I am not mistaken; there have been and there are many and mighty strivings against the Spirit of God. It is a spectacle over which an angel might weep, if there could be tears in heaven,—

man, feeble man, child of the dust, and crushed before the moth, strives with Almighty God. Who has not done it? how many are doing it yet? And while man does it in his thoughtlessness, he hears not, or if he hears, he heeds not, the sound which comes from the distance and falls upon the ear in tones so solemn and distinct, and with a cadence so dreadful, "My Spirit shall not always strive with man." He heeds it not, but goes on his way resisting the Holy Ghost. Thus he hastens on to a condition of hopelessness and helplessness. Quick as the mind can act, he speeds him onward. Every stifled conviction accelerates his movements. Every Sabbath's light but lights him forward. Every message of the truth, every argument and appeal of the sanctuary which falls upon his ear, and reaches his spirit, serve but to quicken his progress. Ere long the crisis comes. In an unlooked for moment the grieved and insulted Spirit spreads his wings for a final flight, and as he goes, he leaves upon the soul a seal which neither earth, nor heaven, nor hell, can break. The die is then cast, the work is done, the decision is recorded. "Let him alone," is the sentence which has gone forth, and the man is lost. Thenceforward his career is one of growing sinfulness. Thenceforward his state is one of spiritual sleep, profound as that of the grave, undisturbed by any Sabbath argument, unbroken by any threatening omen, unaffected by the approaching realities of another world; and though he may live amid scenes of spiritual beauty, and though the refreshing showers of heavenly grace may brighten and give new verdure to the moral landscape around him—there he is—a spot blasted by heaven's fire, which can never be cultivated, a tree scathed by heaven's lightning, ready to be cut down as fuel for the burning. I may seem to you to speak strongly, but oh! how lame and feeble are my words to give expression to the sentiment which God has uttered, "Woe unto them when I depart from them."

Subject of the Spirit's influences—my dying unconverted fellow-sinner—have you a troubled conscience, a thoughtful mind, an anxious soul? The Holy Ghost is with you now—he is moving upon that heart—you have within you, and around you the evidences of his presence and power. "Now is" your "accepted time, now is your day of salvation." "To-day," as the Holy Ghost saith, "if you will hear his voice, harden not your heart."

"Quench not the Spirit of the Lord,
The Holy One from heaven,
The Comforter, beloved, adored,
To man in mercy given.

"Quench not the Spirit of the Lord,
He will not always strive;
O, tremble at that awful word!
Sinner, awake and live!

"Quench not the Spirit of the Lord,
It is thy only hope;
O, let his aid be now implored,
Let prayer be lifted up."

THE SIN AGAINST THE HOLY GHOST.

"Wherefore I say unto you, all manner of sin and blasphemy shall be forgiven unto men; but the blasphemy against the Holy Ghost shall not be forgiven unto men. And whosoever speaketh a word against the Son of man, it shall be forgiven him, but whosoever speaketh against the Holy Ghost, it shall not be forgiven him, neither in this world, neither in the world to come."—MATTHEW xii. 31, 32.

IT is needless for me to say, my brethren, that the Son of God never would have uttered the words of my text, nor would the inspired evangelist have put them upon this permanent record, did they not contain truth of deepest interest to ourselves, and suggest lessons for our profitable study. For one I cannot sympathize with those who imagine that God has purposely thrown a veil of mystery over the sin of which our Saviour speaks, that men ignorant of its precise nature might be careful in reference to spiritual influences, and so be kept from an approximation to its guilt. I cannot bring myself to believe, that God has revealed any thing to us which he did not intend we should understand, or that there is any truth upon these sacred pages, affecting our character and interest, which is not in itself perfectly intelligible to the docile learner. Granting the truth of all that may be said concerning the mysteries of the Bible, yet you will remember that these mysteries appertain to the facts of the Christian system, their nature and modes, which are not matters of revelation, and never to the doctrines of the system, which are revealed truths requiring our faith and obedience, and demanding, therefore, an intelligent apprehension of them. With these views, therefore, I am not, as I come before you with this subject to-day, to be considered a vain and speculating theorist, nor am I to be classed among those whom an idle and prurient curiosity tempts to pry into the unveiled secrecies of the Infinite mind. Rather let me have your attention, as one who believes there is truth here, of vast moment to ourselves, truth perfectly intelligible, and which he wishes to set before you as part of the counsel of God, pointing out our duty and warning us of our danger.

The difficulty, if difficulty there is about our subject, grows, I imagine, out of the different and conflicting theories which have been brought forward in its explanation, according as their various authors have had different ends in view to guide their investigations, and control their reasonings. With these theories we have nothing to do; we will not stop even to mention them; we would rather dispossess our minds of their influences, and come and study the sacred oracles upon this point as though we were approaching them for the first time to ascertain their meaning. With such a spirit then, I ask my hearers to accompany me to-day.

Now, when we look at the language of Jesus Christ, the obvious truth upon the face of it, is, that it is possible for a man to put himself in a position where forgiveness never can reach him; and he does so by sinning not against Jesus Christ, but by sinning against the Holy Ghost. Here is the fact; no words could more plainly express it, and as a naked fact it is perfectly intelligible. But you ask me to explain it; to point out, if possible, those of its features which constitute its malignity, and exclude it from forgiveness, and to shew those workings of the human mind by which a man reaches a position of such absolute hopelessless. We acknowledge the propriety of the demand you make upon us, and we claim your strict attention to the effort we make to meet it.

Indulge me then, if you please, in two or three preliminary remarks which may serve as preparatives to, and guides in the discussion upon which we are about to enter.

The Bible then, we remark in the first place, is eminently a practical book; it is not a volume of theories to amuse the speculative, nor are its contents designed to excite or to satisfy the appetites of the inquisitive and the curious. Its statements all have a direct bearing upon human character; its doctrines are the points whence the lines of Christian conduct are drawn. Its obvious aim is to make men holy. It is meant "for reproof, for correction, for instruction in righteousness, that the man of God may be perfect, thoroughly furnished unto every good work." As the value of every truth, in any department of human knowledge, is derived from its adaptation to the end it is calculated to subserve, the value of any religious principle is derived from its bearing upon the concerns of practical godliness; and, if it is true, that he does not rightly understand the gospel who does not feel its moral influence, it is no less true that he does not understand any particular doctrine of the gospel, in whose mind that doctrine is not immediately connected with some practical results. Grant this point, and there is no difficulty in disposing of not a few of the theories in reference to our present subject, which have been given to the world; for of the vast majority of them, we may affirm, that they are profitable neither for doctrine, nor for reproof, nor for instruction; profitable for nothing, but to shew the ingenuity of their authors, and gratify a taste for the wonderful on the part of the curious.

My second remark is, that the Bible, as a whole, is throughout consistent with itself. It is one of the strong arguments for its divinity, that though its truths have been revealed at "sundry times, and in divers manners," yet they are perfectly harmonious. Acuteness, and learning, and labour have been pressed into the service of its enemies, in order, if possible, to discover some contradiction or inconsistency, but in vain. There may be, indeed, principles herein revealed, the perfect consistency of which with each other, we, on account of our shortsightedness, may not be able to make manifest, but there are none between which the most powerful mind has been able to show the slightest opposition. As in the system of the universe every planet has its own orbit, and every star its own position, and all roll on in perfect harmony, no one affecting, so as to disturb the precision of another's movement, to the production of one general result; so in the system of God's revelation, every truth has its proper bearing, every doctrine its appropriate place in its relation to the rest, no one clashing with or neutralizing the influence of the other, but all combining to bring about one grand end. Hence there is no safer rule of Scriptural interpretation than that which grows out of the consistency of Scripture doctrines; no view of one part of the word of God can be correct which clashes with a true view of any other part of the word of God.

It is worthy of remark, moreover, concerning this revelation of truth, that its distinctive features, or fundamental doctrines, are presented so fully, that "the wayfaring man, though a fool, need not err" regarding them. They are like lines of light running through the Bible, illuminating all, and explaining all. No man who is willing to give to the interests of his deathless spirit a tithe even of the attention which he knows they justly demand, need remain in doubt about the revelations of the Bible concerning the essentials of vital godliness, nor commit a mistake as to the method it discloses for securing everlasting life.

All the statements and principles of the word of God, grow out of two or three great fundamental facts. Its different doctrines are but the presentation of these simple, undeniable facts, in their different relations, whether to God or to man, whether to the past, the present, or the future, whether to the world which is, or the world which is to come. And as in studying the more abstruse and complicated problems of any human science, we derive our light and our help from its axioms, its postulates, its first principles, so in order to enlighten what may seem dark, and explain what may seem difficult of comprehension on the pages of this inspired testimony, we must borrow light and help from its essential doctrines, those which are revealed so plainly, and exhibited so fully, that their meaning cannot be but through wilful ness mistaken.

And now, as under the influence of these remarks, and under the guardianship of this great law of scriptural interpretation, we approach the task of explanation which is set before us, let us see if we cannot discover some principle, so plainly revealed, and lying so directly upon the face of the Bible that no one can mistake its meaning or avoid its perception, which may shed its light upon the apparent intricacies of our subject, and afford us help in our effort to solve its mysteries. Is there one central point of light in the Bible which we may always so keep in view as to prevent us from being entangled in the thickets, or swamped in the quagmires of human speculation? Is there one raised position which commands the whole field of Christian truth? I think there is; and upon that light I fix my eye, and upon that position I plant my feet. I have it here, my brethren, in this simple truth, which shines out with irresistible power of conviction upon every page of the Bible, that *the forgiveness of sin and eternal life through Jesus Christ, is offered to every man to whom the gospel is made known.* That offer is based upon the atonement of the Son of God, on that wondrous sacrifice, whose blood, we are told, "cleanseth us from all sin." This is the peculiar glory of the gospel as a system of relief for fallen man; that it excepts none from an interest in its provisions, excludes none from its pardons, because of the greatness of his guilt. It meets the apostate sons and daughters of an apostate parent, whatever the position they may occupy on the graduated scale of human sinfulness, with the only help for the highest, and a sufficient help for the lowest. The uprightness of one will not do away the necessity of his pardon; the abandonment of the other will not of itself prevent his forgiveness. The offer is limited not by the character of its subjects, but by the value of the sacrifice out of which it grows; and, therefore, it is that we can go with the gospel to the farthest outcast from God, and say to him, "Come, now, and let us reason together; though your sins were as scarlet, they shall be white as snow; though they were red as crimson, they shall be as wool." Strictly speaking, then, there is no such thing as a sin in its own nature unpardonable, because there are no limits to the value of that blood which cleanses from sin. There is not a case of transgression, magnify it as you may, which redeeming mercy cannot reach, nor a sin of a dye so deep, as to neutralize the purifying efficacy of a Redeemer's atonement. The unpardoned sinner carries his oppressive load of guilt upon the conscience, and at last sinks under its weight to a deep perdition, not because God could not, or would not save him, but because he refuses to avail himself of the ample provision which a God of infinite wisdom and mercy has made for his relief.

While in view of this first element of truth, we must claim that no sin whatever is in its own nature unpardonable, we must at the same time admit that there is a sin, which, in point of fact, never has forgiveness. There is a guilt—there may be none of those outward deformities about it, which make us shrink from its exhibition—yet of such a nature that in point of fact, the cleansing blood of the Redeemer never reaches it. Its subjects, (they are found, believe me, in the ranks of our gospel-hearing population,) its subjects have placed themselves in such a position that they never will know the power of a Saviour's atonement, except as it is to them "a savor of death unto death," and increases the weight and the woe of their final condemnation.

Now, we have here a principle and a fact, and they are both presented in the Bible, and presented so distinctly that we can neither controvert the one, nor question the other. No sin can transcend the infinite value, and the cleansing efficacy of a Saviour's blood; but the sin against the Holy Ghost never hath forgiveness. There may be, at first sight, an apparent, but a careful examination will show that there is no real contradiction between them; and hence no explanation of the sin in question can be the correct one which clashes, in the least degree, with this fundamental principle, that "the blood of Jesus Christ cleanseth us from all sin."

We bring in then, at this point, another principle of the Bible, no less clearly announced, no less indisputable than the former, which may serve to carry us one step farther forward in our investigation. It relates to the necessity of repentance and faith in Jesus Christ, in order to the forgiveness of any sin. "Repent ye, and believe the gospel; Repent, that your sins may be forgiven," are the plain Scriptural statements of the only terms upon which mercy coming through the atonement is dispensed unto the children of men. Thus the limitations of God's pardoning love are regulated by the contrition and faith of its recipients. Repentance and forgiveness always go hand in hand throughout the Bible, and human experience. The least sin unconfessed and unforsaken, shuts a man out from hope. The greatest sin, if sincerely and honestly mourned over and acknowledged, is no barrier to a full forgiveness.

I suppose, that up to this point, I have carried the assent of all my hearers along with me, because I have been dealing with the first and simplest elements, the axioms, if I may so call them, of revealed truth.

Let us come then with these as our guides, to the record before us, and see whether we cannot make plain its apparent mysteries. You will find, if you give a careful attention to the words of our Saviour, that there is a broad and palpable distinction between sin against the Son of man and sin against the Holy Ghost. Strange, you may say, that it should be so, but no less true that it is so. There must be some reason for the distinction, and in that reason, if we can discover it, we shall find, if I mistake not, the key to our subject. Now, in our estimate of human sinfulness, we have been accustomed to take our measures of it solely from the personal dignity of him whose laws have been transgressed, and whose authority has been resisted; and, if this is our only rule of judgment, then, I confess, that the sin against the Holy Ghost is perfectly inexplicable; for I cannot find from the Scriptures, that in point of personal dignity there is any difference between the Son and the Holy Ghost. And in view of those who imagine that they can discover a difference, the mystery of our subject must be deeper and more impenetrable, placing as they do the Spirit in a position of inferiority to the Son, according to which arrangement, if iniquity as to its demerit is to be measured by the personal dignity of Him who is sinned against, the sin against the Son must be more heinous than the sin against the Spirit. But as I read the testimony of inspiration, the Father is God, the Son is God, the Holy Ghost is God. The scriptural doctrine of the Trinity, as I understand it, is that of three personal subsistences of one and the same God, "the same in substance, equal in power and glory." I bring up this doctrine here not to illustrate it; not to defend it, but merely for the purpose of shewing that the reason of the difference between sin against the Son, and the sin against the Holy Ghost, is not to be found in a difference of personal dignity between them, making this the measure of sin's heinousness. There is no more criminality in one sin than in another; for what in this sense is said against the Son is said against God, as truly as what is said against the Holy Ghost.

But is there no other measure of human sinfulness? Is there not something due to office as well as character? Is there not thrown around the chief magistrate an authority which does not belong to him as a private citizen? Is a child no more guilty when he spurns the counsel and tramples upon the command of a parent than when he spurns the counsel and tramples upon the will of a stranger; and that though in point of personal dignity, the parent and the stranger may stand upon an equal footing, or if there is any difference, in this respect, between them, it may be even in favour of the stranger?

Now I find the reason of the difference between the sin against the Son and the sin against the Spirit, in the different offices which they respectively exercise in the great work of redeeming man from sin and death. Here is the key with which I would unlock the mysteries of this unpardonable transgression. The office of the Son, as we are taught in the Scriptures, is to make an atonement for sin—the office of the Spirit is to apply that atonement. The Holy Ghost is the great agent of the Gospel, who brings nigh to us its blessings, its pardons, and its hopes, as he brings us to that state of mind, that repentance and faith, without which we can never receive them. Hence, in the discharge of his work, according to the promise of the Saviour, he convinces "the world of sin, of righteousness, and of judgment." He brings truth, in its clearness and power, before the mind, and opens the mind to receive it. He sets the obligations of the truth before the view, and quickens the conscience to feel them. When the facts of the gospel come home to the mind and heart, as great and solemn and stirring realities, the Holy Ghost is there. When conscious guilt troubles the spirit, and fear takes hold upon one, so as to force from him the anxious inquiry, "What shall I do to be saved?" the Spirit of God is there. When the cross of Christ, girt with its bow of promise and of hope, and yet red with the blood of atonement, meets the eye, and the soul bows and casts itself, humbled, penitent, and believing, at the Redeemer's feet, the Holy Ghost is there. Thus, without his influences, we see no evil in sin, and no beauty in the cross; without his influences, we know not the remonstrances of a gospel-stirred conscience, nor the peace-speaking power of atoning blood. Conviction, it is his gift; repentance, faith, they are his gifts. His design is to bring us to the experience of the former, and to the exercise of the latter, and thus to place us in that moral position, where alone the blood of Christ, in its efficacy, and the forgiveness of God in its fulness and freeness, can possibly reach us.

Now, when you say of Jesus Christ, that he is "as a root out of dry ground, without form or comeliness," you sin against the Son of man, and it shall be forgiven you; but when you resist the influences of the Holy Ghost, which would convince you of sin, of righteousness and judgment, and place you where you can see a Redeemer's beauty, and feel the power of his cross, and rely upon his atonement, then you sin against the Holy Ghost, and it shall never be forgiven—and that not because the blood of Christ will not cleanse us from all sin, but because by our opposition to the Spirit's influences, we put ourselves in a position, where that blood can never reach to cleanse us.

Hence, in view of the principles above illustrated, we reach our conclusion. The sin against the Holy Ghost, which never hath forgiveness, seems to be such a resistance to all his spiritual influences, to all his invitations, to all his pleadings, to all his remonstrances—such a wilful blinding of the mind to all the revelations of spiritual things which he makes to the soul, such a wanton stifling of all the convictions of conscience, which he kindles, as grieves him in all his kindness, and quenches him in all his light, neutralizes him in all his power, and drives him away from the soul for ever. When the Spirit of the living God has for the last time knocked at the door of the human heart, made his last appeal to the human conscience, and moved for the last time without effect upon the human soul, and then takes his final flight, and leaves man to himself, then we say, the work is done—the soul is irrecoverably lost—as the man never will be brought to repentance, so he will never be forgiven. He has resisted God in the closest approach he can make to the human spirit, he has resisted him in view of the clearest light, he has resisted the most effective instrumentality and the most powerful motives ministered by the Holy Ghost. He is sealed up for judgment—and the moment the cup of his iniquity begins to run over, he will be delivered up to its dreadful and undying penalties.

I am not ignorant of the fact, that the view which I have given of my subject, differs from some usually adopted, all of which find the sin in question in some overt act, such for example as the ascription of the miracles of our Saviour to Satanic influence, and some of which consider it as peculiar to the days of miraculous agency. Now we admit that it was an overt act on the part of the Pharisees which drew this solemn language from the lips of our Lord; it was "because they said he had an unclean spirit." The conclusion, however, that it requires words to commit this crime, or that the Pharisees had been guilty of it, are entirely too broad for the premises. Words are nothing, separate from the thought and feeling which they express—an overt act is nothing, separate from the moral principle it embodies. The heart is the seat of moral character, and the sphere of divine legislation; and where the temper of mind involved in any overt act exists, there, in the sight of God, is the sin, even though it found no outward expression; and existing there, it shuts a man out from hope, as truly as though it had found a public manifestation. We cannot surely be mistaken here, when we find Jesus Christ, in this very context, acting as his own interpreter, telling us that "for every idle" or malicious "word, man shall give account in the day of judgment;" that "by our words we shall be justified and by our words we shall be condemned," because "out of the abundance of the heart the mouth speaketh." The persons who were now addressed, had unquestionably displayed a bitter hostility to the truth, and a determination to resist it, in opposition to the most convincing evidence; and the words of our Saviour had undoubtedly reference to this, their moral temper and spirit—and yet we should be slow to charge them with the sin in question. That they were in danger, in great danger of passing over the line which would separate them from the prisoners of hope, is admitted, but that they had actually crossed that line there is no certain evidence in the narrative to prove—rather do we suppose that our Saviour, perceiving their temper, their fixed determination to resist all the light and moral influence which could be shed down upon them, was uttering the language of warning in view of the scenes of Pentecostal times, which were close at hand, when the

Holy Ghost was to descend, as the peculiar agent of the gospel dispensation—the last and crowning evidence of the divinity of the Redeemer's mission and kingdom.

We place then our subject with this explanation before you, simply remarking in view of what we have said, that if you would discover this "sin against the Holy Ghost," you must look for it in the temper of the human heart, its determined and effectual resistance to the promised influences of the Spirit of God. The degree of that resistance, and the extent to which it must be carried in order to convict a man of this transgression, we shall not undertake to define. We leave that point to the determination of him who can measure guilt much better than we can, and who knows how far he can consistently go, in his means to reclaim the sinner to his forsaken love and obedience.

But, my brethren, if the principles we have laid down are true, and the explanation which they have furnished of our doctrine is correct, there are some lessons taught us we would do well to study, and a practical bearing of our subject which we dare not overlook. If I am right in my positions, then it is evident that "the sin against the Holy Ghost" does not consist in any one individual act. You must not attempt to find it in this sinful thought or that sinful thought, in this or that unholy deed. You must not attempt to find it in any sin, no matter how great it may have been, which has filled the soul with contrition, and has been followed by deep repentance. You must not find it in any thing, the recollection of which penetrates the heart with a sense of its own vileness, loathsomeness, and shame. You can never find it amid tears of repentance and confessions of sin, but you must find it in a settled habit of the soul, a habit of determined resistance to God in the nearest approaches he can make to the conscience and the heart—a habit of mind to which repentance is a stranger, which knows nothing of the pangs of ingenuous sorrow, which locks up the secret places of feeling and of tears in the human soul against all the appeals of the Holy Ghost, which can breast itself in proud defiance to the whole moral armament of heaven, and binds the spirit with the stronger than adamantine chains of a confirmed and eternal impenitence. Never should I think to find the victims of this *damning transgression* among those who fear that they are its subjects; such a fear never can coexist with that callousness of conscience and insensibility to spiritual things, which are inseparable from the sin against the Holy Ghost. No, I would find it among those who fear it least. I would seek for its distinctive features among those who, year after year, have crowded our sanctuaries, where truth has been ministered weekly in the demonstration of the Spirit; who have listened to arguments, to which though they could not answer them, they have refused to yield, and have resisted "the powers of the world to come," as they threw their mighty influences over the soul. The ice has been gathering round their hearts, under the beams of the Sun of Righteousness; the iron has turned to steel, under the action of the fire which should have melted it, and the stone has become adamant under the strokes of the hammer which should have broken it to pieces. The influences of the truth play around them, but find no permanent lodgement in their minds; and they pursue their wonted path of worldliness and sin, clinging to their spiritual idolatry, unawed by all that is fearful, unmoved by all that is tender, unaffected by all that is startling, unhumbled by all that is touching in the disclosures which have been made by a God of truth and of love. Within the circle, around which these are travelling, you will find the subjects of the unpardonable sin.

If I am right in the view which I have given, then does my subject come home to all of us with peculiar emphasis; I speak not to one within these sanctuary walls, who has not a deep and eternal interest in the theme upon which I have been dwelling. In these days of spiritual declension, when worldly influences seem to be coming over the church of God like a flood, quenching the fire upon its altars, and sweeping away the landmarks which define its limits, there is danger that not a few who have professed the name of Christ, may be led away to a returnless distance from the peace and hope of the gospel. The Apostle Paul appears to have taken his hint from our present subject, when he gave utterance to his impressive warning, "It is impossible for those who were once enlightened, and have tasted of the heavenly gift, and were made partakers of the Holy Ghost, and have tasted the good word of God, and the powers of the world to come; if they shall fall away, to renew them again unto repentance, seeing they crucify to themselves the Son of God afresh, and put him to an open shame." "If we sin wilfully after that we have received a knowledge of the truth, there remaineth no more sacrifice for sin." The catastrophe in man's moral history, then, of which we speak, is placed in connection with a neglect of gospel privileges, as the means through which the Spirit of God operates, an undervaluing or abuse of which is consequently a resistance to his influences which forfeits them forever. Hence all declensions from the life and power of godliness tend to this very result. With these declensions you will find uniformly associated an insensibility of conscience, and a listlessness in reference to spiritual things. It is this insensibility which makes the matter so alarming. Decline in religion, like decline in nature, blinds us to its symptoms. There is, perhaps, no disease which indicates less the fatal errand upon which it is sent, none which like this presents to its subject such flattering promises. It gives to the eye a peculiar brilliancy, and to the cheek an appearance of health, filling the heart with hope, and suffusing it with life, when the winding sheet has already been woven, and the shades of death are fast falling upon the pathway. Thus the road which leads to a spiritual abandonment, is a gradual descent, travelled at first by an easy and imperceptible though constantly accelerated progress. Its stages are first, indifference;

then carnality of spirit, concealed under a constant attention to the forms of religion, and then, an open departure from the life and power of godliness, and a final renunciation of the vows as well as the spirit of religion.

> "The fearful soul that tires and faints,
> And walks the ways of God no more,
> Is but esteemed almost a saint,
> And makes his own destruction sure."

We do not indeed pretend to say of every one who may be thus described, that he has placed himself forever beyond the reach of those spiritual influences by which alone he can be recalled to repentance. God forbid that we should write down any man as lost, while the pulse, though feeble, yet beats, and the eye, though dim, yet moves; but oh! if our subject has any meaning, it tells us that the man who is grieving the Spirit of God, by departing from his ways, is treading upon dangerous ground, because ground enchanted by the wiles and witcheries of sin; and it will be owing to the wondrous grace of God, if he does not pass the line which separates him from hope forever, while in the midst of his carnal security, he is crying peace to his infatuated spirit. Our only security, my Christian brethren, is found in a life of growing piety, in a constant walk with God, and separation from the world; for as piety declines, we resist and grieve the Spirit, and walk in the path which leads to apostacy and death.

And oh! that all my hearers would remember that they are living under "the ministration of the

Spirit." Strangers to his influences we are not; the quickened conscience, and the beating heart, the wakened anxiety, and the starting tear, are the demonstrations of the power of the Holy Ghost. That blessed Comforter, with whose gracious influences our best, and brightest, and only spiritual hopes are connected, moves over the soul, and gives in its view a reality and impressiveness to the truth of God. Solemn and interesting are our circumstances as the subjects of his agency; and I would bring the influence of my subject, this morning, to bear upon those whose memory of the past, or whose consciousness of the present, testifies to ineffectual, because resisted strivings of the Holy Ghost. There is such a thing, believe me, my brethren, as putting one's self in a position where neither repentance nor forgiveness can ever be reached, because there is such a thing as resisting the Spirit of God, until he takes a final leave of the soul. I cannot calculate the amount of resistance which will place a man in a condition in which his forgiveness will be impossible, but I can correct a dreadful delusion, under which the human mind often labours. I mean the delusion that a man fruitlessly plied with the influences of the gospel, may go on, just as he is, and that at some future time the way of repentance will be as open to him, as it was when first he was conscious of the movement of the Spirit of God upon his soul. It is a terrible statement, but a true one, calculated to awaken the salutary and deep anxiety of every unconverted hearer of the gospel. The day of grace does not always run on parallel with human life, to its utmost limit; a man may be abandoned by God's spirit at any time, as having been sufficiently striven with, and admonished, and warned. And thus, in this case, when the day arrives which may have been marked out in his chronology as a fit day for repentance, a day the anticipations of which have served as anodynes to all his spiritual fears, when it arrives it may pass by as a day of little or no anxiety. The mortification has commenced, and the pain has departed, and spiritual death is there; or if not this, if an approaching catastrophe startles him, he may be terrified by the phantom of wrath, and yet not be induced to seek for mercy. He may have faith enough to believe in a certain perdition, but not faith enough to cling to the only deliverer. Oh! where is this mysterious line of God's forbearance? I know not. One may stand on one side of it, at one moment, and cross it the next. One may reach it after years of walking; another, while his step has lost nothing of its youthful spring. But if there be one who remembers the seasons of the Spirit's power within his soul; if there be one who cannot compute (because their number is so large) his stifled convictions; if there be one who in view of the truth of God, has thought oft and deeply upon the concerns of his soul; if there be one who, though he could not resist the evidence of the truth, brought home to him by the messenger of the truth in his Sabbath argument, has yet often resisted the truth itself, oh! surely we may say of him, that he is standing on the mysterious threshold, to cross which is to enter upon a region of hopelessness and death. And a conscience every day getting weaker, because the unseen author of its remonstrances is every day lifting a feebler voice, shall be to him the proof of my assertion. Look at it for a moment. Conscience will have its last conviction; the Son of God will knock for the last time at the door of the heart; the Spirit of truth will move for the last time over the soul. Amid all these convictions, and knockings, and strivings, some one must be the last. Oh! ye to whom I have preached so long, so earnestly, and so fruitlessly, how near are ye to your last opportunity; and if it should pass unimproved, will it not be true of you, that you will be crushed by the very weight of your mercies; that privileges which God meant for blessings, shall prove the heaviest curses; and the influences of the Spirit of God, which should have prepared you for a crown, and fitted you for joy, will help only to build your prison and fan your flames. Quench not, I pray you, the Holy Spirit.

JUDAS ISCARIOT; OR, THE CONSEQUENCES OF A WORLDLY SPIRIT.

"It had been good for that man if he had never been born."—MATTHEW xxvi. 24.

THE words of the text which we have just read to you are no more remarkable for the preciseness of their statement than for the perspicuity of their meaning. They form one of those propositions we occasionally meet with which carry along with them their own interpretation and proof. We understand them perfectly, we feel their truth the moment they are uttered; no ingenuity of criticism can extort from them any but one sentiment, no process of special pleading can pervert or neutralize their inherent evidence of truth. They form, as my hearers are all aware, the prophetic history (if I may use such language,) which our Saviour has written of the man who betrayed him—the inspired epitaph written over the grave of Judas Iscariot. Among candid readers of the Bible there is, I believe, but one opinion concerning the destiny of this false and apostate disciple. We feel in reference to him as we feel in reference to no other man who has figured upon the theatre of the world, and then passed off the stage to enter upon a scene of retribution; you may take the greatest monster of wickedness whom God ever flung into the world seemingly to curse it, whose actions were but a catalogue of the blackest vices in the calendar of crime, whose every foot-print was stained with blood; who, in fact, seemed to be but the personification of the spirit of evil; yet when you think of him as gone, you do not think of him as you think of Judas Iscariot. Of all men who have ever passed through this scene of probation to their reward, he is the only one of whom you can say without hesitation, he is lost; and if you undertake to analyse this feeling, and trace it to its source, you cannot possibly explain it, except as originating in this language of Jesus Christ concerning him, "It had been good for that man if he had never been born." The moment you read these words, you feel—you cannot help feeling—that the person of whom they may be affirmed is lost, and not only so, but irreparably lost; that his destiny is one of conscious misery without mitigation, and without end. It is by this simple statement of the Master, and by nothing else, that we are driven to the conclusion which seems to be well nigh universal concerning the betrayer of his Lord, that whatever there may be for others, for him there is and can be no redemption. The mental process by which we are forced to this conclusion is so rapid that we do not always perceive distinctly the steps by which we reach it; it is, therefore, our object upon the present occasion to subject it to an examination preparatory to applying the principles herein involved, that you may perceive how it is reached by means of several almost self-evident consecutive truths. Grant this proposition concerning any man, that it would have been better for him never to have been born; and I see not how it is possible for the human mind to escape the conclusion that his destiny must be one of interminable suffering, without contradicting some of its intuitive, I had almost said, instinctive perceptions. When we make this plain, I think we shall have reached a general principle, in which many a man in our day has a deep and eternal interest.

I begin then my subject with a statement which no one, I suppose, will dispute. Existence is a blessing; every man desires it; the love of life is an essential element of our being. There is a felt horror at the thought of passing into nothingness, which forms one of the finest arguments of natural theology in favour of the immortality of the human spirit; and yet, if we examine our consciousness upon this point distinctly, we shall discover that our desires do not terminate upon life in itself considered, but upon the good, or the enjoyment which is supposed to be connected with it. Strip life of all enjoyment, and it ceases to be an object of desire. Thus we cling instinctively to the good of existence, and shrink as instinctively from the evil of its loss, which we look upon as inseparable from annihilation; if you could separate existence from every thing in the shape of happiness and sorrow, it would have no properties whatever by means of which we could determine its value. And upon this supposition, it would be a matter of entire indifference to every man, and the question whether he would be or cease to be would be one which would not call up a single thought. It is evident, therefore, that life is desirable, or otherwise, according to the amount of happiness or misery which it brings along with it. If this is true, then it is no less true that the good of life must preponderate over the evil to make it an object of desire. If we could suppose a case in which the happiness and misery of a being exactly balanced each other in every respect, we would have the case of a being to whom it would be perfectly immaterial whether he continues or ceases to be; for he gains nothing by living, and loses nothing by being blotted from existence. It is only as the one preponderates over the other, that there is room for the question, whether it is good or otherwise for a man that he has ever been born? If there is more happiness than misery, then we cling to life with an unyielding tenacity; if there is more misery than happiness, annihilation has no horrors.

True it is, you may tell me, that there have been men whose portion seemed to be nothing but misery, or if this is an overcharged statement, whose hours of comfort, not to say enjoyment, were very few, interspersed here and there among their long continued seasons of sorrow, pain and agony, who have yet clung to life with a tenacity quite as remarkable as that of those whose circumstances have been exactly the reverse, who seem to be contradictions of my doctrine, and conclusive proofs of the desirableness of existence in itself, irrespective of all its attributes. Even admitting the statement to be correct, (supposing as it does the possibility of such an acquaintance on our part with all the circumstances of another, as will enable us to determine accurately the question of his experience,) it is seen at once that the statement is a partial one, since it confines our observation to present circumstances, and leaves altogether out of view the mighty influence of hope. Find me a human being whose life is a life of unmingled sorrow, and who withal has no hope of a favourable change, and I will find you one for whom annihilation has no horrors, and who can say with perfect sincerity, "It had been better for me if I had never been born."

Hence, in studying a question like the present, we never reach a correct conclusion except as we take into view the whole of existence, and form our judgment from the sum total of human experience, as the aggregate of enjoyment or suffering may seem to preponderate. You may trace the course of a man from the cradle to the grave, and you may be satisfied that not one ray of light has ever beamed upon his pathway from its commencement to its close upon earth; that every hour has been one of suffering, that every moment has been one of agony. Yet, if when he reaches the close of his earthly career, he is ushered upon a scene of uninterrupted, eternal blessedness, it were idle to say, it had been good for him had he never been born, and for this simple reason; however great his evils may have been, his actual good is more than sufficient to overbalance the whole of them. So, on the other hand, if you could find a man whose existence is one of joy, whose every hour is one of gladness, whose every moment is one of unalloyed bliss, so that not a single cloud lowers on his pathway, nor a single event occurs to interrupt the even current of his happiness, yet if you suppose that at the end of his earthly career, all his enjoyment is at an end, and that he plunges into the darkness, and anguish, and despair of eternal night, it is true of him that "it had been better for him if he had never been born," because, however great has been his good, the actual evil of his experience will more than counterbalance it all.

If we are safe thus far, we take another position. In the present state of things, good, at least in human estimation, overbalances evil, and hence all men wish to live; and for one I am satisfied that men's apprehensions in this respect are in accordance with truth. There is more good than evil in this world, take it all together. As there are more beauties than deformities in nature, so there is more happiness than misery in human experience. If it were otherwise, this world would no longer be a world of probation, but a world of retribution. My experience may not appear to you to bear out this statement—and your experience may to me seem to contradict it—but every man's experience proves it to his own mind. The reason of these diverse appearances is perfectly obvious. We do not know either the elements or sources of each other's joys and sorrows. What might elevate me might be no source of happiness to you—and what might depress you might not in the least degree affect me, and perhaps might administer to my enjoyment. I may have joys which you cannot appreciate, and you may have sorrows to which I am an utter stranger. Place me in your circumstances, or place you in my circumstances, and it is quite possible, that in the experience of both of us consequent upon this change, the evil might overbalance the good; but take man as he is, and judge of him in view of his actual capacities, and the circumstances in which Providence has placed him, and the good overbalances the evil in the present life, so that if death were to terminate human existence, it could not be said of any man, " it had been good for him if he had never been born." Such, at least, is the unanimous practical decision of our race, or if there are exceptions, they are anomalies which we cannot explain. Who will pretend to give a rational explanation of suicide? Who does not feel that it is in itself evidence of a morbid, unhealthy, unnatural state of mind; that it is the act of one, who for the time being has lost the balance of his reasoning powers, and under the influence of a temporary hallucination is unable to look at things in their true light, and judge of them by a proper standard.

Now I take these positions as unquestioned and

unquestionable, and throw their light upon the sentiment of my text, and ask if we can form any adequate idea of the condition of the man, of whom it may with truth be said, "It had been better for him if he had never been born." The sentence speaks volumes to the mind. Without a figure, it is more imposing, more striking, more terrific, than a cluster of a thousand frightful images could make it. It gives a bare outline of human destiny, and leaves the imagination to run wild, as it fills up the picture with forbidding and horrid creations. What does it mean? Can it be that it designs to affirm annihilation of the human spirit? Then it affirms a positive untruth; for if the person whose condition it describes, has been what we usually term a happy man in this world, then he has actually gained something by his existence. If he has shared in the common allotments of humanity, still, since his enjoyment has exceeded in amount his suffering, he is yet a gainer, because the annihilation which is to put an end to his happiness, is to put an end to his suffering also. Or, if you can find a man in whose experience evil preponderates over good, if hope remains and gilds the prospect of the future with its beautiful and flattering, though too often delusive hues, he cannot understand the sentiment in reference to himself. No! while hope remains, annihilation has no charms for him; he had rather be than not be.

We cannot avoid the conclusion, my brethren, that in these words Jesus Christ has given us a meaningless sentence, if he does not convey the idea that there is to be, consequent upon this life, a state of positive, and necessary, and perpetuated existence. Man is to live, and live on, with all his susceptibilities and capacities of pleasure and of pain. The human mind is to be alive to every thing that affects its relations, and the sensibilities are to be quick to apprehend every thing that touches the experience. Man will understand himself perfectly; be conscious of his losses as well as his gains. Carrying with him into a future scene all the elements and laws of his nature, he will be a living, thinking, feeling, anticipating being. It must be so; he cannot prevent it; he can no more check the current of his existence, as it continues to roll on, than he could originate it in the first instance. He can no more of himself cease to be, than he could of himself begin to be. The question of his existence is, by a necessity of nature, entirely beyond his control. The power which creates is the only power equivalent to destroy. Man may modify substances, and change their form; but he can annihilate nothing. He may change the circumstances or mode of his existence, but he cannot by any possibility destroy it. If he could, he would be omnipotent. If he could, then it would not be true of any man that "it had been better for him if he had never been born," because, since existence, separate from its good or evil, is a matter of no moment, and since man in the present state, is a subject of more good than evil, no matter how severe the sufferings of another world would be, he might, by annihilating himself, terminate at once all his experience of pain. How then could the sentiment of my text be true of any man, if the moment a scene of unmingled misery were entered, he could blot himself at once from existence? Hence, our first conclusion is, that man always must be a subject of positive, sensitive, necessary existence.

Equally indispensable is it, in our apprehension, to make good the sentiment of the text, that man's circumstances hereafter must involve greater suffering than can be found in any condition of existence in this world; for if in the estimation of man, existence is preferable to non-existence; if while any enjoyment remains he would rather live for the sake of that enjoyment, than not live, the conclusion is inevitable, that no condition could justify our Saviour's language, but one reft of all enjoyment, one of unmitigated and uninterrupted suffering. Oh! I read in the words of the Son of God —I wonder how any man can fail to read it—the utter hopelessness of the lost. Give me hope, and no argument can convince me of the desirableness of annihilation; nothing but an utter despair can ever commend it to the wishes of the heart. The present moment may be one of unalleviated sorrow. There may be nothing in any of our actual experiences, to foster the desire of life. There may be every thing to force us to say, "I loathe it, I would not live always." But when hope sheds its influence over the mind, and leads me to balance expected good against actual, present evil, then I shrink back (I cannot help it) from the thought of destruction. Hang round a man in every direc tion the emblems of sorrow, to correspond with his inward experience, and let hope remain, and his spirit is cheered and sustained, and no argument can convince him that annihilation is a blessing Nothing can justify the language of the text, but a condition of absolute despair. The position is incontrovertible, existence is a blessing, if wretchedness stops short of immortality. A man may wear away millions of ages in the experience of woe; he may have heaped upon him torment after torment; there may be no abatement, but rather an increase of misery, as century crowds upon century, till imagination fails in telling up the period; yet if there is to break upon him a moment of deliverance, to be succeeded by an eternity of rest and joy, it is good for him that he has been born. At whatever point his sufferings may terminate, there will remain for him an immeasurably longer season for the enjoyment of happiness, than had been consumed in his agony, which will make him feel that the boon of existence demands from him the most glowing gratitude. If perdition is to be but temporary, and the gates of the eternal prison-house, which close upon the lost, are ever to be thrown open, so that its inmates may go free, every one of them will feel so. I care not what may have been a man's misdoings and sufferings upon the earth, his life may have been uncheered by a single smile, his history may have been but one black and biting calamity, he may have gone down an accursed thing to the pit of despair, a period which we cannot compass, may have been spent amid the penal fires of a fierce retribution, yet let this be the close of the appalling tale, that he is emancipated, his crimes are purged away, his vast debt cancelled, and I am sure, in view of the well-known principles of human nature, that as he sees an eternity of peace opening brightly before him, he will join as cheerfully and as loudly as any in the words of the general thanksgiving, "We bless thee for our creation." It is telling me, then, that sorrow is to be eternal, to tell me of a man, that "it had been good for him if he had never been born."

And now, my brethren, if we have the meaning of our Saviour's proposition distinctly before us, let us turn our attention to another question, Where does it apply? How far does it reach?

If we should confine the sentiment of my text strictly to the immediate connections in which the Master has placed it, no one, perhaps, would question its propriety. We have such an estimate of the character of Judas Iscariot, that we think no punishment too severe for him; while there are other forms of wickedness, in reference to which we do not hesitate to say of the man who manifests them, that annihilation would be the greatest blessing God could send him. But I feel that in the sentiments I am about to advance, I shall go far beyond the ordinary apprehensions, and come into collision with the feelings of the majority; but I design only to walk in the light which Jesus Christ has shed upon my pathway, and in doing so I come to the conclusion, that if the proposition of my text is justifiable and true in the case of Judas Iscariot, it is no less justifiable and true in the case of many a man who thinks he has the least possible interest in it. I am sure, my brethren, that we are blinded in this matter. We look at the act, the terrible act, the damning act of this traitor, and say no judgment is too severe for him. But what was that act—what character, what meaning had it, if you divorce it from the controlling temper of mind which it served to develope. In a moral point of view it is nothing, except as an expression of feeling; and when the feeling exists and controls one, there is the guilt, though its outward expression may be constrained and regulated, or even prevented by independent providential circumstances; precisely as in the eye of God, he who hateth his brother is as truly a murderer as though he had imbrued his hands in his blood. Long before this act was committed, the Master called Judas Iscariot a devil; he was a devil before as really as after he had given his master the traitorous kiss.

Be not startled at the assertion which now I make, that so far as his outward life was concerned, in a worldly point of view, this traitor was an irreproachable man. The Saviour would not have selected him, the other disciples could not have associated with him if he had been otherwise. They who were on terms of intimacy with him gave him their implicit confidence. He had won upon their hearts, and so unsuspecting was their trust, that they did not understand their Master's reference when at the last supper he gave Iscariot the sop, thereby pointing him out distinctly as his betrayer. Yet he was a radically ungodly man, because his controlling spirit was *an inordinate love of money.* This was the element of his character; the parent of his crime, the cause of his doom.

It is a home question in this age of ours—I know it—are there none like him? When you see a man all of whose energies are consecrated to money, who looks upon every thing and determines the value of every thing in view of its relation to this one object, who is dead to all claims but those which it enforces, and cares not what interests he sacrifices, or what law, divine or human, he tramples under foot in obeying them, how far think you does he stand in the eye of God below Judas Iscariot in the scale of moral character?

Or, when you see a man who will break through no restraints, who will sacrifice no private interests, who will, so far as his outward life is concerned, subject himself to no penal enactments of civil law, yet will descend to plans from which an honorable spirit will recoil; will be mean, if not dishonest; degrade himself, though he will not break the statute; will act upon any principle, and embark in any plan, legalized by custom, or uncondemned by the world, however contrary it may be to the spirit of the gospel, or destructive to the interests and hopes of his soul; who will act upon a large scale, though in a different form, upon the same principles, which viewed as the life and spirit of the gaming table are odious and detestable, where will you place him?

Bear with me a moment while I cease from particulars, and present a general principle, which every man may apply for himself. I am not afraid, at all, of being classed with those who are eternally crying down wealth, and who speak of the possession of riches as synonymous with certain perdition. My hearers know me too well to suppose me guilty of that wholesale declamation, which originating rather in carnality than in grace, evinces the ignorance, more than the wisdom of its authors. Riches have their use, but there is a point of possession beyond which, if a man go, they are useless; destitute of intrinsic worth, and valuable only on account of the purposes to which they may be applied. When a man reaches that point, where through inability or indisposition, they are not made subservient to useful ends, they are worse than valueless. Now I am perfectly aware that my principle takes a wide sweep, but in view of these general premises it seems to be unquestionable. When a man has no other object than simply to make money, when he has more than he can, or which is the same thing, is willing to apply to useful purposes; when his whole ambition is to see how many pieces of stamped metal he can gather together and call his own; when he has no ultimate purpose in view, but his desires terminate upon property for its own sake, I care not who he may be, what his outward exhibitions of character, or what his visible relations, he is under the influence of the same spirit, which as it controlled a false disciple, led the Redeemer to the ignominy and death of the cross; and we can say of him without hesitation, if he lives and dies under its power, "it had been better for him if he had never been born"—for such a man has lost the control of himself, he has thrown the reins upon the neck of a degrading worldly passion, and he cannot tell what developments of character he yet may make. He is rushing forward blindfolded in his course, and knows not where he may stumble, and over what he may fall; and if left entirely to himself, unrestrained by independent influences, untrammelled and unconfined by any outward circumstances, he will trample upon every thing, and sacrifice every thing upon the altar of his unholy ambition. We will not, however, restrict our principle; we extend it to earthly ambition, whatever may be the peculiar form of its manifestation, or the object it contemplates. The love of money is not the only human passion which blinds the mind, and wars against the kingdom of God and the interests of the human soul. Any earthly lust, if it gains the complete ascendancy, and mounts the throne, as the governing principle of the mind, will do precisely the same thing. If the love of power, or the love of pleasure, had been as rampant in the soul of Judas Iscariot, he would have betrayed his Master at the bidding of either, as certainly as he betrayed him at the bidding of his love of money. It makes no difference what a man's controlling spirit may be, if it is purely worldly and sensual, and at war with God's commandments, it must be broken, subdued, eradicated, or the man is ruined, lost for time and lost for eternity. It is difficult, I know, to commend this truth to the minds of those who are specially interested. The slave of his passions will not believe either in the wickedness of the dominion to which he subjects himself or in the fear of any dangerous results. And when Judas Iscariot attached himself to his Master, and began his career of embezzlement, as he gave full scope to his controlling temper, he never dreamed of the results; he had no conception of the issues to which it would lead him. He would have treated as an idle tale, the prediction which should have shewn him going to the chief priests to barter away his Master's liberty for thirty pieces of silver. It is the characteristic of all sinful passions, that they blind the minds of their victims to their nature and their tendencies. "Is thy servant a dog?" said Hazael, as the prophet Elisha foretold him of the horrid cruelties of which he would be guilty when he came to be king of Syria. "Is thy servant a dog that he should do this thing?" and yet as Henry says, "the dog did it;" and let a man give himself up to the control of any passion, whether it be the love of money, or the love of power, or the love of pleasure, and he is ripe for any thing which his governing spirit may demand for its gratification; he will perform acts, at the bare mention of which his soul would formerly have shuddered, and that without compunction and without remorse. Nay, more than this, he may, without being aware of it, accumulate upon his own conscience, a guilt, in view of which, as seen resting upon another, he actually trembles. Are you a professing Christian, my hearer, and under the influence of some temper hostile to the spirit and requirements of the Master? You are shocked at the treachery of Judas Iscariot. You can see the deep defilement of his soul, and the guilt which no tears of repentance could wash away, and no human conscience could bear, and the thought of an approximation on your part to such a fearful criminality, would convulse your soul with agony. And yet it may be, that he who seeth not as man seeth, may discover in you some of the moral lineaments of the same image, which as seen in Iscariot, are so positively frightful.

I have never betrayed my Master, is the language of many a carnal and worldly disciple who is living solely for the purpose of compassing some ambitious views; and, perhaps, we can discover the reason why he has not done so, in the absence of some sufficiently strong temptation, or in the influence of some outward circumstances, or of some commanding earthly interest; but in the eye of him with whom principles are actions, and in view of whose spiritual government the wish is put upon a level with the overt act, who determines the guilt of sin not from its actual effects, but from its tendencies and from what would be its results if circumstances favoured its full development; what difference does it make with him in his estimate of character, that the opportunity of crime is absent when the will to perpetrate it is ascendant in the soul? The spirit of Iscariot, though not acted out, stamps the soul with Iscariot's guilt. The controlling temper fixes the character; "as a man thinketh in his heart, so is he."

"I have not, oh! I could not, like the traitor, betray my Master." To the man who, under the confessed dominion of a worldly spirit, uses this language to certify his innocence, I would propound the question, Have you commended him to those around you? Can you honestly say, that in your ardent pursuit of the world, you have as ardently pursued the kingdom of God and his righteousness? That there has been nothing in your manifested character, nothing in your plans and enterprises originating in, matured, and carried out by an absorbing spirit of earthliness, which has calumniated the gospel, and weakened the claims of your Master in view of others, if it has not led them to trample under their feet the religion of the gospel? If I cannot acquit myself in view of such inquiries, oh! surely I cannot complain if I am put on a par with the bribed apostate, as one who in prophetic language has "wounded Christ in the house of his friends."

Judas Iscariot was "the son of perdition," and I will not deny that his crime was peculiarly aggravated by the confidence which was reposed in him, and which he basely betrayed. We should be greatly at fault, however, if we supposed that this constituted the essence of his sin. If I understand his crime, it was a sacrifice of his Master upon the altar of his unhallowed ambition. His sole purpose was to gratify his love of money. An injury to his Master, so far from entering into his design, was utterly foreign to his thoughts. Precisely like him in all the essential ingredients of his sin is every man who has no other end in view than to subserve some worldly or sinful desire; who at its bidding can throw behind him all a Redeemer's claims, and trample on all a Redeemer's commandments. No! no, he does not mean to injure Christ, or to disparage Christ's claims; he means only to gratify his own desires, and if he cannot do the latter without doing the former, he will do both. This is the spirit of which Judas Iscariot was but the embodiment—are there none, my brethren, like him? Is not every man like him who cannot be religious, because religion will interfere with some of his plans of earthly aggrandizement, and call him to sacrifice some of his earthly desires? And wherever there is such a man, and this spirit cannot be subdued, "It had been better for him that he had never been born." There is no parade of words nor clustering of images in this language in which Christ sets forth the doom of uncrucified carnality. And yet while it is perfectly simple, there is not a human being who dares to grapple with the representation, or is equal to the task of unfolding its meaning. The futurity which will furnish the explanation is all midnight. The eye of the soul which enters upon it will open upon darkness. God, who is all light, is before it; but it is darkness. Eternity, that unbroken day in which h ere are no sunsets, is before it, and yet it is darkness; it is all fire, yet all darkness; a flame which consumes but never illuminates. My brethren, if ye have not sacrificed all for Christ, the dark mountains upon which you will stumble and fall are before you. If you would look, you might already see them in your horizon, like iron masses covered with sackcloth. Oh! give yourselves speedily to Christ, and then with new hearts and a right spirit you will see the Sun of Righteousness, which has not yet gone down in your firmament, skirting the edge of that black rampart with beams of gold; and then, as despair gives way to hope, instead of lifting up the wail, "Oh! that we had never been born," you will be able to raise the rapturous shout, "We bless thee, O God, for our creation." It will be with you hereafter, as now you love the world or the Saviour most.

JUDAS ISCARIOT; OR, THE POWER OF CONSCIENCE.

"Then Judas, which had betrayed him, when he saw that he was condemned, repented himself, and brought again the thirty pieces of silver to the chief priests and elders, saying, I have sinned in that I have betrayed the innocent blood."—MATTHEW xxvii. 3, 4.

IT is not among the least interesting facts which this passage brings to our notice, that the betrayer of his Master could not possibly become his accuser; that he who could be prevailed upon by bribery to play the traitor, could not in any way be induced to testify against him whom he had surrendered into the hands of his enemies. Nay, more than this, he is constrained to publish his own infamy in witnessing to his Master's innocence. It would have been a great gain to the chief priests and rulers of the Jews, could they by any means have wrung from one of the intimate associates of Christ, any thing respecting his character and designs, upon the ground of which they might have proceeded against him as a malefactor or disturber of the public peace. They who gave thirty pieces of silver to secure his person, would unquestionably have given much more for evidence to justify their procedures against him; and he who was base enough to betray him, we should naturally suppose base enough to play into their hands, even if he should be compelled to do so at the expense of truth.

Now you perceive that we might take advantage of this fact, to set before you one of the most logical and conclusive demonstrations of Christ's truth and righteousness, which can possibly be constructed. Judas Iscariot was one of the Redeemer's most intimate associates, and must have been well acquainted with his private acts. If Christ, therefore, had been a deceiver, and performed his miracles by collusion, the traitor must have known the deception, and this would, at least, have relieved his self-condemnation and remorse. But it is perfectly evident that the galling thing to the mind of the betrayer, was the full conviction of his Master's innocence. Had he known any thing to the contrary, oh! surely, in self-justification, he would have told it; or even should he have kept it to himself, (a supposition very unnatural,) its knowledge would have preserved for him a comparative quiet, or at least saved him from suicide. Such is a mere outline of the argument, the more valuable because it is indirect.

It is not, however, to this point that we turn your attention this morning. The question which will open the subject upon which we design to discourse, relates to the wondrous influence which constrained the mind of the traitor, not only preventing him from giving testimony against his

Master, but wringing from him reluctant evidence in his favour. It was not the baseness of perjury which deterred him, for a man who could with cool and calm deliberation break such obligations as those which bound Judas to the Redeemer, was equal to any wickedness, however great. It was not earthly interest which deterred him; for in an earthly point of view, he had better have carried the matter through, than have committed suicide. We must look, therefore, for an exponent of his conduct to some unseen influence which swayed his mind, an influence well nigh omnipotent; and what could it have been but the simple influence of conscience? The acting of conscience, then, as seen in the history of this man, shall furnish us with our subject this morning, while we attempt to gather up some of the lessons which this history furnishes, and impress them upon our minds.

There are three lights in which we look at Judas Iscariot, each furnishing us with its distinct doctrine upon the subject of conscience. We see him wrought up into agony by some mysterious influence which derives its meaning and power from the future. We hear him acknowledging the truth. We find him stripped of every thing like an apology for his crime, and we thus reach the following views: Conscience, the herald of the future; conscience, the advocate of truth; conscience, an answer to every excuse for transgression. An exhibition of these views will accomplish my design.

I. I am perfectly aware, my brethren, that there

have been advanced, in behalf of this inward mon itor, claims which never can be made good. Attributes have been ascribed to it which it never possessed, and its powers have been enlarged and magnified, to an extent far surpassing any thing which facts will warrant. The advocates of mere natural religion, have used it as an argument against the necessity of the Bible, by putting it in the place, and making it subserve all the purposes of a special revelation from God. While we cannot sympathize at all with this position concerning it, yet when we find how accurately it distinguishes between right and wrong, how solemn and impressive are the warnings which it utters against the commission of the one, and how delightful is the sense of satisfaction connected with the doing of the other, we cannot but feel that its subject so far carries about with him teachings from heaven, that you cannot predicate of him an entire ignorance of the will of God, and of the consequences of obedience and disobedience. For this is the peculiarity which distinguishes conscience from every other faculty of the mind—that it takes hold upon the hopes and fears of another life, and works with them as its instruments. Its power over the soul springs from anticipation—the element of its reward is hope—the element of its punishment is fear. Its reward is thus the expectation of reward; its punishment the expectation of punishment. In proportion as a man can blind himself to the realities of the future, he can neutralize its influence; and if he could work himself up, by any means, to a state of total unbelief as to a coming world, he would be an entire stranger to all its inflictions. Hence it is, that atheism and infidelity resolve the influence of conscience into superstitious fears—an explanation unworthy of a thinking mind, putting as it does the effect for the cause; the fears of which they speak as originating conscience admitting of no solution but one which brings in conscience as their source. Hence they reason perpetually in a circle, explaining conscience by man's unfounded fears, and man's unfounded fears by conscience; thus assuming every thing and proving nothing. Every man is a witness to himself of the truth of my general position; for as all have been subjects of the approval of conscience, when they have hearkened to its voice, and have suffered in consequence of their resistance to its dictates, they carry the evidence within them that it draws its resources not from the present but from the future, and acts upon men by hope and fear; and if so, then it preaches beyond all contradiction and all question, another state of being; a state of retribution, in which the Supreme moral Governor will recompense actions wrought on the earth. It is thus that we explain the experience of Judas. There was nothing in present circumstances to harm him. Would the men in whose hands he had played, wreak their vengeance upon one who had become their co-worker, and had afforded them such signal assistance in accomplishing their designs? His Master was now subject to his enemies; the traitor saw his condemnation certain, and he could fear nothing from one whose tongue was shortly to be palsied, and whose limbs were shortly to be stiffened in death. No, it was remorse which now preyed upon him—remorse springing from the apprehended certain connection between the past and present, and the future. It was conscience, making every event the herald of judgment, and every shadow the minister of retribution. He could almost read the record of his crime, made by one who would not let it pass unavenged; and though he had gained what he coveted, and held in his hands the wages of unrighteousness with which he meant to satisfy his avaricious soul, there was a boding form, unseen by others, yet flitting distinctly before his mind, which no enchantment could will, and no menace force from the scene. And thus he was a witness to himself, as are all others, in their wrong doing, witnesses to themselves, that this world is under the government of a God who may allow wickedness for a time to be successful, yet gives a boding of judgment, and an earnest of retribution in the dread imagery of wrath which conscience arrays before the spirit.

It is worthy of observation here that these actings of conscience are perfectly independent; they are not the fruits of reasoning, they spring from no logic, they result from no lengthened investigation into the propriety and fitness of things. Men may reason in order to stifle conviction, they may excite their passions into a storm in order to drown its voice, but this is after its testimony has been given; they can do nothing beforehand to prevent that testimony. Unlike those propositions which result from reasoning, the verdict of conscience does not knock at the door of the mind, and sue for admittance; conscience is part of the mind itself, and acts within, bidden or unbidden. If it were otherwise, and we had to make out the being of a God, and a future state of rewards and punishments, by a process of rational deduction, man might meet argument by argument, and proof by proof, and contend, and equivocate, and practice a thousand subleties to get rid of the force of evidence. But it is not so; for when conscience speaks there is no room for evasion, no room for subtleties; conscience in reality is the commencement of judgment itself; and what quibble, or equivocation, or argument can stand before a plain fact?

And thus it is that every man who does wrong and fears the consequences (and no man can divorce such wrong doing from such fears,) carries within him evidence which he cannot overthrow or gainsay to the being of God, and the retributive character of his moral government. I care not who he may be, or what may be his pretensions; he may tell me that he does not believe in God; he may tell me that he sees no evidence of his existence in the traces of design which are every where stamped upon the works of nature; but there is a voice whose testimony to this fact rings in his own bosom, and while conscience speaks, and the forebodings of wrath keep company with unrepented and unforsaken transgression, and the path of him who goes on in the way of evil is crossed and recrossed by images of woe and desolation, though you should shut up the Bible, and blot out from the universe of created things every thing which tells us of a God mindful of the works of his hands, still there would be proof enough left that we live under the government of a ruler who is the avenger of wickedness; and not a subject of that government could ever, in view of his experience, plead ignorance in extenuation of crime.

II. Now, if we have made good our first position, which presents conscience as an evidence of our accountability and future existence, we proceed another step in our illustration, to ascertain the bearing of its testimony upon other questions of truth and duty. The world in which we live is full of error, both of principle and practice, and we cannot but admire the pertinacity with which men will often cling to falsehood, and the ingenuity with which they will reason out its defence. We question very strongly whether man is ever, in the first instance, brought intelligently to the adoption of error, or can ever adduce evidence in its favour which will perfectly, in all circumstances, satisfy his own mind. Where a man's opinions are purely speculative, relating merely to questions of natural science, we do not mean to say that his errors, necessarily, involve moral delinquency. He may be too hasty in his conclusions, or deduce his results from an imperfect or partial examination of facts; we may doubt his wisdom, and withhold our confidence in his judgment, without throwing any imputation upon his heart; but it is vastly different with moral questions. Here, in all cases where the means of arriving at a knowledge of the truth are possessed, the advocacy of error of opinion is usually associated with depraved inclinations, which call for falsehood in their justification. It is, I am aware, a startling doctrine that which I now advocate, that sin or vice, in some form, is the parent of wrong moral principles; that man does not become an Atheist, a Deist, or an enemy of any cardinal doctrine of revealed truth, except as depraved inclination makes it one's interest that there should be no God, and no revelation. And the evidence of my doctrine is found in this, that almost all errors of this kind, however boldly they may be put forth as purely rational truths, however long they may have been held, however pertinaciously and skilfully they may have been defended, give way at once to the influence of conscience. And yet conscience has not to do directly with opinions, but only with practice, and with opinions as they spring from, or are necessarily connected with practice. Conscience never will set a man right in his purely theoretical views on many subjects; it will never expose his errors in astronomy, or physiology, or natural or simply intellectual science; but let him adopt a radically false principle in morals, and he cannot hold it a moment when conscience begins powerfully to act. It shows him the error of his opinions by rebuking the sinful desires or plans in which such opinions originate. I know not what principles Judas Iscariot may have adopted as his principles of action while he was carrying on his designs against his Master. He must, however, have had some distinctly formed views under the influence of which he thought he might, in his circumstances, go forward properly, or at least safely; and yet no sooner does the emergency arise which awakens conscience, than all his finely arranged theories are completely blown away, and a single rebuke of this inward monitor furnishes a complete refutation of all his unanswerable arguments.

There is a parallel, and if any thing, a more strongly marked case, illustrative of our general idea, given in the history of Herod, the Tetrarch of Galilee, and murderer of John the Baptist. No sooner did the fame of Christ spread abroad, than Herod, however unwilling to be disturbed again by the presence of a prophet, yet knowing that there was a worker of miracles abroad in the land, was constrained to express an opinion concerning him; and of all opinions, none could be more inconsistent with his professed faith. "It is John," said he, "whom I have beheaded: he is risen from the dead." Now by what process of reasoning could he reach such a conclusion? Where was the apparent likelihood that Jesus Christ was John the Baptist? What correspondence was there between Jesus working miracles, and John who wrought no miracles? Herod, moreover, was a Sadducee, and according to his professed creed, death was the end of man; there is no resurrection, no angel, no spirit. How, then, came Herod to advance an opinion in such direct opposition to his professed creed? Do you suppose that in the midst of his voluptuousness, this corrupt prince had been re-examining the articles of his faith, and as a result of such new examination, was renouncing as erroneous, doctrines which he formerly held as true? Had he been studying the law and the prophets, think you, analyzing the arguments in favour of the soul's immortality and the body's resurrection, and in view of the evidence which flashed upon his mind, had he come to a conclusion which completely overthrew every article of what he once considered his rational faith? How was it that the marvellous stories which came to his ears concerning the wonder working of Jesus Christ, wrought such an entire revolution in all his theoretical opinions? How but by starting conscience, which, when once awaked, raised the spectre of the murdered John, and made it impossible for him to hide from his view his dreadful guilt, under the pressure of which he could no longer hold his false principles? He had probably never reasoned at all about the doctrines of his creed; like most other errorists, he had taken them for granted, because they suited his inclinations; it was marvellously convenient for him to disbelieve in futurity, in a resurrection, and a judgment to come, because his vices made it desirable that he should perish with the brute. But no sooner did conscience begin to act, than all his speculations or hopes vanish, and Herod trembles in view of that futurity at which he was wont to smile, and that judgment to come, which he had been wont to think was nothing but a dream. We put, then, Herod in company with Judas Iscariot, as shewing how completely conscience can refute all the false reasonings of a sinful mind, and, therefore, evidence of this truth, which men seldom believe, that when man arrays himself against any plain, essential doctrine of God's word, he has not in reality a particle of confidence in one of the positions he assumes.

And it is precisely so, my brethren, with every one whose depraved inclinations lead him to the adoption or advocacy of error. A man may blind his power of perception, and pervert his understanding, but he never can permanently stifle his conscience with bad logic. While his circumstances are such as do not put his theory to the proof, he may, perhaps, succeed by his ingenuity in maintaining error. But whenever conscience rebukes him, or he is called to any great risk on the strength of his opinion, his agitation will show that he has no confidence in it, and in the course he pursues he will positively contradict his professed faith. Every day, every hour, is heaving into being illustrations of the general remark. We have upon record the fact of atheists, in an hour of peril, forgetful of their avowed system, calling for help upon God, whom they had, as they thought, reasoned out of existence. Place such a man in circumstances of danger, in the midst of peril-stricken companions, and do you tell me that he will look with cool contempt upon the agitation of his fellows, and preach atheism to them in the midst of their terrors? or will he not, sympathizing with them in their fears, join them in supplicating in the tempest, the Deity whom he denied in the calm? Yes, and we have not only heard of, we have seen men on their death-beds, who during their whole lives had treated the religion of the gospel as a fable, calling vehemently upon Christ for forgiveness, as though their theories gave way when the soul came to be separated from the body. And it was not reason that silenced their arguments, nor any external evidence which produced such deep conviction of error. It was nothing but conscience, which all along had been gently whispering remonstrances, and was only waiting the opportunity which then arrived, of giving full play to its terrors, to throw to the winds every flimsy argument, and wring from the man a contradiction of himself. Oh! it is wonderful, this power of conscience, whereby it extorts from one a denial of those doctrines with which he had laboured to deceive others and himself, and forces him to become a witness to the very truth he had endeavoured to disprove; and as every man possesses this attribute of mind—I care not who he may be—how astute a reasoner, if he becomes an advocate of error, conscience will prove too much for his logic. He may suffer himself to be carried away by any of the thousand philosophical speculations which go to overthrow the testimony of the Bible, and cut men loose from its restraints; he may think himself very rational in smiling at the simple verities of the word of God, and giving himself to a course of life which those verities forbid; but while we know that he can only smother conscience, but can no more kill it than he can annihilate himself; we know, also, that there is a time coming, when it will raise itself with a superhuman might, and preach to him, and compel him to preach to others the doctrines which he now passes by in silence, or reprobates with scorn. There may be no prophet in the land armed with tremendous powers, to strike terror into those whose creeds have been found to patronize their sins, yet when the hour of peril arrives, or the dread footstep of approaching death is heard, then conscience will be more than the voice of any earthly prophet; however magnificent his endowments, and withering his demonstrations, conscience will be more to awaken, and agitate, and confound the spirit by bringing up to view contradicted truth. And if any man who rejects the gospel and adopts error, tells me that he does not believe in this energy of conscience; that his faith is the result of patient and calm investigation, and that he is not to be disturbed by any prophecy of conviction and ruin coming together, I will not stop to reason with him, but simply remind him, that he carries about with him continually a power precisely like that which Judas illustrated, who, when he saw that Jesus was condemned, threw away the gains of his false reasoning, and wicked though cunning policy, confessed his iniquity, and died, a self-immolated witness to the reality and power of conscience.

III. There is yet another view we are called to take of our subject. There are many men in our world perfectly sound in their principles, who are wholly unsound in their practice. In many of the courses which they pursue, they can but feel, with the light they enjoy, that they are trampling under foot some of the divine commandments. And they differ from those to whom we have al ready alluded, in that, while the latter deny or reason away the principles which stand in opposition to their desires, the former admit the truth of the principles themselves, but find a justification of their neglect or disobedience of them, in some of their peculiar circumstances. It is not every man, who with all the aid a sinful and deceitful heart may furnish, is able to work himself up to the adoption of speculative atheism, or to assume the position of the theoretical skeptic. The testimony to the being of God, which is seen every where upon the spreadings of creation, and to the retributive character of his moral administration, which is presented in the daily and hourly developments of Providence; and the evidence which throngs around this revelation of truth, is too clear, too abundant, too conclusive to be gainsayed, or set aside or evaded—and yet there is many a man, who admitting the being of God, can yet find, as he thinks, sufficient reason to justify his disobedience; and admitting the reality of the gospel and the propriety of its claims, can yet justify his rejection of them. These are your apologists for acknowledged transgression. Set their impenitence and their sins clearly before them, and you need no argument to demonstrate their impropriety and guilt—they are confessed at once—and yet there are not wanting extenuating pleas. Their situation is peculiar, their circumstances are peculiar, their temptations have been peculiarly strong and trying; so that, what they can but confess to be abstractly a crime, is in view of all the considerations they can adduce in their case, no crime at all. Judas Iscariot was unquestionably a very plausible reasoner. However abandoned we may consider him to have been, we cannot imagine him so far lost to all sense of right, as to defend treachery to his Master, as an act in itself proper; but then, he had doubts about his Master's course. He felt that Jesus Christ was too slow in his movements, that he suffered too many opportunities to pass, of which he might have availed himself, to establish his claims and manifest his glory; he was, therefore, but forcing him into a situation where no possible harm could befal him, and where he would be compelled, in self-defence, to make, as he easily could, such a manifestation of his character as would completely triumph over incredulity, and bear down all opposition. Moreover, if, after he had bargained with the chief priests and rulers, conscience should smite him, he felt that he was committed; he had entered into engagements which were binding upon him, and which he could not innocently violate. Very much in the same way Herod the tretrarch seems to have reasoned. He felt that it was wrong to murder John the Baptist, but how could he escape the obligation of his rash and inconsiderate oath? His wickedness, therefore, in his case, was not only proper, but necessary. Thus both Judas and Herod extenuated their iniquities, by considering them as forced upon them by imperative circumstances. And now the point at which I wish you to look, is this: Conscience is too good a casuist to admit of any such apology. In both of these cases, conscience must have remonstrated, though its subjects were setting flimsy sophisms against the imperious sense of right, and persuading themselves that they were acting upon good and sound principles in what they did. But it required only some unexpected event, to give conscience power enough to demolish the false logic, and scare the guilty by a full exhibition of the atrociousness of their crimes. Hence, when Herod apprehended danger, he did not fall back upon his oath, and say there was no alternative, circumstances were imperative. Judas, when he saw that Christ was condemned, did not fall back upon his intentions and declare that he meant right, and aimed only at good. No! truth spake out with terrible emphasis, and its tone and tenor made them both tremble; and Herod could not help looking upon Christ as an avenger of his crime, and Judas, under the weight of conscious guilt, went and hanged himself.

And precisely like them, in our own day, are the men (oh! how large is their number) who flatter themselves that they have some good apology for their sins; that peculiar circumstances render that excusable, which otherwise would be criminal. Precisely like them, are they who think they may safely neglect duty and trespass upon right. When

I see a man violating truth, or practicing deception, or going aside from the straight line of uprightness, because apparently good of any kind may thus be gained or evil avoided—when I see a professing Christian compromising principle, or justifying conformity to the world, on the ground that it is allowable in his peculiar circumstances—when I find a man out of the kingdom of Christ, admitting that he ought to be a Christian, yet unwilling to submit at once to the requirements of the gospel, thinking that he may, in view of some peculiarity in his situation, not only safely, but even rightly procrastinate his decision upon the subject, I know that he is endowed with a power precisely like that which convulsed the spirit of Iscariot with an intolerable agony, and which only awaits the opportunity which the Providence of God, sooner or later, will furnish, of rising in the full majesty and terror of its might, and pouring down upon its wretched victim the full measure of its overwhelming and withering malediction.

These hearts of ours, my brethren, are very ingenious in covering over sin. Never are our wits so sharp, as when our transgressions are to be excused. But oh! let us learn from the case before us, that all the wretched meshes in which we may entangle conscience, will sooner or later break away, as a thread of tow, when it touches the fire. God regulates the movements of conscience, and God allows of no apology for sin. He can forgive it; he can forget it; he can blot it out as a cloud and a thick cloud; he can bury it in the depths of the sea; he can carry it away, so that no more mention shall be made of it; but he never, no never can excuse it. And the man who is in the habit of apologizing for sin, and soothing himself with the thought that he cannot well avoid doing what he is doing—and that what he cannot well avoid doing, he cannot be very guilty in doing—may be sure that the time is coming, when conscience shall awake, and cause the earth seemingly to ring again, as though the footsteps of the avenger were approaching, and make him start and quake, as it peoples the scene around him with the ghosts and images of his iniquities.

It is a solemn truth which I am uttering, and a fearful and real consummation I am portending. Judas trembled and was overwhelmed when the full guilt of his treachery burst upon his mind, as he saw his Master condemned; and the man who rejects Christ now, and treats him with scorn, and instead of forsaking his sins, extenuates and apologizes for them, may be sure, that if not before, he will be startled by the trumpet peal of judgment; and then all his sophistry will leave him, and all his apologies will vanish, and as the great white throne is set, and the judge descends, there will be a cry of agony, "This is Jesus whom I crucified; hide me from the presence of the Lamb."

It is perfectly idle for any man to say all this is fable, for every man knows better. As no one can be found who is not a subject of compunctions of conscience, there is no one who does not carry within him a prophet which portends precisely such an issue. There is a process continually going on of retribution—of reward for right and punishment for wrong—showing us what kind of a government is that of God, under which we live; and however desperate a man's struggles with himself may be, he cannot get entirely rid of this process. There is a tribunal set up every day in the human bosom, and a judge there, and sentence pronounced there; aye, more than this, carried into effect there. But then, when you come to analyze the nature of these inflictions, you find that they consist in dread, and therefore no man can get rid of the evidence of a dreadful scene in the future. The certainty of the fact itself, then, of which we speak, no man who reads at all the workings of his own mind, can doubt. If you ask when, where, how, I give you but the same answer which our Saviour gave to a similar question, proposed by his disciples, when he had been predicting terrible judgments: "Wheresoever the body is, there will the eagles be gathered together." Wherever there is prey, there is the bird of prey. Vengeance seems to follow the sinner as by a kind of instinct. He may cross the ocean, ascend the mountain, dive into the cavern, but he can never hide himself from conscience, which like the eagle, hovering over its prey, is ready at any moment to pounce upon its victim. The commission of sin seems to produce the bird of prey. No sooner is the act performed, but the fatal flap of its wing is heard. And who, in view of this fact, can doubt that every subject of unrepented and unforsaken sin, must sooner or later fall under a ministry of vengeance, whose terrors are prefigured in the painful premonitions already felt? Wh› can escape? Who can evade the scrutiny which must be carried on, and the sentence which must be passed in the solitudes of every human heart? Some time or other, the antitypes to these convictions must come. Man must reach the substance of these dreadful symbols, enter upon the inheritance, of which he has already the earnest. If we are right in our views, then if man is a sinner, conscience is ever at hand, like a bird of prey, with an eye that scathes, and a beak that lacerates—and if not before, when man falls, no matter how, no matter where, no matter when, there it will be instantly upon him, as though it had been watching its moment, hovering over his dwelling, tracking his steps by night and by day, by sea and land. This is conscience. Woe to the man who falls its prey—he may fly, but it flies with him—it is in him, it is an eternal part of himself. My impenitent and unforgiven hearer, the eagle is upon thee—hie to the refuge which God has furnished in the Redeemer's cross.

HISTORY OF SAUL.

"Now Samuel was dead, and all Israel had lamented him, and buried him in Ramah, even in his own city. And Saul had put away those that had familiar spirits, and the wizards, out of the land. And the Philistines gathered themselves together, and came and pitched in Shunem: and Saul gathered all Israel together, and they pitched in Gilboa. And when Saul saw the host of the Philistines, he was afraid, and his heart greatly trembled. And when Saul enquired of the LORD, the LORD answered him not, neither by dreams, nor by Urim, nor by prophets. Then Saul said unto his servants, Seek me a woman that hath a familiar spirit, that I may go to her, and inquire of her. And his servants said to him, Behold, *there is* a woman that hath a familiar spirit at Endor. And Saul disguised himself, and put on other raiment, and he went, and two men with him, and they came to the woman by night: and he said, I pray thee, divine unto me by the familiar spirit, and bring me *him* up whom I shall name unto thee. And the woman said unto him, Behold, thou knowest what Saul hath done, how he hath cut off those that have familiar spirits, and the wizards, out of the land: wherefore then layest thou a snare for my life, to cause me to die? And Saul sware to her by the LORD, saying, *as* the LORD liveth, there shall no punishment happen to thee for this thing. Then said the woman, Whom shall I bring up unto thee? And he said, Bring me up Samuel. And when the woman saw Samuel, she cried with a loud voice: and the woman spake to Saul, saying, Why hast thou deceived me? for thou *art* Saul. And the king said unto her, Be not afraid: for what sawest thou? And the woman said unto Saul, I saw gods ascending out of the earth. And he said unto her, What form *is* he of? And she said, An old man cometh up; and he *is* covered with a mantle. And Saul perceived that it *was* Samuel, and he stooped with *his* face to the ground, and bowed himself. And Samuel said to Saul, Why hast thou disquieted me, to bring me up? And Saul answered, I am sore distressed; for the Philistines make war against me, and God is departed from me, and answereth me no more, neither by prophets nor by dreams: therefore I have called thee, that thou mayest make known unto me what I shall do. Then said Samuel, Wherefore then dost thou ask of me, seeing the LORD is departed from thee, and is become thine enemy? And the LORD hath done to him, as he spake by me: for the LORD hath rent the kingdom out of thine hand, and given it to thy neighbour, *even* to David: Because thou obeyedst not the voice of the LORD ,nor executedst his fierce wrath upon Amalek, therefore hath the LORD done this thing unto thee this day. Moreover, the LORD will also deliver Israel with thee into the hand of the Philistines: and to-morrow *shalt* thou and thy sons *be* with me: the LORD also shall deliver the hosts of Israel into the hand of the Philistines."—FIRST BOOK OF SAMUEL xxviii. 3-19.

OUR discourse this morning is designed to be historical. We take for its subject the history, more particularly its closing scenes, of Saul, the king of Israel, contained in the chapter we have read to you, on some accounts among the most remarkable, as it certainly is among the most instructive biographies upon the sacred page. There is, indeed, a wildness in some of its parts, there is a mixture of the strange and supernatural which excites attention and awakens curiosity; and we would avail ourselves of these features the more easily to fasten the mind upon those great practical lessons which are interwoven with the story, and for the sake of which it has been preserved upon the inspired record among the things which "were written for our knowledge." The mysterious and unearthly circumstances connected with the story can in themselves minister only to an unprofitable excitement of the feelings, and might be passed over almost without notice, were it not that there are truths here which relate to the conscience, which cannot be brought out fully to view, but in canvassing those remarkable incidents which to many give its only interest to the narrative.

If the history is remarkable, I cannot say that it is peculiar. I doubt not that many a man living can see, in the features of this first king of Israel, his own moral lineaments—while I am sure that the principles upon which he acted are receiving now, in new forms indeed, their daily illustrations; and the course which he pursued is, in all its essential points, the same with that which not a few all around us are treading, perhaps unconsciously to themselves. With this view of the narrative, and this explanation of my purposes, I ask my hearers to come with me to its study. I wish to give the outlines of the history, and then present the moral lessons it suggests.

The commencement of the reign of Saul was full of promise. His character as a son marked by filial submission and obedience, seemed to fit him for a sovereign, (as they only who have learned to obey understand rightly how to govern,) while the meekness with which he bore his honours, and the vigour with which he entered upon his duties, were ominous of a happy course both to himself and his people. Gifted as a man with all those qualities of head and heart requisite to the discharge of his office, nothing seems to have been wanting to complete his character, and ensure prosperity, but the influence of fixed religious principle. We are among the number of those who look upon a deep and controlling sense of responsibility to God as essential to permanent security and success in any department or sphere of human action. The subjects of official trusts, men upon whom are devolved the weighty interests and concerns of a nation, need, above all others, its directing influence. No amount of energy, no degree of political sagacity, no shrewdness or cunning, no skill, however consummate, of managing men, and availing one's self of passing circumstances, can atone for the absence of a spirit which leads one to do right in the sight of God, or supply its place among the elements of permanent prosperity.

Of this fixed religious principle, the king of Israel seems to have been entirely destitute. There is no evidence, in any of his doings, that he was a man whose heart was right with God. We are told, indeed, that he became another man—that "God gave him another heart." And there is unquestionable evidence that a great change came over his views and feelings, over his abilities and his inclinations, so that forgetting his former employments, his mind, as it was fixed upon the duties of his new office, expanded in those qualities which become a general and a monarch. We have no doubt that, called suddenly as he was to his royal station, he was endowed with high courage and nobility of spirit, which did not before belong him, because they were uncalled for in the circumstances in which he had moved; and in reference to these new mental developments, it is said, that "God gave him another heart." His whole subsequent history, however, shews that he had never been renewed in the spirit of his mind—even amid the apparent solicitude for God's honour which he sometimes assumed, you can discover nothing like the influence of religious principle—nothing but what is often common in our own day, a deference to religious externals, which the nature of his office or public opinion seemed to demand.

The wisdom, and prudence, and courage, which marked the commencement of his administration, won the hearts of his subjects, and secured the complete triumph of their arms. Never were a people apparently in more prosperous circumstances at home, and abroad never did a monarch occupy a prouder position.

His elevation and success, however, seemed too much for his unbalanced and ungoverned spirit to bear, and in a very little while, his proud and unsanctified nature developed itself; his conduct changed, and he began to decline almost as rapidly as he had previously advanced. In disobedience to the positive command of God, his impatient spirit led him to assume the functions of the prophet, and offer the peace-offering and burnt offering before he went out against the Philistines. The excuses he advanced, when reproved for his disobedience, so far from evincing any sense of his wrong doing, showed a disposition to defend, what in his conscience he knew to have been wrong. The success which was granted him in battle, notwithstanding his rebellion, served only to harden his heart; and he went on in his course of almost reckless impiety, until, in the case of Amelek, he suffered personal and selfish considerations to sway him, and in opposition to the express order of God through his prophet, spared the king of Amalek and the richest of the booty, destroying only that which was refuse and useless. He now seems to have passed the point of Divine forbearance. Though for many years thereafter he remained upon the throne, his history is one of crime and suffering. Deprived of the counsels and admonitions of Samuel the prophet, who now entirely left him, troubled by an evil spirit which came upon him in judgment from God, he appears to have been given up altogether to his own devices, and the unchecked dominion of those evil passions which first led him astray from the path of duty.

We now find the once wise and prudent and happy king, an abandoned man; a fierce, dark, melancholy man, a terror to himself and to those around him. But in his distress he turned not to the Lord. Like too many, in our own day, who when disappointment and sorrow come upon them, turn to the cup, the viol and the song, Saul instead of seeking relief in prayer for his troubled mind, sought it in the melody which the son of Jesse swept from his harp-strings. But soon his source of comfort became one of pain. Now all the bitterness of his spirit seemed to vent itself upon the youth whose music had partially relieved his melancholy—to destroy him became his controlling, ungovernable passion, and though at times, when David, the object of his malice, manifested the most generous forbearance, there seemed to be about Saul some symptoms of remorse, some bursts of better feelings, these were but pauses in the storm, which seemed thereafter to rage with greater violence, and make the closing part of the monarch's life darker and darker, without a single indication of that true repentance, which even then might have averted his coming doom.

And now we reach the end, where we find the lessons upon which we wish mainly to dwell.

The Philistines are gathered together against Israel. Samuel, who had been the king's counsellor and friend, is dead, and all the circumstances in which Saul was placed, conspire to harass him, and fill him with the most gloomy forebodings. Completely at a loss, his own wisdom, his own prudence and skill at fault, not knowing in which direction to turn, he betook himself to God; and here we have one of those cases which have been put upon record by way of warning, to check that presumption of the human heart, which leads man to suppose that at any time he may make his peace with heaven; one of those cases which go to show that there is a time, when, though we may seek God, we cannot find him, though we call upon him he will not hear us. Saul consulted God in his extremity, but it was too late; he answered him not, neither by dreams, nor by visions, nor by the prophets. We do not mean to say that if Saul had sought God by true repentance and unfeigned humiliation, he would not have found him. We do not think we have a right to say of any man in this world, that he is beyond the reach of pardon, if whatever may have been his past life, there is at any time a renunciation of sin, and true repentance. But of this contrition Saul knew nothing. No sense of the wrong he had done moved him, but simply a sense of the peril to which he was exposed. He was the same unprincipled man now, that he was when he spared the king of Amalek, or persecuted David; therefore God heard him not; the sentence of judgment had gone forth, the king must be left to himself, and the mighty must be gathered and fall at Gilboa. And now it is that the wickedness of his heart fully developed itself. Hear this man whom God had raised up to be king; this man whom Samuel, the prophet, had instructed; this man who knew truth and duty, hear him, and see to what lengths of wickedness one forsaken of the Spirit of God will go. "Seek me a woman that hath a familiar spirit, that I may go to her and inquire of her." If you are acquainted with the Old Testament records, you are not ignorant of the severity of God's laws against every thing like witchcraft. "Thou shalt not suffer a witch to live," were the words of God to Moses, when giving him the code of laws by which the Israelites were to be governed; and by this code Saul in the former part of his reign had been governed, and in his measures had carried out the spirit of this law to the letter. Without stopping to inquire into the motive of his unrelenting war against all who dealt in divination and necromancy, it is enough to know that he was not influenced by any abhorrence of the crime as a violation of the laws of God, since we find him now, in his anxiety to pry into the future, having recourse to the very arts which he once sought to abolish; and herein he presents the melancholy picture of man forsaken of God, giving himself up to the most desperate wickedness.

In reference to these practices to which the king now resorted, and to which God had affixed the penalty of death, I cannot coincide in opinion with those who think that they were nothing more than jugglery and deceit, and that sorcery was little if any thing else, than skilful imposition. I cannot find in this view a justification of the really sanguinary laws which were enacted against them. I cannot bring myself to the belief, that under the Jewish dispensation, mere sleight of hand was a crime punishable with death, and I am forced to the conviction that there was more than trick in those who professed to have intercourse with the spiritual world; and without pretending to know or divine any of the secrets of necromancy, I cannot escape the conclusion that there was some combination between human beings and impure spirits. Nor is there any thing unphilosophical or irrational in such an opinion. It is no more absurd, no more difficult of credence, than are the demoniacal possessions recorded in the New Testament, the reality of which is put past all doubt by the evidence sustaining it. If I may venture on a suggestion here somewhat explanatory of this matter, (and no suggestion is out of place which tends to throw light upon the sacred page,) it is this: The devil is said to be the god of this world, and in the ages of heathenism he reigned without a rival; the whole system of idolatry, with its impious dogmas, its profane rites, its mysterious oracles, was his work, by means of which he was permitted to exercise his power over his deluded subjects, and to the overthrow of this system, when Christianity was fully introduced, I believe that our Saviour referred, when he said, "I saw Satan as lightning fall from heaven;" and now we can see why the practice of sorcery and necromancy was a capital offence under the Jewish law, as it tended to subvert the very foundations of the system, bringing in idolatry with its infamous rites, against the universal prevalence of which it was the design of God, by means of the institutions of Moses, to protect mankind. It was not merely a spiritual, but also a political offence; it was an attack upon the first principles of their civil policy; it was treason against the government of the nation.

While, however, I take this position, I am not to be understood as intimating that evil agencies could go beyond the permission of God, could infringe upon the prerogative of the Creator, or communicate any information or power which transcended the reach of the creature. They might unquestionably reveal many hidden transactions of the past, but they could never penetrate into the secrets of the future. With much of human artifice in the divination and necromancy of ancient times, there was, as appears clearly proved by the testimony of Scripture, mingled not a little which surpassed human power, which seems conclusively to establish something like supernatural machination.

It was to an adept in such arts that Saul resorted. Instead of being humbled because God heard him not, he became desperate in his measures, and resolved as he could not obtain an answer from above, to seek one from beneath. Herein he filled up the measure of his wickedness; he forsakes utterly the God, by whom he had been raised to power, becomes a transgressor of the law he had sworn to preserve inviolate, a traitor to the government whose honour and integrity he was solemnly pledged to maintain.

And now for the sequel. Disguised, and at the dead of night, the wretched and guilty king goes to Endor, to consult with the wizard who resided there, and he invokes her to bring up from the grave the prophet Samuel—and here there is an abruptness in the sacred narrative, as though God would prevent us from prying too deeply into such unhallowed mysteries. What the process of necromancy was in this case we know not, but an old man covered with a mantle rises up out of the earth, and Saul recognizing Samuel, bowed his face to the ground.

And who is this shrouded personage who rises up, seemingly in obedience to the necromancer's art? We are aware of the very common interpretation, that Satan here assumed the form of the prophet, and that this spectral thing was the evil spirit with whom the woman of Endor was in communion; but from this view of the case we dissent. We believe that it was really the form of Samuel by which the king was now confronted, and yet we do not believe that his appearance had any thing to do as a result with the witch's incantations. We cannot for one moment harbour the opinion, that the souls of the righteous, after being delivered from the burden of the flesh, are to any degree under the control of evil agency, so that they may be summoned back again to the world—and yet here was the form of Samuel which stood before Saul. If it was not so, the inspired narrative would not have spoken of the apparition as Samuel. There is nothing in the language used to suggest a doubt, but every thing to induce the belief that it was Samuel who appeared, and Samuel who spoke, a fact which must militate against the truthfulness of the record, if it was an evil spirit, and not the prophet, who addressed the king.

The sorceress, too, no less than her guest, was surprised, startled and terrified by the mysterious form which rose up out of the earth. Evidently she expected no such apparition, and it is idle to suppose that she would have been so surprised, if the appearance corresponded with her expectations. We suppose that in the midst of the proceedings God himself interfered, and before the necromancer had completed her arrangements, he sent the dead prophet with his message of woe. We are confirmed in this opinion by the fact that the apparition delivered a prophecy of the future, which was verified to the letter by the events, and herein transcended all human power. It is the prerogative of God alone to foretell things to come, and the accuracy of the uttered prediction forbids any other supposition, but that the old man clothed with a mantle, was Samuel himself, commissioned of God to revisit the earth and pronounce the doom of the obdurate king.

It was a wonderful and thrilling scene which followed. How reproachfully must the well remembered voice of him who had been so grieved and distressed while living have fallen upon the ear of the guilty monarch. What madness in Saul to think that by unhallowed means he could gain from God's prophet what God himself refused to bestow; what could he look for in such circumstances, but the utterance of reproof, and the predictions of vengeance? The Lord has become thine enemy, says the prophet; because of thy wickedness thou art forsaken and abandoned. The cup of thine iniquity is filled up; thine end is come; to-morrow thou and thy sons shall be with me; and the prophet disappears, and Saul is overwhelmed. And yet, though he had heard his death-knell rung in his ears, he rècovers from his shock, and goes out on the morrow to the battle. But his bravery availed him nothing; the edict had gone forth against him; his sons fall on Gilboa; he himself is among the wounded, and even yet his pride and haughtiness of spirit prevail, and to prevent his death by the hand of the uncircumcised he falls upon his own sword, and rushes, a guilty suicide, into the presence of that God whom be had so greatly insulted, and by whom he had been utterly forsaken.

Thus perished one who promised fair in the commencement of his course. Naturally unstable, arrogant, and impetuous, and destitute of all religious principle, rapidly, when he followed the bent of his passions, did he tread the downward path; shewing us that, however happy may be a man's beginning, there is no security for a happy continuance and end, but in an abiding determination to do right, and an abiding sense of dependence upon God; and when without these a man yields to temptation, he goes not by steps, but by strides, from one degree of infatuation and recklessness to another, until with a hardened heart and seared conscience he rushes madly upon ruin, and perishes, at last, in his own corruption.

We have already said that we do not look upon this history, however remarkable, as by any means singular. If in the course which Saul pursued he stood alone, if there were none like him now, or none in danger of becoming like him, the story would be to us without its moral, and without its warning; but we believe that there are not a few even in our day in whom the same sinfulness of the human heart is acting itself out, modified, indeed, in its form by external circumstances.

I. We advert here, then, by way of instruction, to one peculiarity of Saul's course, as evincing his growing wickedness. I mean his becoming a patron of the sin of which before he had been the opponent. Whatever the ascendancy which sorcery had once over him—and it was unquestionably great—still he had professed his conviction of its sinfulness, and had endeavoured to expel it from the land; and now he gives evidence of his growing depravity, and his rapidly approaching ruin, as he favours the very sin against which he had once determinedly set himself. Herein he is like the man of whom our Saviour speaks, when he wishes to describe a desperate moral condition, from whom the evil spirit had gone out, but to whom he had returned, making "his last state worse than the first;" and who is not taught by this striking narrative, the peril of the man, who having been checked in an evil course, gives himself up thereafter to the influence of sin? The slave of his appetite, who has felt his degradation, and resolves to obtain the mastery, and after a temporary abstinence returns to his former course, becomes more degraded than he was before; and the man whose conscience has been acted upon by the Spirit of God, and who has roused himself from his security, and then again given himself up to carelessness, only proves himself farther than ever from all spiritual impressions. There must be, in such cases, as there was in that of Saul, a grand victory achieved over conscience, and a great despite done to the Holy Ghost, and so the breach widened between the soul and God, rendering all ordinary means useless for the purpose of recovery.

I would that all who are not fully determined upon a rejection of the gospel; who are not past the wavering point upon the subject of religion, but are yet halting between two opinions, to look at Saul, as he goes to commune with the witch of Endor, and learn from him a lesson of their danger. If there are those who have their hours of anxiety, their seasons of spiritual disquietude, when, obeying some secret impulse which is not of an earthly origin, they essay to break away from their sins and practice righteousness, and yet return to their former ways of folly and transgression, we bid them mark this monarch of Israel, as under cover of the night he approaches the scene of unhallowed incantations; and as they see him again tampering with that which he once endeavoured to destroy, what is he doing but that with which they themselves may be justly charged, returning to the sin which had been forsaken; and what is the very worst feature of the case, as indicating the erasure of all good impressions, and a searedness of conscience, finding comfort for the mind in that which had occasioned disquietude? And as it was with Saul, so may we expect to find it with every one who acts like him; there will be a reprobate mind, and a rapid hastening to destruction.

II. I would have you observe, however, in order to bring out a second lesson from this narrative, that it was not until after Saul had consulted God, and God had refused to answer him by dreams, or the Urim and Thummim, or the prophets, that he betook himself to the sorceress. We need hardly repeat here, what has already been said, that it was not unfeignedly and with full purpose of heart that Saul sought the Lord; had he done so, even in his then desperate condition, he would have found pardon and succour: but, with an unhumbled heart, and with the same impatience of spirit which marked him when he disobeyed God, by invading the priest's office and offering sacrifice, now, because he did not at once receive an answer according to his wishes, he flies to find in necromancy what he could not find in waiting upon the Lord. And herein I think he is not unlike many in our own day, upon whose minds some serious impressions have been made, and who failing to find relief immediately from their spiritual anxiety in the duties of religion, seek it in other and forbidden things. I doubt not that there are many, especially among our youth, who seek to allay their mental uneasiness by indulging in the pleasures, and engrossing themselves with the occupations of earth. Unable at all times to repress the pleadings of conscience, those pleadings prevail upon them for a time to give themselves to the study of the word of God, and to secret prayer; but very soon relief is sought from their urgency in the business and amusements of the world.

We protest, in view of the narrative we have spread before you, against all such means of allaying one's moral disquietude. The man who tells us that he has tried by the relinquishment of sinful practices, by prayer, and the study of the word of God, and tried in vain to obtain comfort, and now must search for it among the things of this life, is acting over again the part of Saul, who because there was no answer at once from the Lord to his impatient and unhumbled spirit, fled to the cave of the sorceress, to be beguiled and deceived. Such a man feels that he is in peril, that he is environed by many forms of danger, but rather than meet boldly the difficulties of his case, and follow steadily and determinedly what he knows to be the will of the Almighty, he hastens to drink of the cup which shall render him insensible, and be soothed by charms and spells into forgetfulness of his condition.

If there is one of my hearers who has been at all aroused to a sense of his spiritual condition, as unreconciled to God, we would endeavour to arrest the fatal determination of turning to the delusions and enchantments of earth, for that peace which can be found only in the gospel of Jesus Christ. If you would know the issue of such a course, we will play the part of the enchantress ourselves, and summon those who have gone before you, that you may learn from them whether there can be safety and peace in any thing but righteousness. We will summon the dead who were cut down in their wickedness, and they rise up and bemoan their madness, in having been "lovers of pleasure rather than lovers of God;" and as they flit before you, they will tell you that to follow in their footsteps is to rush headlong upon destruction. We will summon those who lived the life, and died the death of the righteous, and as they pass before you in their beauty and their joy, they exhort you to "lay aside every weight and the sin which doth most easily beset you," and the air is filled with sweet sounds of which this is the melody: "Blessed are the dead who die in the Lord."

If there is one who is determined to act over again the part of the monarch of Israel, who went down for comfort to the cave of the sorceress—if there is one, who in place of waiting upon God, and seeking peace of conscience by believing upon Jesus Christ, is determined to try the allurements and fascinations of the things of time and sense, we would meet him on the way, and bid him pause while we bring up the dead, and lay bare the secrets of the future. You think of delighting yourself in the things of earth, and in forgetfulness of your Maker. We tell you what it will be, as we have learned it from communion with the dead, as their words are given to us upon the sacred page. We tell you what thousands before you have found out from sad, bitter experience, that whatever may be the fascinations of earthly pleasure, however the mind may be amused for awhile with worldly pursuits, yet to yield ourself up to sensual gratifications and to secular business, is to make shipwreck of every thing. Thus, while you give yourself up to the deceptions of the world, hoping that it may soothe you with visions of peace, and delight you with dreams of gladness, we rise up before you at the bidding of God, and prophesy of evil—certain, irremediable evil—but not of this alone, for herein is a wonderful difference between the scene at Endor, and the scene through which we are now passing in the sanctuary. While Samuel had but one message to deliver, and that one which told only of destruction, we have indeed to speak of ruin, if a man will not "seek first the kingdom of God and his righteousness;" but we have also to say that God waiteth to be gracious, and that if a man will but renounce that which cannot satisfy, he shall have in its place "a peace which passeth all understanding," and "life for evermore."

III. I cannot but advert, in conclusion, to the touching fact that when Saul wished counsel, it was from Samuel that he wished to receive it; often had the prophet boldly reproved the king, and had, indeed, so offended him by his faithfulness, that for years previous to the prophet's death there had been no intercourse between them. The king had his creatures about him, whom instead of Samuel he had consulted in reference to the affairs of his kingdom; and yet Saul could not help feeling that the reprover and not the flatterer was the best friend he ever had; and, therefore, in his days of distress and perplexity, he earnestly desired the presence of the intrepid counsellor whom in his prosperous hours he had hated and scorned. What a testimony to the worth of one who will tell us of our faults, and not leave us undisturbed in our sins. What a warning that we should prize him while present, lest we live to wish his services when they can no longer be obtained.

How often, my brethren, does it happen in the history of men that they wish to bring back from the grave a friend, a father, or a mother whose advice they had despised, in order that they might enjoy the benefit of the counsel which they once slighted and scorned. If, in such circumstances, they could go to the cave of some sorceress; they would say not, "Bring me up the companion who cheered me in my thoughtlessness, and was with me in the revel and the dance," but "bring me up my father who told me that 'the way of transgressors was hard,' or my mother, who with weeping eyes and broken voice warned me against the paths of folly and sin." It is when men have learned from wretched experience that there is no peace in the paths of ungodliness, that memory recalls the domestic fireside, and the customary seats around it, and dwells upon the look, and tone, and gesture of those who impressed upon them the truths of the Bible; and then there rises in the mind the passing thought, "Oh! that we could call them back again, to profit as we might do now by their slighted instructions and counsels."

My brethren, if there are any of you who in spite of the reproofs and warnings of which you have been the subjects are giving yourselves up to the world, "walking in the way of sinners," or sitting, perhaps, in the seat of the scornful, "there are evil days coming when sorrows shall be multiplied," and you will know what were the feelings of the king of Israel when he said to the woman of Endor, "bring me up Samuel." But of what avail such feelings, even could they be gratified? Saul had his wish; and Samuel came not with words of consolation, but with this message, "to-morrow thou and thy sons shall be with me in the dark, cold grave." For if a man has neglected the Lord, and continued to resist the strivings of his Spirit until, as in the case of Saul, God has departed from him, of what avail to him could be the return of a departed friend? He who remembers with anguish how he despised the command of his father, and forsook the law of his mother, around whom gather the Philistines in his hour of extremity, who feels that he must pay the penalty of his transgression, how could he be profited if the earth should open, and some well remembered form come up covered with a mantle? If a man has neglected God till his last hour, and cannot then find him, though he earnestly seeks him, they who watched over him and prayed for him may be summoned to his bedside, but they could speak no consolation; they could but remind him of the sins he had committed, the opportunities he had squandered, and the mercies he had scorned.

May not that remembered friend be one who reproved and admonished from the sacred desk; week after week, and year after year, he may have busily plied his instructions and appeals. He dies, perhaps; and you who have been offended by his urgency are well pleased to be freed from his home strokes and his pointed remonstrances; but you will think of him again when you feel that the world is slipping from your grasp, and that you have not laid hold upon eternal life. You will think of him again as you toss upon your sick bed, and have no hope that your sins are forgiven. You might, perhaps, wish him back again to instruct and to guide you; but what could you expect to hear from his lips? What could a God-forgetting, and now a God-forgotten man expect to hear? Sore pressed he might say, "God answereth me no more," and when he said so, this must be the answer: "Why hast thou disquieted me to bring me up? Wherefore dost thou ask of me seeing the Lord is departed from thee, and is become thine enemy." God forbid that it should be so with any who hear me to-day; but, remember, I pray you, such must be the end of him who, never having made his peace with God, is haunted, at last, by the memories of opportunities which have been lost, and counsels which have been despised.

ABUSED PRIVILEGES.

"For thou *art* not sent to a people of a strange speech, and of an hard language, *but* to the house of Israel: not to many people of a strange speech, and of an hard language, whose words thou canst not understand: surely, had I sent thee to them, they would have hearkened unto thee. But the house of Israel will not hearken unto thee; for they will not hearken unto me: for all the house of Israel *are* impudent and hard-hearted."—EZEKIEL iii. 5, 6, 7.

WHEN we read the first two of these verses which we have selected for our text, they seem to speak of the peculiarly favourable and happy circumstances of the prophet, so far as the sphere of his official labour was concerned. The contrast is very great between his condition and that of one whose engagement in the same work of delivering the counsels of the Lord, involved a banishment from his country, a residence in an unhealthy clime, and an association with rude and ignorant and inhospitable tribes. The scene of the prophet's ministry was at home, among his kinsmen and friends, to whom he was united by strong and enduring ties, and among whom, as well by reason of long acquaintanceship as of office, he occupied a station of comfort and of influence. Now if we should suppose, concerning the prophet, or concerning any other man in similar circumstances, that he must necessarily be a stranger to all the trials of a ministerial life, we should show that we are drawing our conclusions from very partial premises, from an altogether one-sided view; and if we but read the concluding verse of our text, we should discover an idea which throws a new light upon his position, and appears to teach us that his trials are greater than they would have been, had God thrown him among a strange, untutored people, where he could have looked for none of the comforts of home, and none of the joys of an enlightened companionship. We do not by any means consider of small importance, the sacrifices which are made by one who penetrates into the dark places of the earth to preach to their benighted tenantry the unsearchable riches of Christ. There is on his part a relinquishment of substantial good; there is an amount of pains-taking, and self-denial, and suffering, which experience alone will enable one rightly to calculate; and to these sacrifices, and endurances, and privations, the man who labours in other circumstances, may be an entire stranger. And yet it is a very superficial examination, leading to very erroneous results, which in judging of a man's position, looks no farther than these his external relations; for it is seen at once, that the most important element to a right standard of judgment, the end a man has in view, is left entirely out of the account. I take it for granted that this principle is unquestionable, that a man's position is to be estimated as favourable or unfavourable, not in the light simply of some of its adventitious circumstances, but in the light rather of its relations to the great object of his existence upon which his heart is set. We take an example or two for illustration. The great object of the warrior is military renown; and when he traverses inhospitable regions, and submits to the privations of the camp, and exposes himself to the dangers of the battle-field, he makes many, and substantial, and painful sacrifices; but when you think of his object, and see him returning covered with the glory of his military successes, oh! surely, his position has been far more enviable, his circumstances far more desirable, than those of one who has never moved from the comforts of the domestic fireside, and never been exposed to any of the dangers of flood or field, or had an opportunity of signalizing himself by any public achievement. The man whose object is wealth, domesticates himself in a sickly climate, and in associations of all others most unfriendly to personal comfort; and herein he suffers evils to which a man who remains among his kinsmen and his friends, is an entire stranger; but when he returns from his wanderings, bringing with him as his reward his large possessions, they in whose eyes wealth is the chief good, do not think of comparing to its disadvantage, his position with that one, who, though he may have experienced but few discomforts, has yet scarce attained a competency; and the reason is obvious. The success in the one case is more than an equivalent for all the toils necessary to secure it; and the failure in the other case is not compensated by the personal comforts, for the sake of which it has been submitted to.

In applying this rule of judgment, then, to the subject which in this discourse we have undertaken to handle, I would ask my hearers, in the *first place*, to form a right estimate of the great end of ministerial labour, and keep their eyes fixed steadily upon it. It will not be denied by those who have with any degree of care looked at the subject, that the work in which as ambassadors of Jesus Christ we are engaged, is a work of no little painstaking and toil. The amount of intellectual effort which the full proof of one's ministry demands, and the degree of mental anxiety which it involves, the earnestness of endeavour which a right spirit brings to the work beforehand, the solicitude while actually engaged in putting forth efforts, and the intense and eager expectation, or the painful, saddening fear of results, are not surpassed, if, indeed, they are equalled in any department of human life, or in any sphere of human industry. The result contemplated as the reward of all our wearisome endeavours, is not any earthly advantage, is not any station of earthly influence, is not any amount, however great, of earthly applause. I know there are minds which ignorance contracts, and prejudice perverts, which seem to think that in our day, at least, the ministry of reconciliation, in the most unfavourable circumstances, receive, in an earthly point of view, a very fair equivalent for all their expenditure of time, and talent, and heart; but all my hearers, I am sure, will concede this fact, that there is no man of mind enough, and industry enough, and heart enough for an able and faithful minister of the New Testament, who could not, in many other spheres of human effort, with far less of toil, reach a higher position, and secure greater distinction, and gather to himself a larger amount of earthly good than he can ever think of doing, or would ever wish to do in the sphere of labour to which Providence has assigned him. But none of these constitute the result at which our ministry aims; we look in another direction, we have to do with the spritualities of man's existence; our object is to give impressiveness and power to unseen and eternal things. We set ourselves to war with those influences which chain down the thoughts to sense, and give to the affairs of this fleeting life a paramount importance to the scenes of an eternal duration. To elevate, and enlighten, and sanctify the mind, to bring the human spirit back from its sinful and hopeless wanderings, to reclaim man from his spiritual alienation, to break the dominion of sin, to lead the rebellious to submission to God, and the weary and heavy laden to the liberty, and peace, and refreshment of the gospel; these are the objects at which we aim, and the attainment of which is the only reward which we can look upon as, in any light, a compensation for our effort and our toil.

There are, indeed, other incidental and collateral results following our labours. In the unmeasured superiority of a Christian civilization over an untutored barbarism, in the peace and security, in the intellectual and moral development, in the honesties and decencies and courtesies of life, every where seen where religion, in its general influence, is interwoven in the whole texture of society, and cements its fabric, you behold that to which you would be utter strangers, but for the cross of Christ, and the pulpit which illustrates its principles, and enforces its claims; yet notwithstanding all this, which is undeniably the fruit of our ministry, we fall short of our great aim when through our instrumentality sinners are not converted unto God, and men are not presented perfect in Jesus Christ. Now then, we insist upon it, that if you would understand us aright, you must estimate us as you estimate others, precisely as you estimate the man of business, or the man of fame; you must judge of the advantage or disadvantages of our position from its bearing upon the great end we have in view. This rule of judgment, then, we shall endeavour to apply.

And here it will be admitted, that he who (to borrow the language of my text) labours with "the house of Israel," is in a position, in many respects far more desirable than he who goes "to a people of a strange speech and of a hard language." I would not, for example, detract at all from the admiration which is justly due to the self-denying missionary, who in cutting himself loose from the social circle, in whose sympathies he was wont to live, and in renouncing the comforts of home for the privations and toils of a foreign service, makes a sacrifice of great and substantial good. Here we, it is granted, submit to no such temporal inconvenience, court no such temporal discomforts, expose ourselves to no such temporal dangers; we sit under our own vine and under our own fig-tree, surrounded by those who interchange with us the warmest affections, and in possession of every thing which can administer to the comforts of life. But observe, my brethren, if we judge men in the light solely of these considerations, we have a defective and therefore a false standard; and our conclusion will be very wide of the mark. The question is, not who has the most comforts around him of a personal character—not who makes the most sacrifices, or submits to the fewest trials—here there is no dispute; but, who occupies the best position, so far as the successful accomplishment of his great end is concerned; whose ministry is likely to produce the greatest results, in sinners brought home to Jesus Christ?

Now, to a superficial observer, even with this standard of judgment, the advantages seem altogether on the side of him who labours with the house of Israel. The man who goes to an untutored population, has a vast amount of preliminary work to do, before he can put himself in the condition which I occupy. I am saved the necessity of establishing the first principles of truth. I am not called upon to begin with the lowest elements of proof, and demonstrate the being and unity of God, and the absurdity of idolatry and polytheism.

This process has all been gone through with already; the fundamental principles at least of the gospel, are established; nay, with its cardinal doctrines, I may suppose my hearers intimately acquainted, from the youngest to the oldest. I believe no one is ignorant, wholly, of the redemption in Christ Jesus, the love of the Saviour, his sacrifice for sin, or in short, of any of the great elemental and distinguishing truths, in which resides the mighty power of the gospel of Jesus Christ. I occupy a more advanced point than another, in circumstances directly the opposite, and it would seem as though my way was clear for the successful accomplishment of my great end, as a minister of Jesus Christ. And I do not say that it may not be so. I do not say, that one in my circumstances may not, by reason of his more favourable opportunities, do more for his Master and win more souls to Christ, than one for whom all this preliminary work has not been accomplished. It may be so, and yet there are reasons for thinking that generally it will not be so; and God, when speaking to the prophet Ezekiel, did not think so. When he told him that he was sending him not to a strange people, but to the house of Israel, he designed to shew him beforehand the fruitlessness of his mission. For, says he, "Surely had I sent thee to a strange people, they would have hearkened unto thee." And here I have an illustration directly in point, furnished by a comparison between the ministry of Ezekiel and the ministry of Jonah. The former went to his work cheerfully, because he was going among his own kinsmen, but when Jonah was commissioned to bear a message to the Ninevites, he shrunk back, because it was such an unpromising task to preach to a people of a strange language, and uninstructed in religion. Yet look at the results. Ezekiel's was a fruitless, and Jonah's a successful ministry—the Ninevites repented, and Israel remained obdurate. And now, we ask the question, as to these two, who occupied the best position, the man who laboured amid the external comforts and encouragements of home, or the man who went forward amid all that was disheartening in the circumstances of a strange association?

There is one consideration, my brethren, which in forming our judgment upon such a subject, we are very apt to overlook, which has nevertheless more to do with the matter, than I had almost said all others combined. When you look at the prophet Ezekiel going to preach to the house of Israel, there is indeed much that is pleasing in the thought that he is going to his own kinsmen, and at first sight, much that is encouraging in the fact that they are not ignorant of the first principles of the oracles of God; but then the house of Israel had been the subjects of frequent inculcations of divine truth, and oft-repeated warnings; prophet after prophet had exhorted them to repentance in vain, and each messenger, as he retired, left them more obdurate than before. They are considered as beyond the reach of means, and the prophet acts upon them but to harden them the more, and render them more inexcusable in their guilt. The fact that they were the house of Israel, a people in covenant with God, blessed with the revelation of his will, and yet unprofited and unsanctified through its truths, this is the reason why the prophet's ministry among them would be less effectual, and his position, therefore, less desirable, than they would have been, had he, like Jonah, been sent to the untaught and idolatrous Gentiles.

And thus it is that we wish you to take into the account, that the likelihood of men obeying the gospel, is usually diminishing in proportion to the frequency with which that gospel is preached to them, and its appeals ministered upon them. I wish you thoroughly to understand me, that you may not misinterpret my meaning, that I am not speaking in the light of one's external relations, but only in the light of one's great end in preaching the gospel, the conversion of sinners unto God, when I say that there may be more to disquiet, and more to discourage, more to alarm, and more to dishearten one, in preaching the gospel to precisely such a congregation as is now before me, than in preaching the gospel to an untutored tribe. That there is not, on the broad face of earth, an audience so unfavourable, an audience out of which there is so little probability of converts being, brought to vital Christianity, as one made up like my own, of a people so thoroughly indoctrinated, and so completely versed in the theory, and in the theory only, of religion.

I will not, my brethren, leave this statement before you, in this its bald and unsupported shape, but will endeavour to furnish you with its proof, and thus prepare your minds for the use, which in the sequel, I intend to make of it. Now since what is true of one person, must be true of an as sembly of those who are precisely like him, and as it is easier to speak of an individual than of masses, we shall take an individual and illustrate, in reference to him, the truth of our doctrine; and it seems almost enough to force conviction, to ask the question: Who is the most promising subject of ministerial effort, the man who hears the gospel for the first time, or the man who unaffected, unmoved, and unchanged, has heard it a thousand times? I do not forget, in propounding this question, that it is a higher than any human influence, which renders the gospel effectual. I do not forget that the Spirit of Omnipotence, who brings the dead to life, and gives to man who has worn the grave-clothes of sin and death, to know the power of a spiritual resurrection, is as mighty at one time as at another; but then, I would have you remember that he works through an appointed instrumentality of means; and when those means have been used oft and in vain, oh! it is not limiting the might of Omnipotence, to speak of the diminished probability of their ultimate success. Certainly there is less hope of a man who has heard month after month, and year after year, our message of reconciliation with God, and yet remained indifferent to the mighty and the stirring interests of his soul, and his immortality, than of the man who is comparatively a stranger to its awakening truths, and has never been influenced in his life by its wondrous and mighty motives; for in coming to a man who has long been familiar with, and yet has withstood all the appeals of a spiritual Christianity, who has given to the Bible the assent of his understanding, and withheld from it the affections of his heart, we feel (and herein is our discouragement) that we are coming to cope with a heart whose hardness has already been more than a match for the instrumentality which breaketh the rock in pieces, and that, therefore, we are but repeating an experiment which has a hundred times failed. Granted that a rock which has under ninety-nine blows showed no signs of yielding, may yet break under the hundreth, yet when there is the same amount of resistance, and only the same engine of attack, there cannot be much hope in renewing that which has often been tried in vain. But then you must go farther, and remember that the amount of resistance is actually increased by the constant action of the power which would overcome it, just as an arch becomes more coherent, and compact, and strong, by the weight you put upon it; and the flood gathers mightier force by means of the very dam which would obstruct its current.

There is in spiritual as well as in natural things the power of familiarity to be taken into the account as affecting man's susceptibility of impression. We may by custom become so insensible to the roar of cannon that our softest slumbers will not be disturbed by its loudest reverberations; and we may grow deaf to all the declarations of the word of God so as not to be startled by one of them. We know it; and how then can it be supposed that there is more prospect of ministerial success with him whom the gospel has completely deafened than with him who has been so far removed from its sound that he has never heard of immortality, nor been offered salvation? Is there any more warrant in Scripture than in reason for the hope that he who has been educated in Christian principles, and plied with the Christian ministry, and is yet a stranger to spiritual religion, will yield to another exhortation, or submit under another sermon? nay, is there as much ground for a hope of success in this case, as in the case of a man who has been deprived of every advantage, that he will hearken to our message delivered in all the first freshness of redemption through the blood of Christ? In the latter case, we have, indeed, to cope with the formidable opposition of ignorance, and it may be of superstition; but, in the former case, we have the mightier and more effectual resistance presented by a combination of enlightened intellects and unaffected hearts.

There is something, my brethren, in a mere nominal Christianity which renders it on some accounts more to be dreaded than the ignorance of untutored nature. As with every other blessing, so it is with religion, the easier it is of access the more lightly is it esteemed, and the more apt is it to be disregarded. Nothing seems too hard for us to endure in order to attain a good which demands a struggle; but how prone are we to become indifferent to that for which when in jeopardy we would have fought most manfully! We have the gospel; we are to reach its benefits not in the face of persecution, nor by surrendering our worldly advantages; and because it is so our circumstances are not so favourable to the spread of a vital Christianity. It does not by any means follow that religion will be ingrafted in the hearts of men, because it is interwoven in the institutions of the country; the very opposite is more likely to be the fact. The blessing may be undervalued, because it is within the reach of all; and while an outward regard to it may be the marked characteristic of a whole community, they may be no less distinguished by a practical indifference to it; and thus a people who have enjoyed the clearest light of the gospel may, as they become hardened under its influences, convert their very privileges into the grounds of their more certain and severer condemnation.

I would not have you forget, at this point, that it is a peculiarity of Christianity, that where its light and instructions are enjoyed, there must be the accompaniment of increased responsibility, and the consequence either of faith in Jesus Christ, or settled opposition to his claims. God's word, where it is faithfully sent forth, never returns to him void, accomplishing nothing either in the way of mercy or of judgment. And so the clearness of gospel light, and the multiplicity of gospel advantages, may be not only the precursors, but the instruments of a general blindness of mind, and deadness of heart. And a people subjected to the well arranged and well plied machinery of religion may, by reason of this fact, be fast falling into that state into which we may suppose the hearers of Ezekiel to have been, which rendered his ministry to them more ineffectual and hopeless than it would have been among a people as ignorant and superstitious as the men of Nineveh, to whom Jonah preached with such effectiveness and success.

It is this peculiarity of Christianity which throws such an unpromising aspect over fields of ministerial labour, which on other accounts seem so easy of cultivation. We enter upon our work with zeal and constancy, but we cannot forget the former unpropitiousness of our labours; though, here and there, there may have been a conversion unto God, shewing that Christ has not altogether left himself without a witness, yet the general state of things is unchanged; and the very soil which former tillage has but rendered more unproductive, is to be subdued into fruitfulness by means which have thus far produced an opposite result. And how can we help feeling that the very circumstances which to a superficial observer render our work so simple and so pleasing, in point of fact render it more perplexed and trying; and that we have in reality less promise of ministerial success than we should have were we coming for the first time to pour the light of the gospel upon the minds of our hearers, and to send home its wondrously stirring motives to their hearts.

So fully convinced am I of the main position of this discourse, that I cannot forego appending to my illustration a reflection of most thrilling interest, and of deepest moment to all who hear me.

In view of the process (spiritual process, I mean,) which is going on in the minds of those who are the subjects of a nominal Christianity, and the results in which in all likelihood that process will issue, what inference ought we to draw relative to our position at the last? This is but the first stage of our being, and we are preparing for another. It is ours to think—and oh! it is a fearful recklessness on our part painfully demonstrative of the truth of my doctrine, that we do not think of it—it is ours to think of that platform of judgment which is soon to be erected, and upon which all of human kind are to be gathered; and when that mighty congregation shall be summoned of every tribe, and kindred, and people under the face of the whole heaven, will there not, must there not be, think you, the uprising of unbaptized thousands, the swarming of many millions, who shall unite their voices in calling to a severer condemnation those for whom the light and privileges of the gospel have accomplished no other end than to develope their more thorough wickedness? We cannot draw aside the curtain of the future, and discover the arrangement which will hereafter be made of all the tribes who shall go up from this world to judgment. But here is the thought with which I would leave the discussion of my subject, and I would that it might sink deep into the minds of all of us: If we stand before the last tribunal unreconciled and unforgiven, and he who is to fix our destinies, shall say, as he points to some untutored savage, "Had I sent unto him, he would have hearkened to me," would we not at once understand his verdict, and would we not ourselves join with all orders of intelligences in applauding his righteous decision?

My dear brethren, I stand before you to-day as a minister of reconciliation, in the spot which Providence has assigned me, and where for more than sixteen years I have been delivering the messages of truth, and ministering the word of eternal life; and as the prospect of returning to the sphere in which I have been called to act, has been before me, I cannot tell you how oft the words which I have chosen for my text, have come home to me almost with the power and distinctness of a new revelation, "Thou art not sent to a people of a strange speech, and of a hard language, but to the house of Israel; not to many people of a strange, and a hard language, whose words thou canst not understand."

I feel it to be a privilege to stand where I do. I should belie my own convictions, and dishonour my own emotions, which constantly struggle for utterance, if I did not express my views of the kindness of Providence in placing me where I am. If kind attention, and Christian sympathy, and evidences of attachment too strong and numerous to be overlooked, and a welcome, in its sincerity and warmth far beyond any thing I had anticipated, give character to one's position, I cannot, in view of these outward circumstances of my case, be sufficiently thankful to him who has ordered my lot. Externally my relations are every thing I would have them to be. He who searches the heart knows I would not change them if I could. Yet while I could not without some such public expression, do justice to my own feelings, I cannot refrain from turning my mind in another direction. I cannot but think of the end of my ministry, which is not personal comfort, which is not personal fame, but which is to "present you all perfect in Christ Jesus;" and the thought often comes with a crushing weight upon my spirit, that the comforts of life, however great, the pleasures of earthly companionship, however many, the joys of social sympathy, however enlightened and effective, never, no, never, no, never, can compensate for an unblessed and fruitless ministry.

Under the influence of this thought, I have thrown my subject out before you, and with a twofold object; first, to show to those of my hearers who have any power at the throne of grace, how much I need an interest in their prayers. You follow with your sympathies and your supplications, the man who leaves his home and goes to an inhospitable clime to preach to some untutored tribe the unsearchable riches of Christ. The peculiar trials of his work, and the hardships of his task, call out your sympathies and your prayers, and I would not have you withhold one of them; he needs, he demands, he has a right to expect them all; and as Christians we ought to be humbled because they are not more earnest and effective in his behalf. But then, my Christian brethren, does he who now addresses you, need them less, in order that he may accomplish the end of his ministry? True, there is about him none, if I may speak so, of the moral romance or chivalry which leads one to abandon home, and give himself to the work of the missionary in foreign lands. But then there is as much of the stern realities of toil and labour, and less prospect of success. You pray for the foreign labourer, that the Spirit of God may accompany him, because his wondrous agency is needed to remove the blindness, and overcome the prejudices, and change the hearts of the idolatrous and superstitious; but is the agency of that Spirit less or more needed, to overcome the opposition not of involuntary, but of wilful blindness; to break the iron, as it is found in its native beds, or the iron which has become more hardened by the thousand fires which have heated it? Who needs your sympathies the most, the man who goes to till the soil which he finds in all the richness of undisturbed nature, or he who goes to cultivate a field whose energies have been exhausted by the very means which have been used to render it productive?

If my ministry in the field which God has set me to cultivate proves an unfruitful one, it will not be for want of laborious and toilsome cultivation; but then I know that it never can be a fruitful one, without your hearty co-operation, and your earnest and most ardent prayers. I lay my subject before you, then, as the ground of my appeal, which I address to you in the language of an apostle: "Brethren, pray for us, that the word of God may have free course, and be glorified."

And you, my dear brethren, who have never yet known "the gospel," as "the power of God unto salvation;" you "for whom I have so greatly longed in the bowels of Jesus Christ;" you will not turn away from one who speaks to you out of the fulness of a Christian pastor's heart. I am not insensible to the interest of the relation which subsists between us as men. I cannot but be thankful to you for all your evidences of attachment, and for the marked attention you have given to my imperfect ministrations. If these were the only legitimate ends of my ministry with you, oh! how rich should I think my returns for all my labours and my toil. I have not an unkind feeling to cherish, nor an unkind thought to utter respecting one of my unconverted hearers, so far as I am personally concerned, but when I speak for my Master, oh! I have much to say against them. They have given an attention to the servant which they have denied to his Lord—they have given their hearts to the messenger, and refused them to Him who sent him. Do I not state the truth concerning you, and how faithless would I be to my trust to wish to leave it so. No, my brethren, no! Christ only is worthy of your love. Christ has been using my feeble instrumentality only that he may gain your hearts, and I would have you look at your peril, as those upon whom that instrumentality has been plied in vain. Oh! beware of the deep guilt and fearful danger of abused privileges. Better to have been born worshippers of the unknown spirit of the mountains, than to have been born under the light of the gospel, and to have neglected Him who has spoken to us by his Son. Then God might have said, "They would have hearkened had they been called;" but now he must say, "I have stretched out my hands to a disobedient people."

Let me then beseech you not to act so as to turn your very advantages into witnesses against you at the judgment; do not, I pray you, suffer yourselves to be crushed by the weight of your mercies. In God's name and in God's strength, from this very moment, turn your privileges to account, and let not these Sabbath hours and these means of grace, a mother's prayers and a father's counsels, the instructions of Providence, and the warnings and appeals of our ministry, which if improved might save you—oh! let them not help to build the prison, and forge the chains, and fan the flames which shall confine and manacle and burn for ever.

www.ingramcontent.com/pod-product-compliance
Lightning Source LLC
LaVergne TN
LVHW021306110826
845150LV00003B/498

* 9 7 8 1 4 2 5 5 5 9 2 4 3 *